D0409765

BILINGUAL EDUCATION

GARLAND REFERENCE LIBRARY
OF SOCIAL SCIENCE
(VOL. 197)

BILINGUAL EDUCATION
A Sourcebook

Alba N. Ambert
Sarah E. Melendez

GARLAND PUBLISHING, INC. • NEW YORK & LONDON
1985

Library of Congress Cataloging in Publication Data

Ambert, Alba N., 1946–
Bilingual education.

(Garland reference library of social science ;
vol. 197)
Includes bibliographies and indexes.
1. Education, Bilingual—United States. I. Melendez,
Sarah E., 1941–   .   II. Title. III. Series: Garland
reference library of social science ; v. 197.
LC3731.A65   1985   371.97   83-48211
ISBN 0-8240-9055-1 (alk. paper)

Cover design by Laurence Walczak

Printed on acid-free, 250-year-life paper
Manufactured in the United States of America

To Yanira, Walter, and Adam,
who live and learn
in a bilingual world.

ACKNOWLEDGMENTS

We would like to express our appreciation to the persons who offered their assistance and support in writing this book. To Pauline White for her fine contributions to the chapters on bilingual models, reading, and the annotated bibliographies. To Diane Hazel for her assistance in preparing the annotated bibliographies on English as a second language and teacher training. To Dennis Sayers who contributed material on bilingual vocational education. To our editor Marie Ellen Larcada for her helpful comments and guidance. To our typists Veronica Alicea, Joan Cook, and Ivette Rivera. And to our families and friends who shared our enthusiasm and travails. To all, thank you.

CONTENTS

INTRODUCTION

The United States is a multilingual nation. 1980 U.S. Census data indicate that nearly 23 million U.S. residents speak a language other than English at home. Of these 11,1 million speak Spanish. Although no breakdown is given on other languages, it is estimated that 25 languages are spoken by at least 100,000 speakers each and 40 to 50 other languages are spoken by fewer than 100,000 persons each in the United States. The Bureau of Census reports that the number of school-aged children (5–17 years old) speaking languages other than English in the home is 4.5 million (2.9 million Spanish and 1.6 million other languages).

If these millions of children enter the educational system with limited knowledge of the language of the schools, their opportunities for an education equal to that of English-speaking children are seriously curtailed. This is why bilingual education is a viable, effective alternative to "sink or swim" practices in which limited-English-proficiency (LEP) children are placed in monolingual English classes in competition with native English-speakers. Without bilingual education programs these children lose one or two years in the acquisition of content knowledge while struggling to learn English. In a bilingual classroom, on the other hand, LEP children learn to read, write, and compute in the native language while they acquire the necessary English-language skills to function effectively in an all-English program. The children's native language is used as a temporary instructional medium in most bilingual programs to teach content area skills (science, social studies, mathematics, etc.) and to ease the children's transition into the English language. English-as-a-second-language (ESL) instruction is an essential component of all bilingual education programs. Eventually children acquire the necessary proficiency in English to compete with native speakers of English in the mainstream classroom.

Bilingual education is a full-fledged educational program which differs from the English language program in two areas: (1) subject matter is taught in a language other than English; and (2) intensive English as a second language instruction is an essential part of the curriculum. As such, bilingual education programs are not compensatory or remedial programs for the educationally "disadvantaged." They are authentic educational programs in which all content-area materials of the English language curriculum are incorporated, but two languages are used as mediums of instruction. Teaching children initially in a language they can understand is sound pedagogical practice.

The conservative wave that is sweeping the nation poses serious challenges to bilingual education. Bilingualism in minority groups is seen as a threat to national hegemony and contrary to Horatio Alger ideology. The recent economic recession created a climate of struggle and rivalry for basic government-funded programs. Nevertheless, Congress continues to fund bilingual education programs and language-minority advocacy groups have organized impressive lobby strategies to ensure the continuation of programs that guarantee the rights of LEP children to learn in a language they can understand. Despite the current attacks and financial constraints, bilingual education is here to stay. For this reason, we offer this book.

Bilingual Education: A Sourcebook was written for teachers, teacher aides, teacher trainers, supervisors, administrators, parents, child advocates, and others interested in bilingual education issues. The book can be used in training educational personnel both at the preservice and inservice levels. It contains eleven chapters which discuss program models, legal issues, English as a second language, reading, assessment, bilingual special education, bilingual vocational education, program evaluation, parental involvement and participation, teachers and teacher training and antibilingualism. Each chapter contains a general analysis of the topic followed by an extensive annotated bibliography in the area of discussion. Three appendices offer further resources and bibliographies in bilingual education. We have included material which is relevant to many language groups. Ambert and Melendez together wrote the first chapter;

Ambert wrote Chapters 2, 4, 5, 6, and 11; Melendez wrote Chapters 3, 7, 8, 9, and 10.

Alba N. Ambert
Hartford, Connecticut
June 1983

Bilingual Education

Chapter 1

BILINGUAL EDUCATION
PROGRAM MODELS

HISTORICAL BACKGROUND

Educational policy regarding language of instruction in
United States schools has fluctuated between philosophies of
maintaining cultural pluralism in a society and cultural
assimilation of the society into a unified group. These shifts
in policy reflect the broad political events which have shaped
the United States' view of itself as a nation and as an international power.

Historical accounts of linguistic minorities in the
United States usually portray America as a nation of immigrants.
Yet when Europeans arrived in North America there were over a
million American Indians speaking several hundred languages
(Brisk, 1981). Spanish-speaking Mexicans were already there
when the United States annexed the territories which would
become Arizona, California, New Mexico, and Texas. After the
Mexican-American War of 1848, Spanish-speaking Mexicans living
in these territories suddenly became linguistic minorities in
their place of birth (Leibowitz, 1980).

In addition to these native populations, what is today the
continental United States was settled by at least seven European
language groups. Spanish, Northern Europeans, English, Germans,
French, and Russians populated the territory. The Spanish were
the first immigrants to arrive and for nearly one hundred years,
they were the only Europeans in the continental United States.
In the sixteenth century they settled an area that stretched
from the Atlantic to the Pacific and from the Gulf of Mexico to
the Mississippi.

> In the early seventeenth century, northern Euro-
> peans entered the New World. The English settled
> in 1607, populating most of the Atlantic coast.
> Germans arrived the next year, settling from New
> York to Georgia, in the Midwest, and even as far
> west as Texas. The French also came to the North
> Atlantic coast--in 1608--moving from what is now

Canada, south of the Midwest and New England.
They also advanced from the Gulf of Mexico, dominating the cultural life of the vast Louisiana
Territory after the Spanish crown began to desert
it in 1682. Dutch and Swedes established colonies
during this period, mainly in New York, Pennsylvania, and Delaware. Finally the Russian occupation of Alaska in 1714 spurred settlements as far
south as the present state of California (Brisk,
p. 5).

The needs of non-English speaking populations were recognized early in the nation's history. The acts of the Continental Congress, from 1774 to 1779, made provisions for the
publication of documents in German to benefit the large German-
speaking population in the country. Federal laws were also
printed in French in 1806, and all laws pertaining to the
Louisiana territory were printed in both English and French by
federal mandate. In fact, New Mexico's first laws were drafted
first in Spanish and then translated into English because there
were very few English-speakers in the state. Before the Decla-
ration of Independence most of these non-English-speaking
groups maintained schools where the native tongue was used as
the language of instruction. These schools were often affili-
ated with religious denominations. (Keller and Van Hooft,
1982; Brisk, 1981; Leibowitz, 1980.)

In the pre-Civil War period there were 1.5 million Germans
who settled in remote areas where they often were a majority.
The German immigrants demanded that the Ohio legislature pass
a law which allowed the use of the German language as a medium
of instruction in public school districts where large numbers
of Germans were living. This law, providing for bilingual
schooling in German and English, was passed in Ohio in 1840
(Leibowitz, 1980).

Between 1840 and 1880 German was accepted as a medium of
instruction in Ohio, French in Louisiana, and Spanish in New
Mexico. Wisconsin passed a law authorizing instruction in a
foreign language for a maximum of one hour a day. By 1852
Cherokees, Creeks, and Seminoles were among the Indian tribes
operating their own schools. The Instituto San Carlos, a
private school with all instruction in Spanish, was established
in Key West, Florida, and later received some support from the
state.

From the colonization period until World War I, schooling
which was bilingual or in languages other than English was
common. Although after independence English became a more
frequently used language in schools, non-English education
continued to coexist with instruction of other languages.
School systems acknowledged the culturally and linguistically
pluralistic nature of American society (Keller and Van Hooft,
1982).

Between 1880 and 1917 there were German-English bilingual

schools in Cincinnati; Indianapolis; Baltimore; New Ulm,
Minnesota; and many other rural areas. In other schools,
German, Norwegian, Czech, Italian, Polish, and Dutch were
taught as subjects although not as mediums of instruction.
The constitution of New Mexico required that teachers be
trained in Spanish to work with Spanish-speaking children
(Keller and Van Hooft, 1982; Leibowitz, 1980; Andersson and
Boyer, 1978).

The onset of World War I fostered sentiments of nationalism
and isolationism in United States society, and existing concepts of cultural pluralism shifted toward the idea of cultural assimilation of all ethnic groups into a common monolingual, monocultural English-speaking society. American
school systems were seen as the appropriate transmitters of
the majority culture and, consequently, tools for the assimilation of immigrants (Kloss, 1977). Immigrants were expected
to learn English, forget their native language, and adopt the
"American way" of life.

Between 1917 and 1950 bilingual education was almost
completely eliminated in the United States, and the study of
foreign languages waned. Keller and Van Hooft (1982) cite
several factors which explain these occurrences: (1) the
advent of mandatory attendance laws for public schools; (2)
the elimination of public funding for church-affiliated schools;
and (3) the isolationism and nationalism which pervaded
American society after World War I (p. 7).

During this period many states implemented English-only
instructional policies. By 1923 thirty-four states passed
laws requiring English to be the only language of instruction.
Some states passed laws forbidding the use of other languages
as instructional mediums.

Two historical events were to cause Americans to reevaluate
existing foreign language policies in the American school system.
The first was the launching of the Sputnik satellite by the
Soviet Union, a country previously considered technologically
backward by United States standards (Mackey and Beebe, 1977).
The second event was Fidel Castro's assumption of power in
Cuba, an event which initiated the immigration of a flood of
educated middle- and upper-class Cubans from their homeland
to the United States. In addition, a communist presence 90
miles from the continental United States was seen as a threat
to national security. These events, as well as the civil rights
movement of the 1960's, influenced the passage of the Bilingual
Education Act of 1968.

During the decade of the 50's, a resurgence of interest in
foreign-language learning occurred, and in 1963 the first bilingual education program in decades was established in a
school district. During this period the National Defense

Education Act was passed by the federal government, authorizing
funds for the study of mathematics, science, and foreign languages. The act specifically emphasized the importance of maintaining the foreign language resources of the country. Cuban
refugees flooded Miami, and in 1961 Dade County started
elementary school programs in Spanish and English-as-a-Second-
Language. In 1963 the Coral Way Elementary School in Dade
County implemented a bilingual program in grades one through
three. From 1964 to 1967 bilingual education programs were
established in Texas, New Mexico, California, Arizona, and New
Jersey. On January 2, 1968, President Lyndon B. Johnson
signed the Bilingual Education Act, or Title VII of the
Elementary and Secondary Education Act, for the development of
programs where two languages are used as instructional mediums
(Keller and Van Hooft, 1982).

BILINGUAL EDUCATION TODAY

        Massachusetts was the first state to mandate bilingual
education in 1971. It required that whenever twenty or more
students of the same language background who were dominant in
that language were present in the same school, a program of
bilingual education was to be instituted. Massachusetts's
Transitional Bilingual Education Act was designed to prepare
students for a monolingual English classroom. Native
language instruction in subject areas is required, as is ESL
instruction. The law stipulated three years as the time in
which students must be mainstreamed although students may be
retained for longer periods if teachers and administrators can
make a convincing case for a need to do so. Local districts
are reimbursed for expenses above the district's per pupil
expenditures.
        By 1981, eleven states had passed laws mandating bi-
lingual education, and nineteen had passed permissive legislation. Most of the states mandating bilingual programs have
followed Massachusetts' lead in requiring programs for twenty
or more students of one language and in establishing a three-
year time limit for mainstreaming. They also provide funds to
help cover the costs of the programs. No law provides for
further instruction in the students' native language after
mainstreaming.
        California requires a bilingual program whenever there
are ten or more students of the same language in the same grade
and in the same school. California law also requires that
forty percent of the students in bilingual classrooms be native
speakers of English.
        Despite the predominance of transitional statutes and

programs, there are other types of programs in existence in
the United States. Texas, for example, does not mandate mainstreaming after three years. Evaluations of Texas programs
reveal that students do best in their fifth and sixth years in
the program.

The bilingual programs on Indian reservations and in
Indian schools are usually maintenance programs, funded by com-
binations of funds from Title VII and the Bureau of Indian
Affairs. There are bilingual programs in Navajo, Cherokee, and
many other languages, in grades kindergarten through high
school.

Dade County in Florida, by adding a grade each year to
continue providing bilingual education to the original students,
now has available bilingual instruction throughout elementary
and secondary grades. Boston, Massachusetts, has a bilingual
school for kindergarten through grade five. Bridgeport,
Connecticut, has a multilingual-multicultural magnet school
for English, Spanish, and Portuguese, which began with kindergarten through second grade and expects to add a grade each
year until grade six. In Bridgeport's magnet school, English-
dominant children can learn Spanish or Portuguese. Hartford's
bilingual school has been operational for over a decade and
provides a maintenance program through grade six. New York
City has several bilingual maintenance schools, one with
French, Creole, and Spanish programs.

Montgomery County in Maryland has an eclectic approach to
teaching students of limited English proficiency, which includes ESL instruction by an itinerant teacher, a transitional
bilingual program, alternative ESL (content area courses
modified for LEP students), tutorials, and a magnet center
with ESL clusters.

The Washington International School, in Washington, D.C.,
has a full bilingual (immersion) program from kindergarten
through twelfth grade. Its graduates are fluent and literate
in French or Spanish and English. The school is private and
is almost fully self-sustaining through tuition.

Ninety percent of the bilingual programs in the United
States are state or local programs and funded with state and/or
local funds. Title VII funds usually provide seed money to try
out a new program, develop curriculum and materials, and train
staff. Many local districts continue funding programs out of
local funds.

In 1980, Title VII funds supported over 950 projects in
40 states, Puerto Rico, and four U.S. territories. The projects
included basic education programs, teacher training, materials
development, technical assistance, evaluation, exemplary programs, vocational education, and research. Over seventy languages were being used including most Southeast Asian languages,

Pacific Island languages, many Native American and Eskimo
languages, and the more expected European and Central and
South American languages.

Six materials development centers prepared materials in
nineteen Asian languages. Eleven fellowship programs granting
master's and doctor's degrees utilized seven languages. The
basic programs included components of pullout ESL instruction,
transitional bilingual education, self-contained bilingual
classrooms, resource centers, self-contained classrooms with
bilingual aides, multilingual/multicultural language maintenance, partial bilingual, full bilingual, individualized instruction, and team teaching.

It is obvious that bilingual education in the United
States means many things. Programs vary in objectives,
methodology, curriculum, materials, and in the number and
amount of non-English languages used. The permutations are
almost limitless.

Perhaps the most controversial area of bilingual education in the United States is the linguistic use and outcome
of bilingual programs which promote academic achievement among
children who are non-native speakers of English. Because of
this predominant focus on language use and outcome, bilingual
education presents a unique challenge to education. Discussions
on program planning, teaching methodology, assessment, curriculum and materials are not only based on considerations of
pedagogical theory and practice but also draw from the body
of literature on psycholinguistics and sociolinguistics.
Broadly stated, the psycholinguistic literature is concerned
with the cognitive processes involved in first and second
language acquisition. The sociolinguistic literature considers the interrelationship of bilingual programming choices
to the language and culture of the local community and the
larger society.

As in the period prior to the First World War, instruction
in the native language is a recognized component of the United
States school system. Today, however, unlike previous pluralistic traditions, the trend of bilingual programming in most
states has been toward assimilation of the ethnic group into
the dominant culture. Thus, instruction in the native language is utilized only until the child acquires sufficient
English language skills to function independently in a monolingual English-speaking classroom.

Kjolseth (1972) describes two sociolinguistic models of
bilingual education: a pluralistic model and an assimilation
model. He views these models as the two extremes of a continuum of program choices in bilingual education. The pluralistic model stresses the incorporation of ethnic and non-
ethnic local language varieties and cultures of the community

in the program. Teacher selection and training and curriculum
development reflect the ethnolinguistic features of the community. Both the ethnic and non-ethnic local language varieties are given equal status in the classroom. The goal of the
bilingual program is to integrate the instruction of ethnic
and non-ethnic groups. Gradually, the ethnic and non-ethnic
standard language varieties are introduced into the curriculum
so that the linguistic outcome is maintenance in the language
varieties. This model is seen as a nine-year program.

The assimilation model is one in which community input
into program development is minimal. The community plays an
advisory role with no decisionmaking power in program planning.
Teacher selection and training and curriculum development reflect only the standard ethnic and non-ethnic language varieties and cultures. Only ethnic students participate as the
program is viewed as a short-term three-year remediation program. In this model, the ethnic language is a means to attain
transition to the non-ethnic standard language as rapidly as
possible.

Given the complexity of linguistic and cultural issues
and educational philosophies, the transition from educational
philosophies to educational practices reflects great diversity
both within and between program models.

Concepts of assimilation and pluralism, when considered
in relationship to bilingual program planning, are reflected
in two types of bilingual programs: transitional bilingual
programs and language maintenance bilingual programs.

Transitional bilingual programs

A transitional bilingual program aims for proficiency in
the English language and uses the students' native language
only until they can learn through English exclusively. Transitional programs are the preferred program model of assimila-
tionists. Although many transitional bilingual programs attempt
to incorporate the culture of the limited-English-speaking
students into the curriculum, the goal of the program is to
facilitate students' transition or transfer into learning
solely in English. At the end of a specified period of time
of participation, usually three years, the students are mainstreamed into a monolingual English language program of instruction. Transitional programs vary in the day-to-day methodology used. A common program model begins content matter instruction in the students' native language (L_1). At the
kindergarten level, for example, children learn concepts of
color, numbers, spatial relationships, etc., in L_1. They also
receive daily instruction in English-as-a-Second Language (L_2).
In addition, kindergarten students receive reading readiness

instruction in L_1. Ideally, reading instruction begins in L_1.

When students reach a specified level of proficiency in
English, their second language (L_2)--the degree required depends on the program and the grade level--subject matter instruction is introduced in English, one subject at a time.
Many programs select math as the first subject since it is
presumed not to rely on verbal communication as much as other
subjects.

Each year or semester, or even sooner, where individualized
instruction is the norm, more content matter is shifted to
English. The goal for most programs is that the students
should be able to learn in a monolingual English classroom in
two or three years.

The most effective transitional bilingual programs have
native speakers of the students' native language (L_1) teaching
in L_1 and native English-speakers teaching in English. Most
programs attempt to incorporate the culture of the target language into the curriculum. That usually translates into obser-
vances of holidays, food tasting, and music. Most programs
provide time for children's integration with English-dominant
children in classes such as art, physical education, and music
and for assembly programs and lunch.

As previously noted, transitional bilingual programs are
the predominant type of program in the United States. Although
there are no state bans against language maintenance programs,
states for the most part are unwilling to make a commitment to
maintenance. Transitional programs are often viewed as compensatory education for educationally disadvantaged students. The
students' limitations in English are viewed as a liability to
be overcome. The students' native language is seen as a tool
or bridge to be used in helping the students make the transition
to monolingual English learning.

Language maintenance bilingual programs

The maintenance bilingual program is the preferred model
for educators who espouse pluralistic education and a pluralistic society. Maintenance programs attempt to develop biliterate bilingualism in language-minority students. Culture
is seen as intrinsically related to language and is, therefore,
an integral part of the maintenance curriculum.

The most significant difference between maintenance and
transitional programs is the desired linguistic outcome: transitional programs are designed to lead students to transfer from
learning content in L_1 to L_2, while maintenance programs are
designed to lead students to learn in two languages and maintain their proficiency in both languages.

As in transitional programs, there is a good deal of

diversity from program to program. Some maintenance programs use the preview (L_1) review (L_2) method, i.e., subject matter is taught in L_1 and reviewed in L_2. Others use an immersion in L_2 approach initially and gradually introduce instruction in L_1. Still others use a team-teaching approach with one teacher teaching some subjects in L_1 and the other teaching the remaining subjects in L_2.

Proponents of maintenance programs believe that two-way, or dual-language, maintenance offers the best chance of achieving language maintenance. In a dual-language program, subject matter is taught in both languages, with equal time given to each. A prominent example of a successful maintenance bilingual school in this country was the Coral Way program in Dade County, Miami, Florida. That program had Spanish-speakers and English-speakers (which made it an enrichment program as well). Children received subject matter instruction in L_1 in the mornings. In the middle of the day, they were brought together for art, music, and physical education, conducted in both languages. The afternoons were devoted to reinforcing in L_2 the concepts that had been taught in the mornings in L_1.

Many of the first programs funded under Title VII were conceived of and implemented as maintenance programs. The district 13 bilingual program in Brooklyn, New York, was a maintanance program for grades K through 6. Approximately half the participants were Black/White and Puerto Rican monolingual English-speaking students. The other half were Puerto Rican monolingual-Spanish-speaking children.

That program was typical of the Title VII programs in New York City in the early seventies. Students began the program in kindergarten with instruction in their native language. The other language was studied every day as a foreign or second language. When children had a minimal level of communicative skills, a subject was taught in L_2, typically math, the reasoning was that math required the least amount of language skill.

Irizarry (1978) describes four major types of programs currently in use in the United States. These programs are classified according to the manner in which they differ in language use and language outcomes.

1. Programs of instruction in which all required courses are taught both in the language of the students of limited-English-speaking ability and in English, and in which instruction is given in the comprehension, speaking, reading, and writing of the non-English language and of English. These programs may have as their principal goals the development and maintenance of both languages or the development of both languages only until the student has achieved a level of English-language ability

which allows him or her to perform at an adequate
level in a classroom where instruction is conducted
solely in English.

2. Programs of instruction in which courses are taught
both in the language of the students of limited-
English-speaking ability for all or a part of the
curriculum, and in English, and in which instruction
is given in the comprehension, speaking, reading,
and writing of English. The major goal of these
programs is the development of the student's English
language ability through the use of both languages
until the student is able to perform at an adequate
level in a program in which instruction is conducted
solely in English.

3. Special English-language programs in which instruction is conducted in English with special English
language instruction for students of limited-English-
speaking ability. These may include English-as-a-
Second-Language programs or High Intensity Language
Training programs. The major goal of these programs
is the development of the student's English language
skills as soon as possible in order to facilitate the
student's transition into the regular school program.

4. Language other than English-as-a-Second-Language
programs in which English-speaking students receive
instruction in the language of the students of
limited-English-speaking ability. These programs
may concentrate on the development of oral skills in
the non-English language, at least at the lower
levels. Instruction in other subjects is conducted
primarily in English. The major goal of these programs is to teach another language to English-
speaking students. (Irizarry, pp. 17-18)

While eligibility for Title VII program funding requires
the use of two languages as mediums of instruction, one notes
in the description offered by Irizarry that English as a Second
Language (ESL) instruction in a monolingual English program is
considered a viable program model in bilingual education. Nevertheless, bilingual educators generally agree that a bilingual
program is one that uses two languages as mediums of instruction
and insist that a program is not a bilingual program unless instruction is conducted in the students' native language and the
dominant language of the school system. The U.S. Office of
Education (1971) defined bilingual education as:

the use of two languages, one of which is English, as
mediums of instruction for the same pupil population in
a well-organized program which encompasses all or part

of the curriculum and includes the study of the
history and culture associated with the mother
tongue. A complete program develops and maintains
the children's self-esteem and a legitimate pride in
both cultures.

The inclusion of a monolingual ESL program model in a
discussion of bilingual education programs appears to stem
from the existence of such programs in reality. This is, in
fact, the case. School systems have implemented intensive ESL
programs in which the child receives academic instruction in a
mainstream classroom for part of the day and language instruction in an ESL classroom for a designated period of time.
These programs have sometimes been mislabeled as immersion programs because the child is "immersed" in language instruction
different from that given to native language speakers. However, immersion models, as developed in the United States and
Canada (Lambert and Tucker, 1972; Cohen, 1974), are two-
language models. The native language is the language of the
school and the second language is the language of instruction
used only in the classroom with non-native speakers.

Decisions to implement a monolingual ESL program appear
to be based on such issues as student population size, student
linguistic abilities, available funding and availability of
qualified native language teachers, native language curriculum
materials and native language assessment instruments, as well
as philosophical opposition in school districts to native
language instruction. Often the goals of a bilingual program
depend on the school districts' philosophy of education as a
means toward cultural pluralism or assimilation. Although
community involvement in the planning and implementation of
bilingual programs is assured to be a common occurrence, the
philosophical stand that prevails in selecting the program
model is usually that of the school authorities, not the community. Diminishing fiscal resources also play an important
role in the choice of an educational program for linguistic
minorities. For the school system unfamiliar with bilingual
education resources, the implementation of a dual-language program offering comparable academic achievement in both languages
may appear to be an overwhelming task. To these school districts a readily available ESL staff may appear to be an ex-
pedient solution to academic program implementation for children
with English-language limitations.

Two research studies support a monolingual ESL approach.
The American Institutes of Research (AIR) (1978) suggest that
children receiving bilingual instruction learn less English
than children receiving instruction in English only. Baker
and de Kanter (1982) prepared a report for the U.S. Department
of Education and concluded that transitional bilingual educa-

tion has proven ineffective, especially when compared to immersion (ESL) type programs. Both studies have been severely
criticized for their methodological flaws (see Chapter 11 and
Cardenas, 1978; Swain, 1979; Willig, 1982). There is a grow-
ing body of literature which indicates that instruction in the
native language facilitates the learning of a second language
in language-minority children (Skutnabb-Kangas and Toukamaa
1976; Cummins, 1979, 1980, 1981; Bhatnager, 1980). An important
issue not addressed by the studies favoring exclusive ESL programs is that the positive effects of bilingual education are
cumulative and not evident until the sixth year of instruction.
This critical factor is not taken into account in many studies
evaluating English-language acquisition in children in bilingual programs.

ESL has a strong and respectable place in bilingual education programs; however, models which program only for English
with the exclusion of the child's native language and culture
may not be and have not proven effective for linguistic minority
groups.

Enrichment bilingual model

A third bilingual education program model has commonly
been referred to as an enrichment program. Enrichment programs provide foreign-language instruction to native-language
speakers.

Cohen and Swain (1976) describe the immersion models implemented in the United States and Canada with majority language students learning in the minority language as enrichment-
type programs. They list 17 characteristics that appear in
all successful immersion programs. The most important of
these include: the program is an "early total immersion" type,
i.e., the students are in kindergarten and first grade and
all instruction, initially, is in L_2; the children are segregated from native speakers of L_2; the teachers are fluent,
native-like speakers of L_2; the teachers never mix languages;
there are no structured L_2 lessons in the early grades; teachers
expect children to acquire L_2 in context; and finally, the
program is voluntary.

The Canadian experimental program in St. Lambert (Lambert
and Tucker, 1972) and the El Marino School program in Culver
City, California (Cohen, 1974) both included the characteristics listed by Cohen and Swain and both programs were successful in teaching L_2 through content matter without academic
retardation. Moreover, students later learned L_1 reading and
language arts at least as well as children in conventional
programs.

The success of immersion programs in North America is due,

to a great extent, to the characteristics of the children, parents, and teachers who participate.

The children in the immersion programs in the United States and Canada were members of the majority-language group. There was no threat to their own language in learning a second language. (Although Anglophones in the Province of Quebec may be in a linguistic minority, English is the majority and official language in Canada, as well as the language of power and prestige, even in Quebec.)

The perceptions and expectations of parents, administrators, and teachers were that the children would add a language to their repertoire and, thereby, enrich their educational experiences as well as their ability to interrelate with their minority-language neighbors. No one involved with the experiments considered the programs as compensatory education for disadvantaged children.

Children enrolled in transitional bilingual programs in the United States, on the other hand, are from minority-language groups. Theirs is not the prestige language but a language to be dropped just as soon as they can learn through the medium of English. This "subtractive" aim has been found to be less effective in second language instruction than an "additive" aim, such as that of the St. Lambert and Culver City programs. In fact, the transfer which is the expected outcome of transitional bilingual education, together with the pressure to teach English before the students' native language skills are fully developed, may militate against students learning English as quickly or as well as they might if their native language were not targeted for neglect upon exit from the program.

The goal of the early immersion programs was to develop biliterate bilinguals. Both languages were accorded equal prestige and status; both languages were used (after the first or second year) as languages of instruction. School districts looking at immersion programs for language-minority students have a very different goal: total language transfer. This cannot be considered immersion, but submersion. The implied message is that the students' native language is not as good as the majority language and that, where and when it is used in a transition-type program, it is merely of temporary value.

The parents of students in the St. Lambert and Culver City experiments were able to provide all the middle-class enrichment, e.g., a good deal of verbal communication in a standard register, that is usually taken for granted in white middle-class homes but missing from low-income or poor minority communities.

It is important to note that although the low-income child

may not speak the standard language variety that is the language of the school, this is not an indication that the linguistic abilities of the child are necessarily impoverished.
On the contrary, the child may possess a rich language repertoire that is not built upon by the school system.

Middle-class parents are also more likely to become involved in the education process, ask questions, and demand
excellence. They will be particularly watchful of an experimental program in which their children are the guinea pigs
to ensure that they are not short-changed by the experiment.

Language-minority parents often lack the sophistication
about the educational system or the English communication
skills to be effective advocates for their children's education.

The students in the experimental early immersion program
were all volunteers. It is very likely that children whose
parents are knowledgeable and sophisticated enough to volunteer
their children for a program they believe will be of benefit
are likely to do well in school anyway.

Parents who are recent arrivals to the United States are
not often aware of the educational options available to their
children.

It behooves educators to look carefully at the characteristics of students for whom immersion programs have been successful. The reality of linguistic minority children in the
United States is radically different from that of middle-class
majority students whose parents voluntarily enroll them in
immersion programs for enrichment purposes. Immersion programs
that do not take into account the important differences described above between students in successful immersion programs
and typical students in transitional bilingual programs in the
United States can begin a new era of "sink or swim."

CONCLUSION

Bilingual education is an approach to educating children
of LEP which can be implemented in many ways. Within the
transitional, maintenance, and enrichment models, there is much
variation. School districts and, sometimes, each program within
school distrcts make decisions on staffing, curriculum, materials, student assignment, and mainstreaming, in accordance
with local educational philosophy, political climate, availability of funds, and, sometimes, parental desires.

The diversity found in bilingual education is, at once,
a strength and a weakness. It allows communities to design
programs to suit their particular needs but also makes discussion about bilingual education and comparison of projects
difficult.

REFERENCES

American Institutes for Research. *Evaluation of the Impact of ESEA Title VII Spanish/English Bilingual Program.* Los Angeles: National Dissemination and Assessment Center, California State University, 1978.

Andersson, T., and M. Boyer. *Bilingual Schooling in the United States.* Austin: National Educational Laboratory Publishers, 1978.

Baker, K., and A. deKanter. "The Effectiveness of Bilingual Education: A Review of the Literature." *Report to the U.S. Department of Education*, 1982.

Bhatnager, J. "Linguistic Behavior and Adjustment of Immigrant Children in French and English Schools in Montreal." *International Journal of Applied Psychology*, 1980, 29:141-158.

Brisk, M.E. "Language Policies in American Education." *Boston University Journal of Education*, 1981, 163:3-15.

Cardenas, J.A. "Response I." In N. Epstein. *Language, Ethnicity and the Schools: Policy Alternatives for Bilingual Education.* Washington, DC: George Washington University Institute for Educational Leadership, 1978.

Cohen, A.D. "Progress Report on the Culver City Spanish Immersion Program: The Third and Fourth Years." *Working Papers in English as a Second Language*, 1974, 9:47-65.

Cohen, A.D., and M. Swain. "Bilingual Education: The Immersion Model in the North American Context." In Alatis and Twaddell (eds.). *ESL and Bilingual Education.* Washington, DC: TESOL, 1976.

Cummins, J. "Linguistic Interdependence and the Educational Development of Bilingual Children." *Review of Educational Research*, 1979, 49:221-251.

Cummins, J. "The Cross-Lingual Dimension of Language Proficiency: Implications for Bilingual Education and the Optimal Age Question." *TESOL Quarterly*, 1980, 14:175-187.

Cummins, J. "Four Misconceptions about Language Proficiency in Bilingual Education." *NABE Journal*, 1981, 5:31-45.

Irizarry, R. *Bilingual Education State and Federal Legislative Mandates, Implications for Program Design and Evaluation.* Los Angeles: National Dissemination and Assessment Center, 1978.

Keller, G.D., and K.S. Van Hooft. "A Chronology of Bilingualism and Bilingual Education in the United States." In J.A. Fishman and G.D. Keller (eds.), *Bilingual Education for Hispanics in the United States.* New York: Teachers College Press, 1982.

Kjolseth, R. "Bilingual Education Programs in the United States: For Assimilation or Pluralism?" In B. Spolsky (ed.), *The Language Education of Minority Children.* Rowley, MA: Newbury House, 1972.

Kloss, H. *The American Bilingual Tradition.* Rowley, MA: Newbury House, 1977.

Lambert, W.E., and G.R. Tucker. *Bilingual Education of Children: The St. Lambert Experiment.* Rowley, MA: Newbury House, 1972.

Leibowitz, A.H. *The Bilingual Education Act: A Legislative Analysis.* Rosslyn, VA: National Clearinghouse for Bilingual Education, 1980.

Mackey, W.F., and V.N. Beebe. *Bilingual Schools for a Bicultural Community: Miami's Adaptation to the Cuban Refugees.* Rowley, MA: Newbury House, 1977.

Skutnabb-Kangas, T., and P. Toukamaa. *Teaching Migrant Children's Mother Tongue and Learning the Language of the Host Country in the Context of the Sociocultural Situation of the Migrant Family.* Helsinki: The Finnish National Commission for UNESCO, 1976.

Swain, M. "Bilingual Education: Research and Its Implications." In C.A. Yorio, K. Perkins, and J. Schachter (eds.), *On TESOL '79: The Learner in Focus.* Washington, DC: TESOL, 1979.

U.S. Office of Education. *Programs under the Bilingual Education Act. Manual for Project Applicants and Grantees.* Washington, DC: Government Printing Office, 1976.

Willig, A.C. "The Effectiveness of Bilingual Education: Review of a Report." *NABE Journal*, 1982, 2:1-19.

ANNOTATED BIBLIOGRAPHY

Andersson, T., and M. Boyer. *Bilingual Schooling in the
United States*. Austin, TX: National Educational Laboratory
Publishers, 1978.

A discussion of bilingualism and bilingual education, including a historical overview, rationale, planning of bilingual programs, and research. Includes an analysis of the
implications of bilingual education for society and education in general. The appendices include the Bilingual
Education Act, guidelines for bilingual education programs,
demographic data, immigration legislation, a typology of
bilingual education teacher qualifications and a directory
of bilingual programs in the United States.

Cordasco, F. (ed.). *Bilingual Schooling in the United States:
A Sourcebook for Educational Personnel*. New York: McGraw-
Hill, 1976.

Discusses the historical background of bilingual schooling
and non-English speakers in the United States; typology and
definitions of bilingual education; language learning and
language teaching; as well as programming, administration
and staff development in bilingual education. Appendices
include an overview of court decisions and legislation
affecting bilingual education; program and project descriptions; and general bibliographical resources.

*ESEAA Title VII Bilingual Education Programs: Directory of
Degree-Oriented Training Grants for Fiscal Year 1981*. Office
of Bilingual Education and Minority Language Affairs (OBEMLA),
U.S. Department of Education, 1981.

Lists 146 training projects representing 36 language groups
and a combined participation of 30 U.S. states and territories. Project information is individually listed according
to state or territory and provides data concerning the name
of the grantee institution, location and contact person,
OBEMLA contact officer, grant number, number of years com-

pleted/negotiated, number of program trainees, degrees conferred, activities and amount of project financial resources
provided.

Fishman, J.A., and G.D. Keller. *Bilingual Education for Hispanic Students in the United States.* New York: Teachers
College Press, 1982.

A collection of papers which focuses on factors that contribute to the educational growth and linguistic development
of Hispanic bilinguals in the United States. Organized into
seven chapters, the studies examine: the chronology of bilingualism and bilingual education in the United States,
definition of bilingual educational goals, issues in
language diversity and language standardization in the
Spanish spoken in the United States, attitudes toward
Spanish and bilingual education, research on bilingual instruction and assessment, and language processing in the
bilingual child.

Gardner, R.C., and W.E. Lambert. *Attitudes and Motivation in
Second-Language Learning.* Rowley, MA: Newbury House, 1972.

The book summarizes a twelve-year research project on the
factors which influence successful second-language learning.
The authors conclude that the motivation of successful second-
language learners is determined by their attitudes toward the
people who speak the language they intend to learn.

Guskin, J.T. "Bilingual Education Community Study: Implementing
Bilingual Education in an Urban Midwestern Context." Paper
presented at the Annual Meeting of the American Educational
Research Association, in Los Angeles, California, April 16,
1981.

Provides an overview of the historical, political, cultural
and linguistic variables which influence the development and
implementation of bilingual education in the midwestern, urban
setting of the Milwaukee Public School System.

Hornby, P.A. (ed.) *Bilingualism: Psychological, Social, and
Educational Implications.* New York: Academic Press, 1977.

Articles included discuss the effects of bilingualism on
intelligence, personality and identity; the effects of bilingualism on an individual's language development, general
cognitive style and capacity for learning. The second part
of the book analyzes the social interaction of bilingual persons as well as linguistic usage in bilingual communities.
The third part looks at bilingualism from a national and

international perspective. The articles in this section
describe the factors which have contributed to the spread of
English as a second language throughout the world, the use
of indigenous languages as mediums of instruction in bilingual societies throughout the world, and the implications
of bilingualism for the individual and society.

Keller, G.D., R.V. Teschner, and S. Viera (eds.). *Bilingualism
in the Bicentennial and Beyond*. New York: Bilingual Press,
1976.

Contains exhaustive analyses of linguistic research on bilingualism, including code-switching in Spanish-English bilinguals, linguistic structures of Spanish-English-speaking
children, and the acquisition of Spanish gender by Spanish-
speaking first-grade children. The application of psycholinguistics, sociolinguistics, and socioanthropology to bilingual education is discussed. Includes annotated bibliography of sources of information and resources useful in
bilingual-bicultural education programs.

Kobrick, J.W. "The Compelling Case for Bilingual Education."
In F. Cordasco (ed.). *Bilingual Schooling in the United
States: A Sourcebook for Educational Personnel*. New York:
McGraw-Hill, 1976.

Discusses efforts made by different communities to establish bilingual education programs. Refers to research done
on the effectiveness of bilingual education programs which
prove bilingual-bicultural education is the greatest educational priority in bilingual communities. Analyzes the Bilingual Education Act in light of its psychological impact.
Discusses state bilingual laws.

Lyons, J.J. "Bilingual Education: The Past and the New Year!"
NABE News, 1983, 6:3.

This article provides an overview of the congressional
activities of the 97th Congress during 1982 as they relate
to federal policies affecting bilingual education. Activities reviewed include: budget cut proposals which would
limit Title IV assistance programs and Title VII bilingual
education programs, proposed legislative amendments to
Title VII, debates concerning the ED-Inspector General's
Texas Title VII Audit Reports. The impact of the November
1982 elections on bilingual education is discussed. Future
congressional debates are expected to be in the area of
federal budget cuts and in the area of reauthorization of
the Bilingual Education Act. Three major arguments against
bilingual education presented to Congress are evaluated.

National organizations supporting bilingual education are
urged to continue their efforts.

Macbeth, R.B. "The Challenge of the Eighties: Southeast Conferences on the Education of Hispanics." Miami, Florida,
May 7-9, 1980.

A report on the 1980 Southeast Conference on the Education
of Hispanics is presented in three parts. Section I is a
compilation of critical topics and recommendations formulated by participants in the conference. The topics concern affirmative action, linguistically and culturally
relevant program delivery, special needs, testing and
research, bilingual instruction, funding, parent/community
involvement, politics, and education. Section II is a
compilation of Hispanic concerns and recommendations as
presented to the United States Secretary of Education.
Section III is a paper on Hispanic parents and the schools.
An overview of the extent of Hispanic parent involvement in
education is provided. A program is outlined which promotes
parental involvement in tutoring their own children in basic
academic skills. This paper gives a series of recommendations for individuals involved in parental programs.

Macedo, D.P. (ed.). *Issues in Portuguese Bilingual Education*.
Cambridge, MA: National Assessment and Dissemination Center,
1980.

Articles included in this book discuss such issues in the
bilingual education of Portuguese speakers as the status of
the Portuguese language, value orientations, culture shock,
testing, reading, ESL teaching strategies, Cape Verdeans,
and Azoreans. Some of the articles are written in Portuguese.

Micheal, C. "Bilingual Education in Ohio: An Overview." ERIC
Document, Arlington, VA, 1982.

Profiles bilingual education programs in the Ohio school
systems of Youngstown, Toledo, Cleveland, and Athens. Current practices in Ohio bilingual education are discussed in
funding, identification and assessment of students, instructional models, curriculum materials, the cultural component
of instruction, parental involvement, and staff development.
Statewide trends in bilingual education are identified and
needs are discussed.

Pialorsi, F. (ed.). *Teaching the Bilingual: New Methods and
Old Traditions*. Tucson: The University of Arizona Press,
1976.

A collection of essays by diverse authors which analyze biculturalism, theoretical bases to bilingual education, and programmatic concerns in the implementation of bilingual education programs.

Rothery, I.C. "Federal Policy in Bilingual Education." *American Education*, 1982, 30:30-40.

The author suggests that federal policy regarding the education of language-minority children has tended to favor bilingual-bicultural programs over alternative educational approaches which emphasize English-language instruction despite lack of conclusive research evidence to support the effectiveness of one instructional approach over another. Mandates established by the Lau Remedies and Title VII legislation are cited as examples of federal measures which have exceeded the position adopted by the Supreme Court in *Lau v. Nichols*.

Saville, M.R., and R.C. Troike. *A Handbook of Bilingual Education*. Washington, DC: TESOL, 1978.

A discussion of the rationale for bilingual education in terms of linguistic, psychological, social and cultural factors. Analyzes bilingual program design, curriculum and teaching methodologies in the areas of language and reading, and offers suggestions for effective program evaluation.

Schneider, S.G. *Revolution or Reform: The 1974 Bilingual Education Act*. New York: Las Americas Publishing, 1976.

A comprehensive case study of the legislative history of the bilingual-bicultural provisions of the Educational Amendments of 1974, Public Law 93-380. Presents and discusses the Senate, House, and administration positions and the interest of lobbyist groups on the philosophy and goals of bilingual-bicultural education as they related to federal legislation and implementation. The merging of various positions into a consensus which resulted in the Bilingual Education Act of 1974 is viewed by the author as a movement of reform of existing law and existing federal practice in the area of bilingual-bicultural education.

Simoes, A. (ed.). *The Bilingual Child: Research and Analysis of Existing Educational Themes*. New York: Academic Press, 1976.

Part I includes articles describing cognitive and effective studies in bilingual-bicultural education: cultural attitude scales to determine whether a program is bicultural as well

as bilingual; social and psychological implications of bilingual literacy; and cognitive style analysis of bilingual
children. Part II includes articles on total and partial
immersion programs, including descriptions of programs in the
United States and Canada. Part III looks at practical applications of bilingual theories, such as applied linguistics
and foreign-language teaching; bilingualism and literacy.
Part IV includes general topics in bilingualism: sociolinguistic perspectives of bilingualism and a review of the
literature in first- and second-language learning.

Spolsky, B. (ed.). *The Language Education of Minority Children*.
Rowley, MA: Newbury House, 1972.

   The book is organized in three parts. The first section
describes the nature of multilingualism and the language
problems of minority children in the United States. The
second section includes articles on different aspects of
bilingualism and bilingual education, such as the rationale
for teaching children in their native language, the relationship between bilingualism and thought, bilingual education
models discussed from a sociolinguistic perspective, and
cultural pluralism in bilingual education. The third section
covers curriculum issues: teaching English as a second language, teaching standard English to Black children in reading
and testing are discussed.

Travis, M. *Bilingual-Bicultural Education in Alaska: An Introduction to Program Development*. Juneau: Alaska State Department of Education, 1980.

   Presents four models of bilingual-bicultural education programs operating in Alaska. The models are: (1) transitional,
(2) full maintenance, (3) partial maintenance, and (4) mono-
literate. Educational program topics, briefly outlined,
include: student eligibility for bilingual-bicultural education, program funding, basic components of program design
and criteria for program evaluation.

Trueba, H.T., and C. Barnett-Mizrahi (eds.). *Bilingual Multicultural Education and the Professional: From Theory to
Practice*. Rowley, MA: Newbury House, 1979.

   Includes an overview of bilingual education; bilingual
education program models; linguistic and cultural considerations in bilingual education; cognitive and affective development of children; teaching of content areas in bilingual programs; theories, methods, techniques and materials for
second-language teaching; and evaluation.

Von Maltitz, F.W. *Living and Learning in Two Languages:*
Bilingual-Bicultural Education in the United States. New
York: McGraw-Hill, 1975.

Offers a historical overview of bilingual education; discusses arguments made for and against bilingual education;
describes bilingual programs discussing the dialectal differences in bilingual populations, such as Cajun, Louisiana
Creole, Creole French; and offers a description of a
Chinese-Spanish-English program in New York City. The
author discusses the rationale behind bilingual-bicultural
education, bilingual education in Puerto Rico, how other
countries deal with linguistic minorities, bilingual education for American Indians and state mandates for bilingual
education.

Willig, A.C. "The Effectiveness of Bilingual Education: Review
of a Report." *NABE Journal*, 1982, 6:1-19.

A critical review of a recent report prepared by Baker and
deKanter for the U.S. Department of Education which concludes that transitional bilingual education has proven
ineffective, especially when compared to immersion-type
programs. Willig discusses the purpose of bilingual education and the nature of bilingual education in relation to
the report's findings. Weaknesses in the statistical review
methodology used in the report are discussed. Described is
an alternative review methodology presently being utilized
in a secondary analysis of data presented in the original
report. Because of the current implementation of a wide
variety of bilingual programs, the author recommends that
further research on the effectiveness of these programs involve a planned variation of design permitting the components
of one bilingual program to be compared to another bilingual
program.

Chapter 2

LEGAL ISSUES

Before the 1960's it was assumed that uniform educational treatment was beneficial to all children. Special educational programs for specific learning needs were virtually unheard of in public school settings. All children were exposed to the learning process through the same materials, curricula, and teaching methodology. This uniformity was especially detrimental to the millions of limited-English-proficiency children receiving instruction in English, a language they could not understand.

To a great extent changes in attitudes concerning the ineffectiveness of teaching non-English-speaking children solely in English were brought to the fore by educators, legislators, community activists, and child advocates who were becoming increasingly aware of the inequality of treatment of language-minority children in education. Children of limited English proficiency (LEP) received discriminatory treatment in schools. They were taught in a language they could not understand with materials which were incomprehensible. Although learning English is crucial to economic and social mobility in this country, educators, legislators, and the courts have agreed that limited-English-proficiency children should receive instruction in a language they can understand while they acquire the English-language skills needed to succeed in American society. Teaching LEP children solely in English is a denial of equal educational opportunity. Legislation and litigation have affirmed the rights of children to a meaningful education.

Specifically, rights of LEP children are guaranteed by law. The sources of these rights are found in a combination of federal and state legislation, their rules of implementation, case law, and in administrative interpretation of legislation and litigation by governmental enforcement agencies. The decades of the 1960s and 1970s were particularly important in the litigation and legislation that have determined today's legal framework of educational programs for LEP children. While

many states have their own provisions for education of LEP
students, the federal courts and the U.S. Congress have provided leadership in these areas and state laws and regulations
have tended to reflect the federal mandates.

Although it did not address the educational rights of LEP
children directly, the landmark *Brown v. Board of Education*
case of 1954 laid the foundation for much of this legal activity. In *Brown*, the Supreme Court ruled that the separation
of schooling according to race is inherently unequal and does
not meet the test of equal protection provided in the Fourteenth
Amendment to the U.S. Constitution. The test of equal protection was later applied to other minority populations--notably
LEP children.

FEDERAL LEGISLATION

The *Civil Rights Act of 1964* was the first major piece of
federal legislation requiring that school districts receiving
federal funding guarantee non-discriminatory treatment on the
basis of race, color or national origin.

Title VI of the Civil Rights Act states:

> No person in the United States shall, on the ground of
> race, color, or national origin, be excluded from
> participation in, be denied the benefits of, or be
> subjected to discrimination under any program or
> activity receiving Federal financial assistance.

The Act requires that school districts receiving federal
assistance ensure access of national-origin minority children
to public education. Interpretations of the Act by the United
States Office for Civil Rights (e.g., OCR's May 25, 1970 Memorandum, 35 Fed. Reg. 11595) led to the requirement that such
school districts had the obligation to provide specialized instruction to LEP students and to guarantee that non-discriminatory testing mechanisms are utilized in evaluating LEP children
for placement purposes. The Act also allows the Office for
Civil Rights to conduct compliance reviews of school districts
receiving federal funds, often requiring that they design an
educational plan to correct civil rights violations. The Civil
Rights Act of 1964 provided the legal basis for the landmark
Lau v. Nichols Supreme Court decision, to be discussed in a
subsequent section.

On May 25, 1970, the Department of Health, Education and
Welfare issued a memorandum to school districts requiring their
compliance with Title VI of the Civil Rights Act of 1964. The
purpose of the memorandum was to clarify HEW policy on issues
related to the responsibility of school districts to provide

equal education opportunity to national-origin minority-group children who were limited in their English proficiency. The memorandum addressed major areas of concern regarding compliance with Title VI.

First, since inability to speak and understand English excludes LEP children from effective participation in educational programs, the school districts were directed to take affirmative steps to remedy language limitations in order to provide access for these students in the educational programs.

Second, school districts were enjoined from assigning national-origin minority-group students to classes for the mentally retarded on the basis of English-language limitations. School districts were furthermore required to provide national-origin minority-group students access to college preparatory courses.

Third, any ability grouping or tracking system used by the school system to remediate the special language needs of national-origin minority-group children must be designed to meet the language-skill needs of these children as soon as possible and must not be used as educational dead-ends or permanent tracking.

Fourth, school districts were held responsible for the adequate notification of national-origin minority-group parents of school activities. Such notification must be provided in the appropriate language--other than English.

The May 25th memorandum further requires that school districts examine current practices in their districts to determine whether they are in compliance with the issues addressed in the memorandum. The May 25th memorandum was significant because it required school districts to provide programs for children experiencing English-language limitations. According to the memorandum, providing identical materials and instruction to all students did not ensure equal educational opportunity. In addition, all school districts receiving any form of federal assistance were held accountable for adherence to this memorandum. Furthermore, the memorandum provided grounds for court actions by national-origin minority-group children and offered valuable information to groups safeguarding student rights.

In 1968 Congress passed Title VII of the Elementary and Secondary School Act, or the *Bilingual Education Act*. Section 702 of this act states:

> In recognition of the special educational needs of the large numbers of children of limited English-speaking ability in the United States, Congress hereby declares it to be the policy of the United States to provide financial assistance to local educational agencies to develop and carry out new and imaginative elementary and secondary school programs designed to meet these

special educational needs. For the purposes of this
title, "children of limited English-speaking ability"
means children who come from environments where the
dominant language is other than English. (20 U.S.C.
880b)

Funds allocated for the Bilingual Education Act of 1968
were to be used for planning and development of bilingual education programs; preservice and inservice training for teachers,
supervisors, counselors, aides, and support staff; and for the
implementation and maintenance of the program.

The distribution of funds would be determined by the
number of children between the ages of three and eighteen
classified as limited-English-speaking. The states demonstrating the greatest need would be accorded priority.

In 1978 the Bilingual Education Act was amended (20 U.S.C.
3222). Section 702 now states that there are large numbers of
children of limited English-speaking ability who have a cultural heritage which differs from that of English-speaking
persons and that a primary way by which children learn is
through the use of their language and cultural heritage.
Therefore, large numbers of children of limited English-
speaking ability have educational needs which can be met by
the methods and techniques of bilingual education. The Congress, through this amendment, declares a policy of establishing equal educational opportunity for all children through bilingual education programs. For this purpose Congress proposed
to provide financial assistance to develop bilingual education
programs at preschool, elementary, and secondary levels to
meet the educational needs of children of limited English-
speaking ability.

The Bilingual Education Act was, therefore, amended to
require specifically bilingual education programs for children
of limited English proficiency in an effort to guarantee equal
educational opportunities to these children. The amendment
also recognizes the importance of a child's native language
and cultural heritage in the learning process. Although the
major thrust of the amendment was to promote the development
and implementation of bilingual programs for children of
limited English-speaking ability, it allows voluntary enrollment in bilingual programs of children whose native language
is English.

The amendment requires that bilingual education programs
be designed to include both English and the native language as
mediums of instruction. Through the study of the history and
culture associated with the native language, the bilingual
programs established must attempt to develop pride in the
students' culture and reinforcement of children's self-esteem.

The amendment broadens the criteria for eligibility to bilingual programs to those "who cannot read, write, or understand English at the level appropriate for their age and grade." The amendment extends eligibility to include American Indians and Alaskan-native students. The monies approved for Indian programs will be handled solely by the applicant and not by other agencies.

The amendment stipulates that bilingual programs in Puerto Rico include children of either limited English or limited Spanish-speaking proficiency.

Funding for bilingual education programs was allocated through 1983 and the amendment now requires that criteria be established by school districts for both entry into and exit from bilingual programs.

The amendment requires the Commissioner of Education and the Director of Bilingual Education to establish and operate a national clearinghouse of information for bilingual education. Material development centers were to be established to develop materials for bilingual programs in the elementary schools as well as materials for institutions of higher education preparing bilingual education professionals.

Since a paucity of adequately trained personnel could present a major obstacle to the development of bilingual programs, the amendment stipulates that 15 percent of each bilingual education grant be used for the preparation of bilingual education personnel and preservice and inservice education. A bilingual education fellowship program was also established.

Proposals for funding require inclusion of a staffing plan specifying the employment of persons who have listening, speaking, reading, and writing abilities in both the English language and the native language of the students with which they would work.

The Amendments of 1974 provide for community participation in bilingual programs. Funding applicants are required to consult with parents of potential bilingual program students prior to submitting an application. Applicants are also required to establish committees composed of parents and secondary school students to participate in the planning, implementation, and evaluation of the bilingual program established.

The Amendments brought a new priority to the Library Services and Constitution Act (LSCA). The LSCA specified that priority for funding would be given to library programs of projects serving areas of high concentrations of limited-English-speaking persons (Education Amendments, 1974).

The Bilingual Education Act requires that an annual report be sent to Congress and the President outlining the present state of bilingual education.

The report would include a national assessment of the
educational needs of children and others of limited
English-speaking ability, an evaluation of Title VII
activities, a description of teacher and other bilingual personnel requirements, and a statement of
next year's extended bilingual education activities
and their cost. (U.S. Civil Rights Commission,
1975, 173)

The Act also requires national surveys to identify the
number of individuals of limited English-speaking ability and
the extent to which federal, state, and local programs were
meeting their linguistic needs. The Act also mandates the
preparation of a five-year plan to extend bilingual education
services to those who were in need of such services as identified by the survey.

The Act requires that applications for assistance include
a description of the evaluation that will be used to assess
the program's progress. The evaluation plan must include a
method for comparing the reading-skill performance, in both
languages, of children participating in the program and an
estimate of the children's progress in the absence of the program. Appropriate tests of statistical significance are required for reporting pre- and post-test results.

At the time of enactment of the *Equal Educational Opportunities Act of 1974*, Congress had become aware of the need
for a national education policy that would address the issue
of equity in education and the major educational reform movements affecting the country. One of these movements was the
quest for bilingual education by language-minority groups. As
mentioned above, in 1968, Congress enacted Title VII of the
Elementary and Secondary Education Act, also known as the Bilingual Education Act, where Congress declared its support
and appropriated funds for demonstration projects in the field
of bilingual education.

By 1974, a significant number of states had also enacted
bilingual legislation, federal courts had ordered the establishment of bilingual programs, and the United States Supreme Court
had confirmed the authority of the government's Office for
Civil Rights to enforce civil rights mandates. The Equal
Educational Opportunities Act includes the codification into
law of the guarantee of equal education rights for language-
minority students and of legal principles declared by the
Supreme Court in the landmark case, *Lau v. Nichols* (to be discussed in a later section).

Section 1701 (1) of the Equal Educational Opportunities
Act states: "All children enrolled in public schools are entitled to equal educational opportunity without regard to race,
color, sex, or national origin...."

Of particular relevance for language minorities, Section 1703 of the Act also states:

No state shall deny equal educational opportunity to an individual on account of his or her race, color, sex, or national origin by ... the failure of an educational agency to take appropriate action to overcome language barriers that impede equal participation by its students in its instructional programs.

Under this section, even school districts not receiving federal funds are obligated to provide adequate educational services to any individual eligible for participation in its programs.

By 1974, federal legislation had vigorously built a structure of legal requirements and funding to develop appropriate programs for children of limited English proficiency. The solidity of this structure would be tested in court cases across the nation.

CASE LAW

State and federal courts have been instrumental in clarifying the educational rights of LEP children. During the 1970s a number of significant cases were litigated that helped define the process by which LEP children were serviced. Litigation has been crucial to the establishment of rights for language-minority children. An overview of key court cases involving the educational rights of language-minority children may help in a better understanding of the issues before the courts.

Lau v. Nichols *(1974)*

A class action suit was filed in the Supreme Court by 1,856 Chinese students of limited English-speaking ability against the San Francisco Unified School District. Plaintiffs claimed that they were not receiving a meaningful education due to the school district's failure to provide them with English-language instruction or other adequate instructional procedures. Plaintiffs argued that this was in direct violation of Section 601 of the Civil Rights Act of 1964 which bans discrimination based on "race, color, or national origin, (in) any program or activity receiving Federal financial assistance...."

The Supreme Court declared that

... there is no equality of treatment merely by providing students with the same facilities, textbooks, teachers, and curriculum; for students who do not understand English are effectively foreclosed from any meaningful education.

In this case, the Supreme Court mandates that school districts must provide limited English proficiency children with "a meaningful opportunity to participate in the public educational program." Although the Court did not suggest one specific solution, it was noted that teaching English to the students who do not speak the language, as well as native-language instruction, was an option, among others. Defendants were ordered to address the problem and rectify the situation.

As we will see, Court decisions since *Lau* have resulted in the establishment of bilingual programs, clarified school districts' responsibilities, and rejected claims of national-origin discrimination (Teitelbaum and Hiller, 1977).

Aspira of New York, Inc. v. Board of Education of the City of New York *(1972)*

In 1972 Aspira, a Puerto Rican self-help organization, filed suit against the New York City Board of Education on behalf of an estimated 182,000 Spanish-speaking students in New York City public schools. Plaintiffs alleged that the school system had failed either to teach Spanish-speaking children in a language they could understand, or to provide them with the English-language skills needed to progress in school.

On August 29, 1974, the parties entered into a consent decree which provided that:

1. The Board of Education would identify and classify those students whose English-language limitations prevent them from effectively participating in the learning process and who can effectively participate in Spanish.

2. By September of 1975, the defendants were to provide all the children described above with: (a) a program to develop their ability to speak, understand, read, and write English; (b) instruction in Spanish in such substantive courses as mathematics, science, and social studies; (c) a program to reinforce and develop the use of Spanish in children entering the school system, and whose assessment of reading readiness in English indicates the need for such development. In addition to, but not at the expense of, the three central elements of the required program, entitled students were to spend maximum class time with other children to avoid isolation from their peers.

3. By September of 1975 the defendants were to provide all elements of the program to all children within the defined class.

4. The Board of Education was to promulgate minimum educational standards to ensure that the program would be provided

to all children within the defined class in each of the community school districts.

5. The defendants were obligated to use their maximum
feasible efforts to obtain and expend the funds required to
implement the program.

In addition to the above stipulations, the consent decree
included agreements on the use, development, and dissemination
of appropriate materials and tests, as well as the recruitment,
training, or retraining of adequate staff. The court did not
accept immersion or pull-out programs as appropriate to the
needs of limited-English-proficiency students (Federal
Supplements, 394).

Although the Aspira case was a major stepping-stone in
the development of bilingual programs in New York City, the
court's ruling limited eligibility to bilingual programs.
Students had to demonstrate stronger language skills in the
native language than in English in order to qualify. This
ruling differed from the *Lau* decision, which based eligibility
solely on limited English-speaking ability (Federal Supplement,
394).

Serna v. Portales Municipal Schools *(1972)*

Chicano students filed suit against the Portales Municipal
School District in New Mexico, arguing that the English-only
program in the school district constituted a denial of their
equal educational opportunity. The court found the school district in violation of the students' constitutional rights to
an equal educational opportunity and ordered the provision of
bilingual instruction.

While an appeal was pending in this case, the Supreme
Court reached a decision on the *Lau* case. Noting the similarities in the two cases, the Tenth Circuit Court of Appeals affirmed the district court's ruling under Title VI but declined
to decide the constitutional claim. In affirming the district
court's Title VI ruling, the Tenth Circuit Court held that the
students had a right to bilingual education and upheld the
district court's adoption of a bilingual instruction plan.

Rios v. Read *(1977)*

Plaintiffs demanded information regarding achievement levels,
tenure in special ESL pullout classes, reading scores, and attendance rates in an effort to evaluate whether the programs
of the Patchogue-Medford school district in Long Island promoted academic progress and fluency in English as a second language. Defendants argued that it could withhold records because *Lau* requires only that a school district take affirmative

steps to meet the needs of non-English-speaking students.

The court acknowledged that the school district offered
a remedial program for limited English-speaking children and
that a bilingual department was established in the district.
Nevertheless, the court rejected the notion that *any* affirmative steps taken by a school district would satisfy *Lau*:

> It is not enough simply to provide a program for dis-
> advantaged children or even to staff the program with
> bilingual teachers; rather, the critical question is
> whether the program is designed to assure as much as
> is reasonably possible the language-deficient child's
> growth in the English language. An inadequate program
> is as harmful to a child who does not speak English
> as no program at all.

The district court, then, extended the *Lau* decision to
include an "effective" program.

Arroyo v. Barbarito *(1975)*

A class action suit filed on behalf of Puerto Rican pupils
with English-language limitations enrolled in the New Haven
public school system. The complaint alleges that the system
has over 2,295 Puerto Rican and other Hispanic students, a
substantial number of whom have "English language deficiencies."
Plaintiffs allege that the schools have "no educational programs, services, and/or personnel equipped to meet the linguistic needs" of these children, "an insufficient number" of programs, or "inadequate or inappropriate" programs. The complaint alleges that defendant's practices violate the Fourteenth
Amendment and Title VI of the Civil Rights Act of 1964. Plaintiffs seek, in part, "(a) comprehensive full-time bilingual
educational program ...," a method for identifying pupils in
need of services and evaluating the progress of those receiving
services, and a program of affirmative action hiring to employ
bilingual personnel.

On April 21, 1977, without objection, the court approved
a class consisting of "all Puerto Rican and other Spanish-
speaking children who attend the public schools of the City of
New Haven, Connecticut, who speak, comprehend, read and write
the English language with difficulty or not at all." It would
not suffice merely to furnish any program but that the services
rendered had to prove effective for the students concerned.

Otero v. Mesa County Valley School District
No. 51 *(1975)*

A class-action suit filed on behalf of Chicano students.
Plaintiffs sought a court mandate for the establishment of
appropriate bilingual programs with a school staff which reflected the cultural and linguistic background of the students.
The main contention in this case was that existing educational
programs designed for white middle-class students accounted
for the poor academic achievement of Chicano students. The
programs provided to them were inappropriate and violated
their rights under Title VI and the Equal Protection Clause.
The court held that the Fourteenth Amendment does not require
school districts to provide bilingual-bicultural programs.
The court added that the low academic performance of Chicano
students was caused by socioeconomic factors and not failings
of the educational program.

Regarding the Title VI claim, the court found that evidence
of serious language deficiency was not presented and that the
school board was "making a real, conscientious effort to recognize, face, and solve any problem which may exist as to any
student."

Ramos v. LaFontaine *(1976)*

A class action suit was filed on behalf of children of
limited English ability against the Hartford Public Schools.
Plaintiffs contend that they are not receiving a meaningful
educational opportunity because they either do not participate
in any bilingual education program or have been placed in programs which are insufficient, inappropriate, or inadequate to
ensure their equal and effective participation in the learning
process. On June 5, 1978, the court approved a consent decree
submitted by the parties. The consent decree orders that
defendants:

1. Formally identify students in need of bilingual education through a language survey, language dominance testing, and
English proficiency testing.

2. Obtain parental approval for bilingual program placements. All communication with parents must be performed by
personnel familiar with the bilingual program.

3. Teaching staff recruited for bilingual programs must
demonstrate their ability to communicate orally and in writing,
in English and Spanish, Portuguese or Italian. A testing instrument will be utilized for this purpose.

4. Assess the staff needs of bilingual programs and recruit the necessary teaching staff to ensure appropriate services to all students identified as children with limited
English proficiency.

5. Develop and implement a plan for community relations
and parent participation that will enable the parents of
limited-English-proficiency students to participate fully in
their children's educational experience. An outreach approach
is to be used, including communications in the appropriate languages, to bring parents into the school in a meaningful
manner.

6. All curriculum requirements for graduation will be
available to limited-English-speaking students. Whenever
minimum competency skills for promotion for non-limited-
English-speaking students are developed and implemented, the
same will be done for students of limited English proficiency.

7. Develop an organizational structure for the development
and coordination of the scope and sequence for the bilingual/
bicultural curriculum.

STATE LEGISLATION

During the early 1960's there were no state-mandated bilingual education programs in this country. On the contrary,
prior to 1968 twenty-one states, including California, New
York, Pennsylvania, and Texas, had approved legislation requiring that all public school instruction be conducted in
English. In seven states teachers could face criminal penal-
ties or revocation of teaching license if they conducted bilingual classes.

The late 1960s was a period of mounting dissatisfaction
with the public school system, especially from the perspective
of language-minority populations. An extensive campaign for
bilingual/bicultural education ensued until 1967, when Senator
Ralph Yarborough of Texas introduced a bill in Congress which
would later become Title VII of the Elementary and Secondary
Act of 1968, or the Bilingual Education Act.

Nevertheless, Title VII funding was limited and only a
handful of bilingual programs could be federally financed.
The pressure grew at state level to enact local bilingual
education legislation to fulfill the needs of limited-English-
proficiency children.

During the latter part of the 1960s a group of community
leaders in Boston, Massachusetts, formed the "Task Force on
Children Out of School" to investigate the school system's
policies toward poor children. Among other things, the task
force found that half of Boston's estimated 10,000 Spanish-
speaking school-aged children were not in school. Boston
community activists and sympathetic legislators worked together
to remedy the situation, and in the fall of 1971 the nation's
first comprehensive state bilingual education law was passed

(Ann. Laws. Mass. Ch. 71A, 1-9). The law states that classes
conducted in English are "inadequate for children of limited
English proficiency and that bilingual education programs are
necessary "to ensure equal educational opportunity to every
child." The Massachusetts bilingual law is not only the first
state bilingual law in the country, but it has stricter provisions than any subsequently approved by other states. The
law requires school districts to take a yearly census of
school-age children within the district who are of "limited
English-speaking ability," to classify the children so identified "according to the language of which they possess a primary
speaking ability." The law also requires the state to offer
a transitional bilingual education program of up to three years
to these children whenever there are 20 or more children of
limited English-speaking ability within a district who speak
a common language other than English. The state provides
financial assistance to compensate for the additional cost of
bilingual programs; up to a maximum of $2.5 million for the
first year, $3.5 million per year for the second and third
years and $6 million per year for the fourth and subsequent
years of programs in transitional bilingual education.

Today twenty states have enacted bilingual education laws
(see Table 1 below). Most bilingual education programs mandated are transitional in nature although some states, such
as Alaska, California, Connecticut, and New Mexico, allow for
language maintenance programs. Most state mandates require
school districts to conduct an annual census to determine the
number of language-minority children in the district and to
notify parents of their children's placement in bilingual programs. Another common feature is the requirement that language-
minority children be integrated with English-speaking children
in courses which do not require English-language proficiency
(such as art, music, and physical education). The laws differ
in important areas, though. Massachusetts and Illinois, for
example, require that only reading and writing in the native
language be taught, while oral comprehension, speaking, reading,
and writing will be taught for English. Texas law states that
all four skill areas will be developed in both the native
language and English.

CONCLUSION

Federal and state legislation, litigation, as well as
administrative policy decisions have clearly established the
rights of limited-English-proficiency children to bilingual
education programs. Legal and educational experts, in agreement with linguistic minority advocates, have repeatedly

stressed that a meaningful education can only be attained in
the language understood by students. Teaching children of
limited English proficiency solely in English without consideration for their native language skills constitutes a denial of
these children's equal educational opportunities.

===
Table 1

STATE LEGISLATION

State	Date Passed	Type of Program
Alaska	1975	Maintenance/Transitional
Arizona	May 1973	Transitional
California	September 1976	Maintenance/Transitional
Colorado	November 1975	Transitional
Connecticut	July 1977	Maintenance/Transitional
Illinois	1973	Transitional
Indiana	1976	Transitional
Louisiana	July 1975	Transitional
Maine	March 1977	Transitional
Massachusetts	November 1971	Transitional
Michigan	October 1974	Transitional
Minnesota	May 1977	Transitional
New Jersey	January 1975	Transitional
New Mexico	April 1973	Maintenance/Transitional
New York	May 1974	Transitional
Oregon	1971	Transitional
Rhode Island	May 1974	Transitional
Texas	June 1973	Transitional
Utah	February 1977	Not stated
Wisconsin	1975	Transitional

===

REFERENCES

Arroyo v. Barbarito. C.A. No. N75-191, D. Conn., 1975.

Aspira v. New York City School Board. DCNY 394 Federal Supplement 1161-1166 (New York, 1975).

Brown v. Board of Education of Topeka. 347 United States Reports, 483-495 (October Term, 1954).

Lau v. Nichols. 414 U.S. Reports, 563-572 (October Term, 1974).

Otero v. Mesa County Valley School District No. 51. 408 Federal Supplement 162-172 (D. Colorado, 1975).

Ramos v. LaFontaine. D. Conn. C.A. No. H-76-38, 1976.

Rio v. Read. 73 Federal Rule Decisions, 589-603, 1977.

Serna v. Portales Municipal Schools. 499 Federal Reporter, 2d, 1147-1154 (10th Cir., 1974).

Tietelbaum, H., and R.J. Hiller. "Bilingual Education: The Legal Mandate." *Harvard Educational Review*, 47:138-170.

U.S. Commission on Civil Rights. *A Better Chance to Learn: Bilingual-Bicultural Education.* Washington, DC: Clearinghouse Publication No. 51, 1975.

ANNOTATED BIBLIOGRAPHY

Alford, A.L. "The Education Amendments of 1978." *American Education*, 1979, 15:6-14.

The author delineates the changes brought about by the Education Amendments of 1978, including emergency school aid programs, strengthening of bilingual education programs and updating the Adult Education Act.

Andersson, T., and M. Boyer. *Bilingual Schooling in the United States*. Austin: National Educational Laboratory Publishers, 1978.

A discussion of bilingualism and bilingual education, including a historical overview, rationale, planning of bilingual programs, and research. Includes an analysis of the implications of bilingual education for society and education in general. The appendices include the Bilingual Education Act, guidelines for bilingual education programs, demographic data, immigration legislation, a typology of bilingual education teacher qualifications and a directory of bilingual programs in the United States.

Arroyo v. Barbarito. C.A. No. N75-191, D. Conn., 1975.

A class action suit filed on behalf of Puerto Rican pupils with English-language limitations enrolled in the New Haven, Connecticut, school system.

Aspira v. New York City School Board. DCNY 394 Federal Supplement 1161-1166 (New York, 1975).

A suit filed on behalf of Spanish-speaking students against the New York City Board of Education.

Ballesteros, D. "Toward an Advantaged Society: Bilingual Education in the 1970's." *National Elementary School Principal*, 1970, 50:25-28.

Presents arguments for bilingual education and a discussion of the Bilingual Education Act of 1968.

Bilingual Education: Current Perspectives--Law. Virginia Center for Applied Linguistics, 1977.

A book containing a legal perspective on bilingual education. It includes a section on the implications of desegregation on bilingual education, as well as court cases.

Brown v. Board of Education of Topeka. 347 United States Reports, 483-495 (October Term, 1954).

The text of the landmark desegregation case, including arguments for plaintiffs and defendants.

Cordasco, F. "The Bilingual Education Act." *Phi Delta Kappan,* 1969, 51:75.

Presents a historical overview of bilingual education and a discussion of the Bilingual Education Act of 1968. Discusses the objectives of bilingual education programs.

Deane, B., and P.A. Zirkel. "The Bilingual Education Mandate." *The American School Board Journal,* 1976, 163:29-32.

Summarizes the struggle for bilingual education. Discusses court cases relevant to bilingual education, such as *Lau v. Nichols, Serva v. Portales, Aspira v. New York City Board of Education* and *Otero v. Mesa County Valley School District No. 51.*

"Education Amendments of 1972." *Georgetown Law Journal,* 1973, 61:1067-1086.

A commentary which reviews the Education Amendments of 1972 by summarizing each title.

"Education Amendments of 1974." *American Library,* 1974, 5: 574-575.

Includes a discussion of the changes made in the Elementary and Secondary Education Act through the 1974 Amendments. Emphasis is on the amendments' effects on laws concerning libraries.

Gee, E.G., and D.J. Sperry. *Education Law and the Public Schools: A Compendium.* Boston: Allyn and Bacon, 1978.

Contains a discussion of the *Lau v. Nichols* case.

Geffert, H., R. Harper, S. Sarmiento, and D. Schember. "The Current Status of U.S. Bilingual Legislation." In *Bilingual Education Series: 4, Virginia*. Center for Applied Linguistics, 1975.

Contains an overview of court decisions and legislation affecting bilingual education. Legislation by states is also reviewed.

Grey, C., S. Convery, and K.M. Fox. "The Current Status of Bilingual Education Legislation: An Update." In *Bilingual Education Series: 9*. Washington, DC: Center for Applied Linguistics, 1981.

Discusses court decisions in bilingual education at state and federal levels.

Guide to State Education Agencies. Virginia: National Clearinghouse for Bilingual Education, 1980.

Discusses state bilingual education legislation, teacher certification, and state agencies.

Irizarry, R.A. *Bilingual Education: State and Federal Legislative Mandates*. Los Angeles: National Dissemination and Assessment Center, undated.

A summary of legislative provisions in bilingual education for each state. Includes a summary of program types, populations served, census mandates, staff training materials, and evaluation reporting.

Kobrick, J.W. "The Compelling Case for Bilingual Education." In Cordasco, F. (ed.). *Bilingual Schooling in the United States: A Sourcebook for Educational Personnel*. New York: McGraw-Hill, 1976.

Discusses the efforts made by different communities to establish bilingual education programs. Refers to research done on the effectiveness of bilingual education programs which prove that bilingual-bicultural education is the greatest educational priority in bilingual communities. Analyzes the Bilingual Education Act in light of its psychological impact. Discusses state bilingual laws.

Lau v. Nichols. 414 U.S. Reports, 563-572 (October Term, 1974).

Class action suit filed in the Supreme Court on behalf of Chinese students of limited English-speaking ability against the San Francisco Unified School District.

Liebowitz, A.H. *The Bilingual Education Act: A Legislative
Analysis*. Rosslyn, VA: National Clearinghouse for Bilingual
Education, 1980.

Explains federal legislation on bilingual education and discusses the historical background of linguistic minorities in
the United States. Analyzes the Bilingual Education Act and
discusses the future directions of bilingual education.

Massachusetts General Laws Annotated. Chapter 71A, 1-9,
189-195.

The Massachusetts Bilingual Education Law.

National Advisory Council on Bilingual Education. *Fourth
Annual Report 1978-79*, September 30, 1979, B3-6.

Discusses the legislative status of bilingual education,
the administration of programs, other federal programs
affecting bilingual education, current federal research,
and state legislation on bilingual education. The appendix
includes legislative changes affecting Title VII.

Otero v. Mesa County Valley School District No. 51. 408
Federal Supplement 162-172 (D. Colorado, 1975).

A class action suit filed on behalf of Chicano students
against the Mesa County Valley School District in Colorado.

Plastino, A.J. "The Legal Status of Bilingual Education in
America's Public Schools: Testing Ground for a Statutory
and Constitutional Interpretation of Equal Protection."
Duquesne Law Review, 1978, 17:473-505.

Discusses the legislative status of bilingual education.
Recent court cases are interpreted.

Pousada, A. "Bilingual Education in the U.S." *Journal of
Communication*, 1979, 29:84-92.

Discusses the Bilingual Education Act of 1968 as part of
the Elementary and Secondary School Act of 1965, the amendments of 1974, and the court cases litigated in bilingual
education.

Ramos v. LaFontaine. D. Conn., C.A. No. H-76-38, 1976.

The text of the class action suit filed on behalf of all
children of limited English ability who are entitled to,
but are not receiving, bilingual education in the public
schools of Hartford, Connecticut.

Rena, A.A. "Action by the 93rd Congress, Bilingual Education
Act." *Today's Education*, 1975, 64:81-82.

Includes an overview of the Education Amendments of 1974.
A discussion of how proposals should be submitted is included.

Rios v. Read. 73 Federal Rules Decisions, 589-603.

Legal suit filed by non-English-speaking students against
the Patchogue-Medford school district in Long Island, New
York.

Roos, P.D. "Bilingual Education: The Hispanic Response to
Unequal Educational Opportunity." *Law and Contemporary
Problems*, 1978, 42:11-140.

This article describes legislation affecting bilingual
education including the Office for Civil Rights' May 25th
Memorandum, commentary on how desegregation affects bilingual education, and a summary of court cases.

Schivarty, B. *Statutory History of the United States Civil
Rights, Part Two*. New York University School of Law: Chelsea
House Publication in association with McGraw-Hill Book
Company, 1970.

Discusses the Civil Rights Act of 1964. The book also
presents legislative history of civil rights in the United
States.

Schneider, S.G. *Revolution or Reform: The 1974 Bilingual
Education Act*. New York: Las Americas Publishing Co., 1976.

A comprehensive case study of the legislative history of
the bilingual-bicultural provisions of the Educational
Amendments of 1974, Public Law 93-380. Presented and discussed are the Senate, House and Administrative positions,
as well as the interest of lobbyist groups on the philosophy
and goals of bilingual-bicultural education as they relate
to federal legislation and implementation. The merging of
various positions into a consensus which resulted in the
Bilingual Education Act of 1974 is viewed by the author as
a movement of reform of existing law and federal practice in
the area of bilingual-bicultural education.

Serna v. Portales Municipal Schools. 499 Federal Reporter, 2d,
1147-1154, 10th Circuit 1974.

A suit filed by Chicano students against the Portales Municipal School District in New Mexico.

Sugarman, D., and E.G. Widess. "Equal Protection for Non-English Speaking School Children: *Lau v. Nichols*." *California Law Review*, 1974, 62:157-182.

This articles provides an in-depth discussion of *Lau v. Nichols* including the interpretation and implications of the Supreme Court's decision.

Tietelbaum, H., and R.J. Hiller. "Bilingual Education: The Legal Mandate." *Harvard Educational Review*, 1977, 47:138-170.

Attorneys Tietelbaum and Hiller review the *Lau v. Nichols* Supreme Court decision which upheld the right of non-English-speaking students to educational programs designed to meet their language needs. In this article the authors point out that winning court cases will not overcome all the obstacles to equitable education. Sluggish federal enforcement of *Lau* remedies and school districts' resistance to establish bilingual programs are some of the hurdles discussed.

U.S. Code Congressional and Administrative News. 92nd Congress, Second Session, 1972, 2:278-281.

The text of the 1972 Education Amendments. Includes a summary of each title amended.

U.S. Code Congressional and Administrative News. 88th Congress, Second Session, 1964, 1:295-319.

The text of the Civil Rights Act of 1964.

U.S. Code. Title 20, 880b, 460.

The text of the Bilingual Education Act.

U.S. Code. Title 20, 3222, 212.

A discussion of the amended Bilingual Education Act of 1975.

U.S Commission on Civil Rights. *A Better Chance to Learn: Bilingual-Bicultural Education*. Washington, DC: Clearinghouse Publication No. 51, 1975.

This book includes a historical overview of bilingualism, equal educational opportunity for students, descriptions of programs and program evaluations. Laws are also included in the appendix as are state policies.

U.S. Office for Civil Rights Memorandum. *Federal Register 18*. July, 1970, 35, 11595-11596.

    Text of the May 25th Memorandum.

United States Statutes at Large. 89th Congress, First Session, 1965, 79:27-58.

    Text of the Elementary and Secondary School Act of 1965.

United States Statutes at Large. 95th Congress, Second Session, 1978, 92:1337-2688.

    Text of the Educational Amendments of 1978.

United States Statutes at Large. 93rd Congress, Second Session, 1974, 88:514-521.

    Includes the text of the Equal Educational Opportunity Act of 1974.

Chapter 3

ENGLISH AS A SECOND LANGUAGE

LANGUAGE-LEARNING THEORIES

The approaches and methods used in teaching second
languages in the United States in the twentieth century have
been based on one or the other of the two major theories of
learning--behaviorist or rationalist.

Behaviorists, of whom B.F. Skinner (1957) and Bloomfield
(1933) are the predominant proponents, maintain that the
learning process is essentially a stimulus-response-reinforcement process. Language learning is like any other learning.
Language is considered to be no more than a set of learned
habits, the acquisition of which requires no thinking or
analysis. In fact, behaviorists do not accept the notion of
mind and thinking, since they cannot be observed. They deal
only with phenomena that can be observed, measured, and described.
Twaddell (1958) summarized the bias toward the empirical
method of behaviorists in terms that make them sound somewhat
absurd: "The scientific method is quite simply the convention
that mind does not exist" (p. 57).

Another tenet of behaviorists that seems quaint today is
that "language is speech, not writing." This led to language
teaching that concentrated on speaking and pronunciation,
almost to the total exclusion of instruction in reading,
writing, and grammar.

Methods of language teaching based on the behaviorist
theories of learning became known as "mim-mem" or mimicry-
memorization. Children learn language by mimicking what they
hear, believe the behaviorists. If they receive positive reinforcement for it, they will repeat the hehavior, i.e., sound,
word, sentence. If there is negative reinforcement (or no
reinforcement, which is seen as negative), the child will not
repeat the behavior. A second-language methodology based on
behaviorism stresses memorization of dialogs and practice
pattern drills. The surface structure and form of the language, as well as the pronunciation, are emphasized. Since

50

meaning and comprehension cannot be observed, described, and measured, they are not considered.

Rationalists, as exemplified by Chomsky (1965), maintain that human beings learn language because they are innately, and uniquely, capable of doing so. They are, in effect, biologically programmed to learn language. Chomsky coined the phrase Language Acquisition Device (LAD). He claimed that humans are innately and uniquely equipped with an ability to acquire language. The fact that all human beings, even retarded children, learn a language is given as evidence of the theory.

Rationalists declare that language learning is a creative activity governed by rules. Children analyze, categorize, and evaluate language and develop rules for how it works. They cannot possibly be mimicking and memorizing since it is almost impossible that they will hear the same utterance twice. In addition, say rationalists, children say things that they have never heard adults say, e.g., "two foots." It is obvious that they have learned the rule for plurals and overgeneralized. They usually correct themselves later in their language development.

A rationalist approach to language teaching stresses meaning and content instead of structure. Instead of mimicry-memorization and drilling, they use natural, meaningful communication. Dependence on memorization only, without learning any rules, can make the language-learning process impossible, since every single structure would have to be memorized. Grammar is taught explicitly since grammar can help the language learner apply what has been learned to new language situations.

In summary, behaviorist theories led to the structural or descriptive school of linguistics, which led to approaches of language teaching that stressed repetition, memorization, positive reinforcement of correct responses, and emphasis on the surface structure of language. The surface structure of language deals with the words and sentences of language, disregarding the meaning. For example, in the sentence, "Visiting relatives can be boring," the utterance can convey two different meanings, depending on which words are stressed. This is of particular significance to the second-language learner who may learn the words and their placement in the sentence and still misunderstand the meaning.

Language-teaching approaches based on rationalist theories stress comprehension and meaning or the deep structure of the language as illustrated in the sentence "Visiting relatives can be boring." Grammar, rules, and analysis are all part of rationalist approach.

SECOND-LANGUAGE ACQUISITION

We have discussed theories of language acquisition which have a bearing on second-language learning. However, there are many issues involved in the learning of a second language. Researchers have attempted to answer such questions as: Is second-language learning similar to first-language acquisition? Do children learn a second language more easily than adults? Is there an optimum age for second-language learning? Is there a best method for teaching a second language?

It is important at this point to distinguish between language acquisition and language learning. A language is acquired in childhood, naturally, through living, without any formal instruction in the language. A language is learned through purposeful instruction. Therefore, it would appear that only children can acquire language. Adults must learn and be taught language. Furthermore, children can and do acquire second and third languages with apparent ease.

Acquisition of two or more languages simultaneously is said to occur before a child has acquired mastery of any one language, usually by the age of three (McLaughlin, 1978). After the age of three, it is considered that a second language is learned, since a child already has one fairly complete language system. This is successive language learning.

Children universally learn language in the same order, i.e., listening, speaking, reading, and writing. Children have been listening to language for almost a year before they begin to produce words. Additionally, they have been listening to complete sentences and yet begin to speak with one-word utterances, progressing to two-word utterances, and so on. Through toddlerhood and early childhood, children are capable of understanding sentences of much greater length and complexity than they are capable of producing.

The strategies children use in learning a second language are similar to those used in acquiring their first language. "This suggests that there is a unity of process that characterizes all language acquisition, whether of a first or second language, at all ages" (McLaughlin, p. 200). Dulay and Burt (1974) and Ervin-Tripp (1974) found that children make errors in learning a second language similar to those they make in acquiring their first language.

Based on the evidence of how apparently easily children learn a second language and on the lateralization of the brain, a hypothesis of a critical period for language learning emerged (Lenneberg, 1967). Assigning specific functions to certain areas of the brain, lateralization, is believed to start at about two and continue until puberty. More recently, researchers have believed that lateralization may be complete as early as 5

(Krashen, 1973). Before lateralization, the native language (L_1) and a second language (L_2) can be acquired without much difficulty and with nativelike pronunciation (Scovel, 1969). At that point, it can be considered acquiring two first or native languages.

Prior to lateralization, the brain has a plasticity which appears to be an enabling factor in first and second language acquisition. This plasticity diminishes with lateralization. The ability of pre-pubertal children to learn a second language free of accent is due to physical development. Speech muscles develop gradually, and plasticity may still be present before puberty.

The theory of lateralization and simple observation of children's language behavior would tend to corroborate the hypothesis that children are better than adults at learning a second language. In a few months, children can communicate sufficiently to function in the playground and, at least orally, in the classroom.

On closer scrutiny, however, the superiority of children's language-learning ability is not quite so impressive. A seven-year-old child needs to learn only 50,000 words to be considered a fluent speaker of a language, while an educated adult needs a vocabulary of more than 200,000 words. A seven-year-old has not developed adult-level sentence length and complexity. A child then is considered bilingual if he or she has learned one fifth of the vocabulary of an adult and can communicate at a seven-year-old level of syntactical and grammatical complexity (Krashen, 1978).

Piagetian developmental theory states that the formal operational stage of cognitive development is reached at puberty. It is then that a child can handle abstractions and formal thinking. If language learning is an analytic, thinking, rule-formation process, then it would appear that the period in which a second-language learner can most benefit from formal language instruction would be post puberty. Durette (1972) found that college students learn languages twice as fast as high school students and five times as fast as nine-year-olds. Burstall (1977) found that adults are faster and more efficient learners of second languages, except for pronunciation, than children. It appears then that there is more involved in second-language learning than lateralization.

Guiora, et al. (1972) talk about a language ego as an identity related to one's language. The development of the ego is intimately related to language, since it is through language that the positive or negative reinforcement needed for ego development is received. If the language ego theory is valid, then it might be expected that young children would have the least difficulty in learning a second language, since

their egos are still evolving in terms of L_1. Adding a new
language at this point poses no particular threat. Adoles-
cence, however, is a time of emotional turmoil and insecurity.
It is at this age that the ego is probably the most vulnerable.
Brown (1980) stated: "Pre-adolescent children of 9 or 10, for
example, are beginning to develop inhibitions, and it is conceivable, though little research evidence is available, that
children of this age who are exposed to a second language will
have more difficulty in learning the second language than
younger children" (p. 54).

It would seem that adults could go either way. If their
ego resolution has been successful, language learning should
be easier. An insecure adult of low self-esteem would probably
have a difficult time learning a second language.

Attitude toward languages, one's own and the target language, is an important factor in language learning. Young
children have had less opportunity to develop negative attitudes toward language than adults. They may not be aware of
all the issues of politics, prestige, nationalism, etc., that
contribute to a person's attitude about a second language.

It is surprising, however, how even children in early
grades can perceive and acquire attitudes about language.
Many of the early Title VII bilingual programs used the two-
way model, with monolingual English-speaking students learning
the native language of the non-English-speaking group (usually
Spanish). One of the recurring issues was the marked difference in the amount of second-language learning between the two
groups: the Spanish-speaking students learned significantly
more English than the reverse.

Although there are many contributing factors to this
phenomenon, such as the constant reinforcement of English outside the classroom, and in the media, the question of attitude
cannot be dismissed. Even children of 5 or 6 quickly learn
that English is the prestige language.

Adult strategies in second-language learning have not
been studied as much as those of children, but it appears that
they "approach a second language systematically and attempt to
form linguistic rules on the basis of whatever linguistic information is available to them--information from both the
native language and from the second language itself" (Brown,
p. 57).

It has been found that adults make many of the same errors
in learning a second language as children do in learning their
first language. This would indicate that they use strategies
for second-language learning similar to those used by children.

Seliger (1978) posits that there may be many critical
periods for language learning "successive and perhaps over-
lapping, lasting probably throughout one's lifetime, each

closing off different acquisition abilities." He states further that "... owing to the loss of plasticity and the closing
of critical periods for whatever language functions, the
learner will not be able to incorporate some aspect of the
second language." He concludes that "much language can still
be acquired by adults, but not to the same degree possible
for children ..." (pp. 16, 18).

A popular theory of second-language learning held that a
person's first language would interfere with his/her attempts
to learn a second language. This led to contrastive analysis
as a tool for anticipating the problem a learner would have
in attempting to learn a second language. It was argued that
knowledge of how the learners' first and second languages are
similar and how they differ would help the teacher anticipate
those features of the new language that would cause difficulty.

Contrastive analysis compares all the structures of the
native and target languages in an attempt to identify all the
structures that are similar and can be transferred, and all
those that are different, or exist in one language and not the
other and might, therefore, cause interference. Where structures are similar (e.g., "m," "p," "b" sounds in Spanish and
English) the learner can transfer the sounds from the native
to the target language. Conversely, the "sh" and "z" sounds
in English do not exist in Spanish, and Spanish-speaking
learners of English traditionally have difficulty with these
sounds.

Contrastive analysis proved to be inadequate to predict
all the errors that a language learner can make. Not all the
errors made by a language learner in L_2 are caused by interference from L_1. Adults sometimes make the same errors in
learning a second language that children do in learning a first
language. They formulate rules as they progress in learning a
language and sometimes overgeneralize, as children do in saying
"two foots."

Error analysis appeared to be a better method for identifying the errors made by language learners. This involves analyzing all the errors made by language learners, not only those
caused by language interference. It revealed that second-
language learners do not make all the errors predicted by contrastive analysis and that not all errors made were due to
native language interference but, in fact, had many sources.

Although error analysis is a useful device for studying
the strategies language learners use in learning a second language, it does not tell very much about the learners' communicative competence. The ultimate reason for learning a language
is to communicate with speakers of the language. This requires
mastery of all the functions of the language.

Both error and contrastive analysis concentrate on the

forms of language, the vocabulary, pronunciation, grammatical structures, that a learner uses. That does not give any information on how much comprehension of the context is taking place. Evelyn Hatch (1978) summarizes the problems inherent in observing only students' ability to use words and sentences correctly. She maintains that a language learner does not necessarily first learn to "manipulate structures" and gradually learn many structures which are then used in communication or discourse. She proposed that the reverse is true: "One learns how to do conversation, one learns how to interact verbally, and out of this interaction, syntactic structures are developed" (p. 404).

Neither contrastive nor error analysis tells us very much about a person's communicative competence--How well does a learner manipulate the functions of language? Can a language learner use the language to exchange information, convey and perceive feelings, persuade, etc.? "We use language in stretches of discourse" (Brown, 1980). The best way to gain understanding of how much mastery of the functions of a second language has been acquired is through discourse analysis.

Discourse analysis is concerned with the psychological, sociocultural, physical, and linguistic features of communication. Issues such as the style of speech a speaker uses in speaking to different audiences (register), non-verbal communication, and the rules of conversation are all within the purview of discourse analysis.

APPROACH TO LANGUAGE INSTRUCTION

The theories of language acquisition and second-language learning have resulted in several approaches and many methods for second-language instruction. We will discuss some of the major approaches and methods.

Although "approach" and "method" are often used interchangeably, there is a worthwhile distinction. An approach is one based on one of the learning theories, i.e., will the approach stress mimicry and memorization or will it stress meaning, process, and grammar? Will grammar be taught formally? How much importance should be placed on pronunciation and on correcting errors? Methods are developed on the basis of the approach to which the developer subscribes.

The twentieth century has been one of change, and often turmoil, for language-teaching methods. There have been numerous methods, each greatly touted, and often hailed as a panacea, until the next one came along. For the most part, each new method built on a previous one, discarding some aspect and replacing it with a new one.

Grammar-translation approach

Classical languages were traditionally taught with the
grammar-translation approach. Students were never expected to
speak or think in the language. They needed only to read
passages in the original and translate them into English.
During the 1950's and 1960's in the United States, many students suffered through foreign-language classes, memorizing
verb conjugations and vocabulary lists with their translations.
The classes were conducted in English, except for the drilling
of the verb conjugations and the reading aloud of short passages. Whole paragraphs were translated from the target language into English. There was little attention paid to understanding the content of the material or to pronunciation.
Often the teachers themselves had decidedly poor command of
the language, particularly of its pronunciation.

Reading approach

This was the preferred approach for students who needed
only to read the target language, either for studying in it
or for reading professional materials, e.g., Ph.D. students.
There is a good deal of reading done in the target language
immediately. The vocabulary is carefully controlled and the
grammar taught is only that which is necessary for understanding the material being read.

Direct approach

This is usually referred to as a method but there are
several methods that fall under this type of teaching, and we
will consider it as an approach. Emerging as a reaction to
the grammar-translation approach, its underlying principle is
that the best way to learn a language is by using it naturally
for communication. The Berlitz method is based on the direct
approach. In the direct approach, material is introduced via
an anecdote or short dialog. The Berlitz method begins by
naming common classroom articles. Questions and answers based
on the dialog or anecdote follow. Classes are conducted solely
in the target language and progress from simple to complex
material. Grammar is taught formally only after the students
have had the opportunity to practice the patterns orally.
The direct approach has been used successfully by the
U.S. Foreign Service and the military to prepare personnel
who must learn basic communication in a short period of time.

The audiolingual approach

Features of the direct method and the habit-formation, stimulus-response-reinforcement of an approach based in behaviorist learning theory are combined in this approach. The audiolingual approach introduces new material in naturalistic dialog. Vocabulary and grammatical structures are carefully controlled and sequenced. Language skills are sequenced, i.e., listening, speaking, reading, and writing. Memorization, via repetition drills, is stressed. Formal grammar is not stressed; instead, grammar is induced from the dialogs. Contrastive analysis of the native and second languages is used extensively. Use is made of audio-visual aids. Classes are conducted primarily in the target language but brief explanations in the native language are sometimes used. Pronunciation is stressed and reinforced with a good deal of teacher praise or correction. Dialog and conversation are sometimes contrived, since vocabulary and grammatical patterns are carefully controlled.

The cognitive approach

The emphasis in this approach is communication. All language skills, listening, speaking, reading, and writing are considered equally important. Pronunciation and memorization are not stressed. Context and meaning are of primary importance. The affective aspects of language learning and teaching, i.e., teacher and pupil attitude, motivation, and classroom interactions are also considered important. The teacher is seen as a facilitator of the language-learning process. Language learning is seen as rule-formation involving thinking, analysis, and evaluation. Therefore, grammar is taught formally. Use of the mother tongue is allowed.

LANGUAGE TEACHING METHODS

There are literally dozens of methods currently in use in foreign and English-as-a-second-language instruction in the United States. We will discuss only the best known or most widely used.

The audiolingual method

This is an approach and a method which is still used. Many commercially produced materials use the audiolingual method described in the previous section.

The silent way

Caleb Gattegno (1978) has developed a teaching method
which has acquired many converts and created many antagonists.
The title stems from the fact that the teacher in a second-
language class is silent a good deal of the time, as much as
ninety percent. Instruction begins with the use of cuisenair
rods (brightly-colored wooden rods of varying lengths). A
lesson will begin with "A rod." This is repeated several
times. "A red rod" follows. From this simple beginning students progress to very complex discourse using the rods to
represent many things, such as cars, houses, etc. During a
first lesson, students have been able to respond to sentences
such as "Take three yellow rods and two green rods and give
them to Joan."

After introducing new vocabulary and patterns, the teacher
remains silent most of the time and directs the class through
sign language that looks like charades. Students also have
the opportunity to play teacher. The teacher does not correct
students, answer their questions, or give positive reinforcement.

Initially, vocabulary is limited. Along with the rods,
phonic charts and word lists in colors to denote identical
sounds are used exclusively. After the basics of the language have been covered, controlled readers are introduced.

The silences in lessons are very active periods when
students are thinking about what they have heard. They must
think and concentrate intensively in order not to miss any-
thing, since the teacher will make a statement only once.
Students must correct themselves and help one another.

The counseling method

Curran (1976) sees the teaching-learning relationship as
essentially similar to the counseling relationship. In fact,
he calls the participants teacher/counselor/knower, and
learner/client. This method is probably the one most concerned about the process and interpersonal relationships in
language learning and teaching. Curran emphasizes that the
teachers' and students' feelings about themselves and about
one another are the primary factor in the teaching-learning
environment. Each must assume a share of the responsibility
for the relationship.

Language learners (clients) sit in a circle. Teachers
(counselors) remain outside the circle. Students are told to
talk about any topic they like. They begin the conversation
in their native language and the teacher then translates what
each student has said into the target language. The students

repeat what the teacher has said in the target language. A
tape is made of the students' repetition of the target language. At the end of the conversation, the tape is played
back and the teacher writes what the students have said on the
board. This provides a text from which vocabulary and grammar
are explained.

This method, with its lack of structure, places control
of learning on the students. The teacher does not question
or give reinforcement, positive or negative. This places
great demands on the teacher, however, since there is no way
to control vocabulary or grammar.

One drawback of this method is that it requires that all
the learners and the knower have a common language. If more
than one language is represented in the learners, then one
"knower" is needed for each language.

Another limitation of the method is that a knower needs
counseling skills as well as knowledge of the two languages.

The total physical response

From close observation of how young children learn language, Asher (1969, 1977) concluded that (a) children spend a
long time listening to language before they speak, and can
understand a good deal more language than they can produce;
(b) that children's bodies are actively involved in their
language learning, i.e., children mainly make statements concerning actions in which they are involved; and (c) most of
the language children hear in their early stages of language
learning are direct commands.

The Total Physical Response, then, stresses the need for
listening to a second language before being required to speak
it. Language is taught through commands that require the student to act or respond physically. Only after the students
have had a good deal of practice in listening and responding
to commands are they asked to speak. Students are asked to
reverse roles and give commands to the teacher and to one
another. This method has the advantage of putting the control
of vocabulary and grammar in the teachers' hands.

There are many other methods of teaching English as a
second language being used in programs throughout the country.
Suggestology uses music to create a mood conducive to language
learning. The Audio-Visual Method uses filmstrips. The Community Learning method is similar to the Counseling Method.

The three methods described in greater detail are those
most widely used in bilingual education programs.

ENGLISH AS A SECOND LANGUAGE IN BILINGUAL
EDUCATION PROGRAMS

None of the methods discussed was developed specifically
for use in bilingual education programs. Each one was concerned with the teaching of a foreign language. Some were
tried with such exotic languages as Swahili and some with such
widely used languages as Spanish.

Until the 1950's, non-English-speaking children arriving
in the United States were placed in mainstream classes where
very little out of the ordinary was done to try to integrate
them into the class. This has been named the "sink or swim"
method. Some sympathetic teachers would assign other students
who spoke the language to explain things to newcomers in their
native language. English as a foreign or second language was
almost exclusively an activity for foreign students in colleges and universities.

School districts were suddenly finding themselves with
large numbers of students, mostly Chicanos in the southwest
and Puerto Ricans in the northeast, who were not learning
English and assimilating. Mexican-American veterans returning
from World War II started the "Little Schools of the 400," an
early-day Headstart-type of program. These schools were set up
to give Chicano children readiness for school by teaching them
"the 400 most common words of American English" (Keller and
Van Hooft, 1982). In New York City, in 1958, the Board of
Education issued the Puerto Rican Study which described the
problems faced by Puerto Rican children in the city's public
schools.

The first approach to teaching new arrivals English was
the pull-out English as a Second Language (ESL) program. Children from several classrooms would be taken out of their classes
in groups of up to ten for one period a day of instruction in
ESL. These programs were unable to have much impact on the
rate of English learning of the students for many reasons.

In New York City, for example, there was usually one ESL
teacher to a school. Some ESL teachers were itinerant, serving
several schools. In those cases, children were pulled out for
instruction only once or twice a week. In light of what is
known about language learning today, it is obvious that this
was not sufficient. In addition, it was often the practice
that when a principal needed an extra teacher to "pinch-hit,"
it was the ESL teacher who was pressed into service and the
children lost a class. In schools where safety was a problem,
the teacher had to go from room to room returning children and
picking up the next group. Very often, fifteen minutes of a
fifty-minute class were wasted in the process.

When proponents of bilingual education began claiming that

ESL alone was not effective, ESL teachers became defensive and vehemently opposed bilingual education. Not only were they defending their profession but their jobs as well. Unfortunately, there is still too much distance between Teaching English to Speakers of Other Languages (TESOL) and bilingual education professionals. Although bilingual educators all agree that an effective program of bilingual education must include a strong ESL component, they point out that an approach based solely on ESL which ignores the student's native language and culture is doomed to failure.

In transitional bilingual programs, the most common in the United States, typical students will begin learning all subjects in their native language and studying ESL for one or more periods a day with an ESL teacher. This is often done on a pull-out basis. The best situations have teachers who have been trained in TESOL. Often, however, the teachers are not certified, nor have they had preparation in TESOL.

As the students' proficiency in English increases, subject matter is introduced in English, thereby increasing the amount of time spent learning English. Most of the ESL instruction is limited to oral English, reading and writing being left to the classroom teacher.

Unfortunately, there is often little communication between the classroom teacher and the ESL teacher. In an ideal situation, they would confer often in order to reinforce each other's teaching. The ESL teacher could include content area vocabulary in the language class.

Since most bilingual programs in the United States are of the transitional model, there is always the felt pressure to teach children to speak, read, and write English in order that they may be mainstreamed in approximately three years. Although there is research evidence to indicate that there is a direct correlation between proficiency in L_1 and achievement in learning L_2 (Skutnabb-Kangas, 1979; Cummins, 1979), bilingual teachers and administrators find that they must push the formal ESL instruction before children have acquired the necessary proficiency in L_1 to achieve maximum benefit from instruction in L_2.

It bears repeating that there is research evidence to indicate that the optimal age for simultaneous acquisition of two languages is from birth to three. After the age of three, language learning appears to be most effective after children have fully mastered their L_1. This creates conflict for bilingual educators when they must adhere to a time schedule for mainstreaming despite what they believe to be sound pedagogical practice. If children of limited English proficiency (LEP) begin their schooling in a bilingual program before they have learned to read their L_1, should they be taught to read L_1 or should they be taught to read L_2 and forego reading in L_1? Sound pedagogy and common sense would indicate that children of 5, 6, or 7 who have appropriate mastery of their L_1 are ready for reading in L_1. Waiting for them to develop comparable mastery of L_2 will delay the learning to read unnecessarily.

It is argued that reading is a skill that once learned does not have to be relearned; students who can read one language will find learning to read a second language fairly easy. The skills of reading, decoding, word attack, comprehension, etc., are said to be transferable. This argument is particularly relevant to Spanish-speaking students, since Spanish has greater sound-symbol correspondence than English and is, therefore, easier to read. It is not clear that the same is true for students of Asian backgrounds whose languages do not use our alphabet.

Cummins (1979) hypothesizes that a threshold level of competence in L_1 is necessary before children are exposed to L_2 in a school situation. When that occurs, and L_2 is introduced in an "additive" mode, i.e., the child will be adding a language, not exchanging (subtractive), a threshold level of bilingualism is reached, which results in positive effects on cognitive growth.

The assumption underlying this hypothesis is that L_1 has provided a child with understanding of linguistic concepts and the development of abstract thinking, which he or she will use in learning L_2. If a child is exposed to formal instruction in L_2 before reaching the developmental level of abstract thinking, it is likely that he or she will not achieve competence in either language.

If bilingual programs were to delay reading in L_2 until children were proficient readers in L_1, many children would not be able to be mainstreamed in three years. Learning a second language and reading in either L_1 or L_2 are subject to individual aptitude. It is well known that not all children learn to read at the same time.

Some children are being taught to read in L_2 before they are proficient readers of L_1. When they lag behind their peers in reading in English upon being mainstreamed, critics of bilingual education declare that it is not effective. Yet, several studies have demonstrated that there is sometimes a lag in one or both languages in children in bilingual programs in the first few years which is usually recovered later, in four or five years.

The issue of reading in L_2 for students who are proficient readers of L_1 is similar. The cognitive approaches to ESL give equal stress to speaking, reading, and writing. Reading, writing, and grammar are often taught immediately, all the skills being integrated in each lesson.

One technique for integrating all the language skills which is effective with both children and adults is the language experience. Students relate an experience, the teacher writes it, the students read it and then copy it.

Adults learning a second language who are literate in L_1 profit from explicit instruction in grammar and from contrastive analysis. Rules for grammar are best presented after students have had some practice using the structures.

While young children seem to learn a second language easily in a "natural" way, i.e., without formal instruction, older children, especially those literate in L_1, adolescents and adults benefit from, and seem to prefer, formal instruction. Some of the methods discussed, particularly those which combine "naturalistic" language learning with formal instruction, are effective with both children and adult language learners. The Total Physical Response and the Silent Way have been effective with children and adults.

TESTING IN ESL

Testing has been and continues to be an important issue in bilingual education and ESL. Except for the few maintenance programs, children are placed in bilingual programs on the basis of an assessment of their language dominance, i.e., their strongest language. After students' dominance is determined, proficiency must be assessed in order to place them in an appropriate class, level, ESL group, etc.

A bilingual person for whom dominance might not be clear could be tested for proficiency in either language, and the language in which he or she is most proficient would be the dominant language.

When a teacher believes a student may be ready for mainstreaming, proficiency is tested again. If the student is deemed proficient enough to profit from instruction in English, he or she is mainstreamed.

Testing in ESL is fraught with all the problems of testing in general and, in addition, with some problems peculiar to bilingual education. In the first place is the question of whether a test truly measures what it purports to. Some tests are oral, others are written; some test vocabulary, etc. Walters (1979) suggests that "A partial solution to this problem is to consider language assessment from the perspective of the entire range of the child's abilities." He continues, "Thus, by broadening the number and type of instruments used to assess language ability, it is possible to increase the accuracy of the assessment" (p. 5).

Another problem with language assessment is that tests
are normed and assume homogeneity. Even if the groups on which
the tests were normed were homogeneous, which is highly unlikely, the students in bilingual education programs represent
different cultural, linguistic, and dialectal groups.

Language tests provide information on students' mastery
of phonological, syntactical and lexical aspects of the language, but tell nothing about their communicative competence.
Testing in ESL is, therefore, moving from discrete point tests,
those focusing on one point at a time, e.g., phonology, vocabulary, etc., to pragmatic or integrative tests. A pragmatic
test "is any procedure or task that causes the learner to
process sequences of elements in a language that conform to
the normal contextual restraints of that language ..." (Oller,
1979, p. 38).

The Bilingual Syntax Measure improves on other commonly
used tests, such as the New York City Language Assessment
Battery, in that it elicits discourse from children instead
of one-word utterances or pointing to an item.

Integrated tests are better at assessing students' ability
to comprehend and produce language. Cloze, dictation, oral
interviews, essay, and translation are examples of pragmatic
tests.

Testing is discussed more fully in Chapter 4.

CONCLUSION

It is very clear from the literature that there is no one
method of teaching ESL that is best, since no method could
possibly fill all the needs and styles of all students and instructors. Issues such as individual aptitude, learning style,
motivation, amount of time spent on learning the language, outside reinforcement, all have an impact on how much language is
learned.

There are themes that reoccur in the literature, however.
Teaching or learning a foreign language is not a pure science.
Like the arts, the skills needed to learn and teach are sometimes abstract. The needs and, therefore, the skills for
learning and teaching are always changing. The methods must
change accordingly.

The ESL students must feel positive about their task of
learning. They must have positive feelings about the value and
pleasure of learning a second language. Negative feelings will
occur; they are normal. The learner and the educator must
accept this. It is the latter's responsibility to lessen this
reality and to create a warm, positive environment, as much as
possible.

Students must know that they can express negative feelings in the learning environment and thus turn their fears and anxieties into positive learning experiences. As the fears are communicated and analyzed, they will ultimately be eliminated through the use of the second language as the agent of discussion. Hence, the second language and the fear of it become the agents of change.

ESL learners must feel good about themselves, their culture, and their native language. They must realize that their own language is as interesting and intellectually challenging as the second language being learned.

An important factor in successful language learning is the amount of time spent on the task. It is preferable to spend one half hour a day on learning L_2 than to spend two hours once a week. In addition, peer relationships with native speakers, out of the classroom, and other direct-contact-learning experiences are essential to learning a second language.

ESL teachers should have had the experience of attempting to learn another language. The understanding of the frustrations, fears, anxieties, difficulties, and joy upon success that is gained from the experience cannot be taught, only lived.

Finally, ESL instructors ought to love people, and enjoy the process of discovering the similarities and differences among them.

REFERENCES

Asher, J.J. *Learning Another Language Through Actions: The Complete Teacher's Guidebook.* California: Sky Oak Productions, 1977.

Asher, J.J. "The Total Physical Response Approach to Second Language Learning." *Modern Language Journal,* 1969, 53:3017.

Bloomfield, L. *Language.* New York: Holt, 1933.

Brown, D.H. *Principles of Language Learning and Teaching.* New Jersey: Prentice-Hall, 1980.

Burstall, C. "Primary French in the Balance." *Foreign Language Annals,* 1977, 10:245-258.

Chomsky, N. *Aspects of the Theory of Syntax.* Cambridge: MIT Press, 1965.

Cummins, J. "Cognitive Academic Language Proficiency, Linguistic Interdependence, the Optimal Age Question and Other Matters." *Working Papers on Bilingualism,* 1979, No. 19.

Cummins, J. "Linguistic Interdependence and the Educational Development of Bilingual Education." *Review of Educational Research,* 1979, 49:222-251.

Curran, C.A. *Counseling-Learning in Second Language.* Illinois: Apple River Press, 1976.

Dulay, H.C., and M.K. Burt. "Natural Sequences in Child Second Language Acquisition." *Language Learning,* 1974, 24:37-53.

Durette, R. "A Five Year FLES Report." *Modern Language Journal,* 1972, 56:23-24.

Ervin-Tripp, S. "Is Second Language Learning Like the First?" *TESOL Quarterly,* 1974, 8:111-127.

Gattegno, C. *Teaching Foreign Languages in School the Silent Way.* New York: Educational Solutions, Inc., 1972, 2nd ed., reprinted, 1978.

Guiora, A.Z., R.C.L. Brannon, and C.Y. Dull. "Empathy and Second Language Learning." *Language Learning*, 1972, 22: 111-130.

Hatch, E. *Second Language Acquisition.* Massachusetts: Newbury House, 1978.

Keller, G.D., and K.S. Van Hooft. "A Chronology of Bilingualism and Bilingual Education in the United States." In J.A. Fishman and G.D. Keller, eds., *Bilingual Education for Hispanic Students in the United States.* New York: Teachers College Press, 1982.

Krashen, S. "Lateralization, Language Learning, and the Critical Period: Some New Evidence." *Language Learning*, 1973, 23:63-74.

Krashen, S. *Principles and Practice in Second Language Acquisition.* New York: Pergamon Press, 1978.

Lenneberg, E.H. *The Biological Foundations of Language.* New York: Wiley & Sons, 1967.

McLaughlin, B. *Second Language Acquisition in Childhood.* New Jersey: Lawrence Erlbaum Associates, 1978.

Oller, J.W., Jr. *Language Tests at School.* London: Longman, 1979.

Scovel, T. "Foreign Accents, Language Acquisition and Cerebral Dominance." *Language Learning*, 1969, 19: 245-254.

Seliger, H.W. "A Multiple Critical Period Hypothesis." In *Second Language Acquisition Research: Issues and Implications.* New York: Academic Press, 1978.

Skinner, B.F. *Verbal Behavior.* New York: Appleton-Century-Crofts, 1957.

Skutnabb-Kangas, T. *Language in the Process of Cultural Assimilation and Structural Incorporation of Linguistic Minorities.* Rosslyn, VA: National Clearinghouse for Bilingual Education, 1979.

Twadell, F.W. "On Defining a Phoneme." In M. Joos (ed.), *Readings in Linguistics: The Development of Descriptive Linguistics in America Since 1925.* New York: American Council of Learned Societies, 1958.

Walters, J. "Language Variation in Assessing Bilingual Children's Communicative Competence." *Bilingual Education Paper Series*, 1979, Vol. 3, No. 3. National Dissemination and Assessment Center, California State University.

ANNOTATED BIBLIOGRAPHY

Andersson, T. *The Pre-school Years*. Evaluation, Dissemination and Assessment Center, California, 1981.

   A study of the experience of three families whose children
   became biliterate before entering school. The author states
   that pre-school children are learning to read but too often
   adults do not notice. The concise text is highly readable
   and practical. Section IV includes specific advice on how
   to encourage young children to read in two languages.

Cazden, C. *Child Language and Education*. Holt, Rinehart and
Winston, New York, 1972.

   A classic on child language, it discusses the nature of
   language and language development, language and thinking,
   and language in school. The appendix provides methods for
   analyzing children's speech.

Celce-Murci, M., and L. McIntosh, eds. *Teaching English as a
Foreign Language*. Newbury House Publishers, Inc., Massachusetts, 1979.

   A book of readings which covers theory and practice of
   ESL in a readable and usable format. The book is grouped
   into four major sections: teaching methods, language skills,
   students, and teachers. The language skills section is particularly useful to the teacher as it provides specific
   activities and techniques.

Clark, R.C. *Language Teaching Techniques: Resource Handbook
No. 1*. Pro Lingua Associates, Vermont, 1980.

   For the second language teacher, 26 techniques for teaching
   communication and grammar. The focus of the techniques is
   the spoken language. For each technique presented, the purpose, a description, and a sample are given. These are followed by a detailed procedure, variations, suggestions, and
   guidelines for writing a similar activity.

Cohen, A.D. *Testing Language Ability in the Classroom*. Newbury House Publishers, Inc., Massachusetts, 1980.

This short volume is intended for teachers who must assess their students' progress. It discusses testing in general, i.e., the test, the test-taker, test-administration and scoring. One chapter is dedicated to quiz and test preparation. Includes a useful glossary and an exclusive reference list.

Diller, K.C., ed. *Individual Differences and Universals in Language Learning Aptitude*. Newbury House Publishers, Inc., Massachusetts, 1981.

These eleven essays contribute to the discussion of the significance of individual aptitude for language learning despite the universals generally accepted. Three major divisions organize the papers: neurolinguistic perspectives, psycholinguistic perspectives, and a philosophic view. Essays discuss the optimum age controversy, genetic influence, strategies for language learning, attitude, and more. The book is for those who wish to be brought up to date on the research, not necessarily for the practitioner seeking techniques.

Donoghue, M.R., and J.P. Kunkle. *Second Languages in Primary Education*. Newbury House Publishers, Inc., Massachusetts, 1979.

Makes a strong case for foreign language programs in elementary education and distinguishes between these and bilingual education programs. Presents the FLES method for oral, reading, and writing skills. Offers useful suggestions for planning the program and includes annotated list of language dominance and proficiency tests.

Finocchiaro, M. *English as a Second Language: From Theory to Practice*. Regents Publishing Co., New York, 1974.

This revised edition includes the theories and methods which have emerged since the original was published. This is a good text for teacher-training programs.

Goldstein, W.L. *Teaching English as a Second Language: An Annotated Bibliography*. Garland Publishing, Inc., New York, 1975.

Lists 852 entries in TESL in seventeen categories, from adult to writing. Of particular interest to ESL teachers are the entries under methodology and teaching aids.

Gonzalez, E.S., and J. Gage. *Second Language Learning Among Children: A Bibliography of Research*. National Clearinghouse for Bilingual Education, Virginia, 1981.

Approximately 90 abstracts of books, papers, and monographs on a wide range of topics in second-language acquisition of children. A good place to begin for anyone doing research on the topic. Although entries are not grouped by topic but merely listed by access number, there are title and author indexes.

Hatch, E.M., ed. *Second Language Acquisition: A Book of Readings*. Newbury House Publishers, Inc., Massachusetts, 1978.

The 26 papers in this book are grouped into three major categories: case studies, experimental studies, and simultaneous acquisition of two languages, children adding a second language and second-language acquisition of older learners.

Heaton, J.B. *Writing English Language Tests*. Longman, London, 1975.

This book is intended for the language classroom teacher. It discusses language testing and the different types of tests used in language teaching. The reader is guided through test and item construction. Includes a good bibliography and practice material.

Izzo, S. *Second Language Learning: A Review of Related Studies*. National Clearinghouse for Bilingual Education, 1981.

Reviews recent studies and poses the question, What factors influence success in second-language learning? Speaking of personal, situational, and linguistic factors Izzo highlights many interesting themes which the lay person and the professional will find relevant in day-to-day practice. The extensive, twelve-page bibliography augments the useful contents of this text.

Joiner, E.G., and P.B. Westphal. *Developing Communication Skills: General Considerations and Specific Techniques*. Newbury House Publishers, Inc., Massachusetts, 1978.

The first seven papers deal in somewhat general terms with the issue of communication in the language classroom and provide illustrations that help clarify the theory. The second set of papers deals with specific techniques for teaching communication. The student preparing to teach second languages or the teacher seeking to improve her or his techniques will find the topics for discussion and/or action useful.

Kaplan, R.B., ed. *On the Scope of Applied Linguistics.* Newbury House Publishers, Inc., Massachusetts, 1980.

This slim volume is a good introduction to applied linguistics. Ten linguists redefine the term and discuss topics such as a search for insight, the scope of linguistics, educational linguistics, and the pursuit of relevance. A good case is made for the inclusion of applied linguistics in the continuing education of L_2 teachers.

Macauley, R. *Generally Speaking: How Children Learn Language.* Newbury House Publishers, Inc., Massachusetts, 1980.

This slim volume traces the development of children's language using a minimum of technical terminology. In addition to discussing the order of child language learning, it discusses attitudes toward language and learning a second language. This is a highly readable introduction to language learning.

Mackey, R., and J.D. Palmer. *Language for Specific Purposes.* Newbury House Publishers, Inc., Massachusetts, 1981.

Of particular relevance to administrators of adult education. The first paper, dealing with developing curriculum for programs of language for specific purpose, traces such development from the policymaking decision to the pre-program development, program development, maintenance, and quality-control stages. Adult basic education and bilingual vocational education administrators will find the practical orientation of the papers useful.

Madsen, H.S., and J.D. Bowen. *Adaptation in Language Teaching.* Newbury House Publishers, Inc., Massachusetts, 1978.

This book will be helpful to language teachers in adapting textbooks and materials to their particular needs. Topics discussed are contextualization, usage problems, language variety, and administrative and pedagogical concerns. Appendices contain very practical material on evaluating textbooks, estimating readability, and adapting materials in context.

Nilsen, D.L., and A.P. Nilsen. *Language Play: An Introduction to Linguistics.* Newbury House Publishers, Inc., Massachusetts, 1978.

Teachers of high school students and adults will find this book useful. After discussing language and language development, it proceeds to discuss language play as a creative and innate activity. Succeeding chapters discuss play with the sounds of language, spelling, work and sentence formation, and much more. This could help make language learning more fun.

Paulston, C.B., and M.N. Bruder. *Teaching English as a Second Language: Techniques and Procedures*. Winthrop Publishers, Inc., Massachusetts, 1976.

Aimed at the classroom teacher and teacher trainer, this book is concerned with the techniques of ESL. The sections are each dedicated to a language skill, grammar, speaking, pronunciation, listening comprehension, reading, and writing. Each chapter contains practical and useful material for the ESL classroom.

Penalosa, F. *Introduction to the Sociology of Language*. Newbury House Publishers, Inc., Massachusetts, 1981.

Intended for graduate and advanced undergraduate students. this is an attempt to present the current understandings in social science and linguistics and their relationship. The material should be read by everyone teaching linguistically and culturally different students. The nature of language, society and culture, multilingualism, and language policy and language conflict are some of the important topics dealt with. The bibliography is extensive.

Richards, J.C., ed. *Understanding Second and Foreign Language Learning: Issues and Approaches*. Newbury House Publishers, Inc., Massachusetts, 1978.

Thirteen papers attempting to bring together current theories and trends in second-language learning and teaching. The book will be most interesting to those studying the teaching and learning of a second language. Teachers of ESL will not find recipes. Each chapter includes an extensive list and good discussion questions.

Rivers, W.M. *Teaching Foreign-Language Skills*. The University of Chicago Press, Illinois, 1968.

This remains a popular text for teacher-training programs in ESL. The author encourages methods that incorporate habit formation and understanding. It covers all the language skills and provides specific techniques.

Selinker, L.E. Tarone, and V. Hanzeli, eds. *English for Academic and Technical Purposes.* Newbury House Publishers, Inc., Massachusetts, 1981.

This book should be of particular interest to those teaching English to adults whose purpose is to study or work in technical pursuits or to pursue higher education in English. The papers are grouped into a section on theory and one on practical applications. The content is quite specific and technical and probably will not be of much interest to the public school teacher.

Stevick, E.W. *Memory, Meaning, and Method: Some Psychological Perspectives on Language Learning.* Newbury House Publishers, Inc., Massachusetts, 1976.

Explores in depth the role of memory and meaning in language learning. The book reads like a review of the literature with its numerous references. Discusses several language teaching methods but is not a "how-to" book. The book ends with six things the author would like to see in a classroom which would improve the climate and learning achieved in any, not just in language, classroom.

Stevick, E.W. *Teaching Languages: A Way and Ways.* Newbury House, Publishers, Inc., Massachusetts, 1980.

Addresses three questions. "Why do some language students succeed and others fail? Why do some language teachers fail and others succeed? What success may the learners and teachers of foreign languages expect?" Stevick's style is to describe his personal experience with the theory or method and then draw his own conclusions.

Thonis, E.W. *Literacy for America's Spanish Speaking Children.* International Reading Association, Delaware, 1971, and Marysville Reading-Learning Center, California, 1976.

Highlights concepts and misconceptions which can direct the educator away from errors of the past toward more successful approaches to effecting literacy or bilteracy in the classroom. The volume is most relevant to the elementary school years. Three issues discussed are: "the nature of the Spanish speaking child in relationship to his success in reading"; the need to group pupils on the basis of skills --"preliterate," "literate" and "functioning illiterate"; and "alternatives for helping the Spanish-speaking pupil achieve literacy levels commensurate with his greatest potential."

Thonis, E.W. *Teaching Reading to Non-English Speakers.*
Collier-Macmillan International, New York, 1980.

Intended for the classroom teacher, the book deals with
three major topics: reading in the vernacular, reading in
English, and appraising pupil progress. Reading in the
vernacular discusses reading as a developmental task. Reading in English treats all kinds of second-language readers,
literate, pre-literate, and illiterate in L_1. Also discussed
is reading in the content areas. The orientation is very
practical. All teachers responsible for teaching reading
to LEP students ought to have it in their libraries.

Winitz, H., ed. *The Comprehension Approach to Foreign Language Instruction.* Newbury House Publishers, Inc., Massachusetts, 1981.

Thirteen papers each arguing that it is necessary to comprehend a second language before one can produce it. The
case is made repeatedly for a long period of listening to
the second language in order to develop the aural comprehension that will later facilitate the speaking. The chapter
by Swaffar and Stephens describes the theoretical and actual
comprehension-based class.

Chapter 4

ASSESSMENT

Test taking is as much a part of American life as watching television. It is estimated that 95 percent of the people living in the United States have taken a standardized test. Furthermore, the testing market is worth $300 million a year. We take tests in schools to determine our ability, to monitor our progress, for possible placement in special programs. We take tests to enter college, to qualify for jobs, to drive our cars. Tests are used to select the fit, the capable, the skilled. Tests are also used to exclude. The ubiquitousness of tests in our society is undeniable and, at times, overwhelming.

In educational settings, tests can be important pedagogical tools. If used with caution, tests can provide invaluable information on students' academic skills, intellectual development, areas of strengths and weaknesses, and adaptive behavior. Unfortunately, tests have frequently been misused to label, stigmatize, track, and deny educational opportunities to minority children. Tests which are standardized on white middle-class populations are administered to minority children and results interpreted without taking into account the differences between the two groups. Minority children, therefore, score low on tests which do not reflect their experiences and values. Once labeled with a low score, minority children, especially those of limited English proficiency, face the probability of placement in classes for the mentally retarded, denial of access to advanced placement, or tracking into low ability groups. In order to neutralize the potential misinterpretation of tests, alternative assessment methods must be developed and implemented to insure nonbiased evaluation of minority children.

This chapter will explore the assessment of limited-English-proficiency (LEP) students in different areas. Intelligence tests, language proficiency assessment, minimal competency testing, and special education testing will be analyzed. Alternative assessment methods will then be discussed, as well as the role of evaluators, school districts and teachers in the assessment process. An annotated selection of tests for LEP students is included, as well as a guide to non-discriminatory assessment.

ASSESSMENT

What exactly is assessment? According to Salvia and Ysseldyke (1978), assessment is a process of collecting data to make decisions about students. These data may be obtained from norm-referenced[1] and criterion-referenced[2] tests, interviews, observations, school records, medical evaluations, and social histories.

Considerable attention has been given to the discriminatory role standardized, norm-referenced tests play in the disproportionately high identification and placement of minority children in low ability groupings, special education classes and minority children's exclusion from programs for the gifted and talented, technical programs, and academic achievement programs. Yet it is the assessment process itself, as much as inherent bias in tests, that affects identification and placement. "Even given a fair test or set of tests, there is considerable evidence that the bias in decision-making would not be ameliorated." (Ysseldyke and Algozzine, 1982, p. 130)

They state:

> Abuse is evident in many areas related to the assessment of children and includes (1) inappropriate and indiscriminate use of tests; (2) bias in the assessment of handicapped children and in the identification as handicapped of children who are not; (3) bias throughout the decision making process; and (4) bias following assessment. (p. 131)

Assessment procedures, then, must be considered in their entirety when analyzing the discriminatory effects of testing on minority children. Tests alone should not be held accountable for bias. The role of the assessor and the assessment process are just as critical.

---

1. Norm-referenced tests are tests which compare an individual's performance to the performance of his or her peers.
2. Criterion-referenced tests measure a person's development of particular skills instead of comparing the person's performance with the performance of others.

INTELLIGENCE TESTING

Claims as to the inappropriateness of intelligence tests for minority children are abundant (deAvila and Havassy, 1974; Gonzalez, 1974; and Mercer, 1971). LEP youngsters tend to perform more poorly than their white middle-class counterparts on standardized tests. Test performance creates a vicious circle in which low test scores result in placement in lower-level groups. Children fail to maximize their potential, their self-concept suffers, and soon they are performing according to test results and teacher expectations (Samuda, 1975). The tests' predictive capacity is not a virtue of the test design. Test results contribute substantially to the self-fulfilling prophecy. To a great extent tests do not predict performance but create elements conducive to specific behavior patterns. This is especially true in tests administered to LEP youngsters in which their true potential is not identified.

A number of factors influence LEP children's low performance on intelligence tests. Language, culture and socioeconomic status are some of the most important variables affecting test performance in this population.

Language

Frequently children of limited English proficiency are evaluated in English. It is obvious that in a situation such as this children's performance will be far below their competence in the areas assessed. At times LEP children may "seem" proficient in English when in fact they have mastered the phonological component of the English language but not the areas of syntax, morphology, and semantics. In cases of minority English-speaking children, the standard English utilized in intelligence tests may be unfamiliar to them. Although they may be able to perform the tasks, they may not be able to understand directions well enough to discern what is expected of them.

Culture

In attempting to develop testing procedures appropriate for children of limited English proficiency, translations of widely used tests have been performed. Translations present a number of problems, though. One of the most salient objections to translations is that intelligence tests are not culturally relevant to the LEP youngster. Test items are geared to the values, beliefs, and experiences of white middle-class

populations. Tests are developed by white middle-class professionals. Translations alone will not eliminate the cultural biases inherent in test items. Problem-solving techniques, vocabulary and experiences reflected in intelligence
tests are culture-specific to Anglo-Saxon populations. As
such, IQ tests are said to be culturally anglocentric
(Gonzalez, 1974).

Socioeconomic Status

The urban and rural poor traditionally score lower than
middle-class youngsters on intelligence tests. Children whose
experiences are different, who have not been exposed to the
values, material goods, and language of the middle-class child
will be at a disadvantage when taking tests that focus on the
values and experiences of a higher socioeconomic group. The
proportion of poverty among ethnic minority families in the
United States is often double the national average (U.S. Commission on Civil Rights, 1976); therefore, LEP children tend
to fall within the level of poverty and are apt to experience
difficulties in understanding test items in intelligence
measures.
It has been amply documented that intelligence tests
reflect the culture, values and language of white middle-class
populations. LEP youngsters who do not share these characteristics are unduly penalized for not having the experiences of
the dominant group.

"Culture-Free" Tests

Claims have been made that certain tests are more valid
when administered to language-minority children. These "culture-free" tests involve simple instructions which can be
easily translated into any language. Examples of "culture-
free" tests are those which require the child to draw different
objects, such as Draw-A-Person, Draw-A-Tree, Draw-A-Family,
etc. This testing procedure purportedly eliminates linguistic
and cultural bias, since the directions to draw a specific
object can be effectively translated. The difficulty arises
when we realize that it is virtually impossible to eliminate
the language variable. Language can affect all tasks, including a drawing activity. An example of this is the Draw-A-
Family Test. When Anglo-American children are instructed to
draw a family, they will draw the typical North American
nuclear family which consists of a father, mother, and two or
three children. A Hispanic child, on the other hand, will

frequently draw the nuclear family and the extended family.
This occurs because the word *familia* refers to all the persons
related to someone, not just the nuclear family (Alvarez, 1977).
An assessor not familiar with this fact may incorrectly interpret the drawing as representing all the persons who live with
the child under one roof.

Drawings can also be affected by children's ability and
experiences in handling paper and pencil. Children with little
or no schooling may produce drawings which reveal very poor integration, and their performance on tests which require copying
geometric figures may indicate serious visual-motor coordination difficulties.

LANGUAGE PROFICIENCY ASSESSMENT

It is uncertain whether language proficiency can be accurately measured using structured tests that sample only selected
discrete items (such as syntax and morphology) or whether proficiency must be measured using a global approach (Ambert and
Dew, 1982). Proponents of the use of structured discrete-point
tests argue that valid information on students' language proficiency is obtainable when samples of specific language skills
are elicited (Bachman and Palmer, 1982). The use of structured
tests has been widely accepted by school districts that wish to
minimize costs. Structured tests are usually easier to administer and require less time to interpret. Nevertheless, it has
been argued that the structured discrete-point language tests
are inaccurate (Oller, 1976). Language proficiency is a complex
skill which cannot be adequately assessed using a single measure,
at a given time, and under specific performance constraints.
Proponents of the global language assessment approach argue that
in order to assess language proficiency accurately, language
samples must be acquired over time in order to assess a student's
wide range of linguistic abilities.

Regardless of the type of assessment deemed appropriate,
central issues to language proficiency measurement remain:

1) The definition given to language proficiency determines the tasks used to measure it. If it is believed that a proficient individual is one who errs
   little in syntax, then the accuracy of syntax production is measured. If it is believed that the
   proficient individual is the person who knows how to
   use languages for different purposes (to persuade,
   to deny, to support, to explain, etc.), then an
   entirely different assessment procedure is constructed.

2) The school's service plan for language minority
   students determines the proficiency areas assessed.
   If the school provides assistance to students who
   are limited speakers of English, then oral proficiency alone will be measured. If, however, services are extended to language minority students who
   are not limited communicatively but are limited in
   their uses of English for academic purposes, then
   literacy skills will also be routinely assessed.
3) The need to assess the native language proficiency
   levels as well as the English proficiency levels is
   determined by the schools' philosophy regarding
   native language use and development. If schools
   consider the use and development of the child's
   native language to be counterproductive to objectives in English, they will include at best a cur-
   sory measure of native language proficiency. On
   the other hand, if they see language proficiency as
   a broad construct--the aggregate of the child's
   abilities in the first and second languages--then
   they will of necessity include comprehensive measures
   of each language. (Ambert and Dew, p. 55)

We see then that consistent language assessment policies
do not exist. Nevertheless, language proficiency tests have
proliferated in the past few years. Most language proficiency
tests focus on a particular aspect of language while not con-
sidering other important linguistic components. Very few instruments attempt to measure students' overall language performance. Children given language proficiency tests are often
categorized according to ability or inability to perform specific linguistic tasks, but the tests rarely offer prescriptive
recommendations. If language difficulties are revealed in test
results, provisions are not made for remediating the language
difficulties discovered.

MINIMAL COMPETENCY TESTING

As school districts follow the trend toward basic skills
improvement and establish minimum standards for promotion and
graduation, the need to scrutinize minimal competency testing
for LEP students becomes apparent.

Minimum competency programs include development of state-
level graduation tests or tests to evaluate students' competency on a grade-to-grade basis. Some minimal competency
programs set a level of minimum competency in reading, math,
and language skills at a particular grade level. Other pro-

grams emphasize survival skills, such as filling out forms, writing checks, etc. Some school districts incorporate both areas into their graduation requirements. Testing to determine levels of proficiency in academic areas has serious implications for linguistic minority students. If minimal competency tests do not reflect the cultural, linguistic, and educational experiences of LEP youngsters, they are most likely to fail. Factors such as timing, use of standard English, irrelevant content, may adversely influence test performance. There may exist differences in the curriculum content between bilingual programs and English programs, differences not reflected in the standard competency tests. These factors may cause children in bilingual programs to fail minimal competency tests developed for students within the standard curriculum program. Translations alone will not remedy the situation.

In some school districts students in bilingual and special education programs are exempt from minimum competency standards and testing. The double standard is thus applied. Bilingual children are considered less capable than children within the standard curriculum to acquire basic skills. Children in bilingual programs are furthermore compared to special needs children in their inability to attain the necessary skills to survive in society. The development of appropriate tests for the bilingual program is a more equitable solution than to exempt linguistic minorities from minimal competency standards and testing.

SPECIAL EDUCATION TESTING

The overrepresentation of minority children in special education programs has been well documented (Massachusetts Advocacy Center, 1978; Mercer, 1971). Placement in special education programs is frequently based on children's performance on intelligence tests. Mercer found that in interpreting IQ test results, evaluators did not consider sociocultural factors which influence students' performance. Minority children were evaluated according to white middle-class standards and placed in special education programs based on their low test scores.

Special education test abuses are many. Often tests are administered in English to children of limited English proficiency. Purportedly bilingual psychologists, who are fluent in the child's native language and unfamiliar with the child's cultural background, perform biased assessments. In other instances the inherent bias in test content will affect a child's performance. LEP children are often referred for special edu-

cation evaluation due to inability to speak English or to
school staff's general lack of sensitivity to linguistic and
cultural differences. Appropriate behavior in the child's
culture may be deemed inappropriate within the culture-deter-
mined values of the school. A child's reticence before an
Anglo authority figure may be termed verbal deficiency, for
example. A LEP youngster may, therefore, be referred for
special education assessment on the basis of linguistic and
cultural differences.

Public Law 94-142 mandates nondiscriminatory testing and
evaluation. The Education for All Handicapped Children Act
(1975) specifically states that children have a right to a
thorough assessment of the nature and degree of specific disability, in a nondiscriminatory manner and with no single
measurement being the sole criterion for evaluation. Evaluation is defined by Public Law 94-142 as:

> procedures used ... to determine whether a child is
> handicapped and the nature and extent of the special
> education and related services that the child needs.
> The term means procedures used selectively with an
> individual child and does not include basic tests
> administered to or procedures used with all children
> in a school, grade or class. (Federal Register,
> August 23, 1977, p. 42494)

Evaluation procedures must meet the following standards,
among others:

(a) Tests and other evaluation materials:
    (1) Are provided and administered in the child's
        native language or other mode of communication,
        unless it is clearly not feasible to do so.
    (2) Have been validated for the specific purpose for
        which they are used; and
    (3) Are administered by trained personnel in con-
        formance with the instructions provided by their
        producer. (Federal Register, 1977, pp. 42494-97)

In special education assessment, a multidisciplinary team
approach is used. This guarantees that the students' assessments will not be fragmented and that educational decisions
are not made solely on the basis of one test result. One
assessment, therefore, will not outweigh placement determination. But if the evaluation team has limited knowledge of the
child's language and culture, the child is still apt to be mis-
diagnosed and inappropriately placed in a special education
program.

A pervasive problem with the multidisciplinary team approach is that in theory all members of the team contribute

equally to decisions made on educational placement. In practice, the psychologist's interpretation and recommendations may be given more weight than the other members'. Although the psychologist often bases recommendations on one or two testing sessions, the teacher's opinion may often be overpowered by the prestige and authority of the psychologist. Special education assessment frequently includes the evaluation of intellectual functioning. Heavy reliance is placed on I.Q. tests, not only during the assessment process, but also in placement decisions. Since I.Q. test results have historically had biasing effects on LEP children, attempts have been made to develop assessment procedures which take into account children's linguistic and cultural backgrounds. Nondiscriminatory testing procedures include score adjustment or test renorming for specific ethnic groups to compensate for test bias, translating existing tests, and the development of "culture-free" instruments. These procedures, unfortunately, have not been successful in eliminating bias.

Inherent racism exists when test norms are adjusted or lowered rather than using a more appropriate test (DeAvila and Havassy, 1974). Translations do not solve the problem of biased assessment because translations alone do not eliminate the cultural content of the test items. "Culture-free" tests are as culture-bound and language-bound as other types of tests.

The testing procedures described do not eliminate bias in assessment. It is essential that in order to offer LEP children the opportunity to perform in testing situations according to their potential, alternative assessment procedures be explored which minimize the biasing effects of traditional testing methods. Four alternatives to I.Q. tests are the Cartoon Conservation Scales (CCS), the System of Multicultural Pluralistic Assessment (SOMPA), the Learning Potential Assessment Device (LPAD), and the Kaufman Assessment Battery for Children (K-ABC).

The Cartoon Conservation Scales (DeAvila, 1976, 1980) is a Piagetian-based assessment which offers information about children's cognitive level not provided by traditional measures of intelligence (DeAvila and Pulos, 1979). It is based on research which indicates that cognitive development is the same for children from diverse cultural backgrounds when assessed by their performance on Piagetian tasks (DeAvila and Havassy, 1975).

Eight Piagetian-based concepts are administered in a pictorial format. Six of the concepts include types of conservation (number, length, substance, distance, horizontality, and volume), and the remaining two concepts include perspective and probability. A cartoon-like format is used with a problem presented in three frames on the upper portion of the page and three

alternative answer frames located on the lower portion of the
page. The child can respond to either written or spoken
material. The child must successfully complete three pre-
training items before starting the test. The test includes
administration procedures in both English and Spanish.

The System of Multicultural Pluralistic Assessment
(Mercer and Lewis, 1978) includes three assessment models: the
medical model, the social system model, and the pluralistic
model. The medical model includes a health history inventory,
visual acuity test, auditory acuity test, weight-to-height
ratio, physical dexterity test and visual—motor perception
test in an effort to identify physical dysfunctions that may
cause learning deficits. The social systems model evaluates
the child's behavior to determine if it meets the social norm
of the groups in which the child participates. It is a multi-
dimensional model with norms for every role in each social
system and it identifies strengths as well as weaknesses.
Measures in the social system model include the Adaptive
Behavior Inventory for Children (ABIC) and the Wechsler Intelligence Scale for Children-Revised (WISC-R). The WISC-R
measures the child's performance in the social system of the
school and the ABIC measures the child's performance in the
family, community, and peer group. The pluralistic model consists of four sociocultural measures: urban acculturation,
socioeconomic status, family structure, and family size. These
factors are used to place the child in a sociocultural group.
Test results are compared with scores of persons from comparable
sociocultural backgrounds (Ambert and Dew, 1982).

The Learning Potential Assessment Device (Feuerstein,
Rand, and Hoffman, 1979) is another alternative to I.Q. tests.
This technique involves determining the child's current level
of functioning, training the child to correct deficits in cognitive functioning, and measuring the extent of change achieved
during the training as well as the degree of training needed to
achieve the modification. The LPAD is a test-train-test method
in which the assessor becomes a teacher and the assessed a
learner. It is designed to tap a child's potential for learning.

In this assessment procedure the examiner takes on a
teacher role and supplies the student with the training needed
to solve the initial problem. Once mastery is achieved, the
student is presented with a series of tasks that represent pro-
gressively more complex modifications of the initial training
task. The factors included in the administration of the LPAD
include actively instructing the examinee, providing detailed
and accurate feedback concerning success and failure, directly
engaging the child in the learning process, encouraging internal
motivation, interpreting for the examinee the meaning of his/
her success and failure, and tailoring the entire test situation

to meet the needs of the individual child (Feuerstein, Miller, Rand and Jensen, 1981; Passow, 1980).

The Kaufman Assessment Battery for Children (Kaufman and Kaufman, 1983) is a measure of intelligence and achievement which separates mental processing ability (intelligence) from acquired factual information (achievement). This differentiation may lead to fairer placement decisions especially for the culturally-different child and the poor achiever who may have experienced limited opportunity and achievement rather than diminished mental capabilities. The separation of intelligence from achievement is intended to reduce the number of children erroneously placed in special education classes. The K-ABC utilizes stimuli which are as nondiscriminatory as possible, that is, material which is familiar to boys and girls from diverse cultural backgrounds. It attempts to assess the way in which children process information in response to stimuli and determine the processing style by which children solve problems best so that this information can be used in teaching the child (Smith, 1982). The K-ABC has a Spanish version which was standardized in Mexico City.

RECOMMENDATIONS FOR THE FUTURE

The assessment of LEP children is fraught with controversy and difficulties. Test contents; evaluators' attitudes and expectations; the students' language, culture, and socioeconomic status; are crucial factors which affect performance. The typical white middle-class experiences may be alien to the child whose world view is totally different. Serious attempts by test developers, teachers, and psychologists must continue in order to provide alternative evaluative methods which will not penalize the LEP student on account of cultural, linguistic, and socioeconomic factors. It is obvious that no one test can fairly evaluate any child. Multifaceted evaluation techniques are necessary to tap into a child's total development. Criterion-referenced tests, medical evaluations, and home environment data are as important as formal educational and psychological evaluations in providing a comprehensive indication of a child's academic performance, level of development, and any other information needed to make appropriate educational decisions. Assessors' attitudes and procedures are equally critical to the student-evaluation process.

CRITERION-REFERENCED TESTS

Criterion-referenced tests provide a good alternative to the cultural and linguistic biases of standardized or norm-referenced tests. In contrast to norm-referenced tests, these compare an individual with some established criterion or performance standard and not with other individuals. In these tests a limited number of very specific behaviors are measured and through their use, we can obtain information on what a child can do and what a child cannot do. They are very useful in assisting teachers in the establishment of educational objectives. The level of a child's performance in a given task as well as the child's deficits in skill mastery are tapped by criterion-referenced measures. It is important that in developing criterion-referenced tests, instructional sequences and specific instructional objectives be available.

OBSERVATION

Systematic observation techniques can also provide invaluable data for the comprehensive evaluation of students and responsible instructional decision-making. Observation is the process of systematically looking at and recording behavior for the purpose of making instructional decisions (Cartwright and Cartwright, 1974, p. 3). Choosing instructional objectives, sequencing objectives and teaching procedures, selecting teaching methods and instructional materials, behavior management, grouping, and progress evaluation can all be aided by systematic observation techniques.
Through systematic observation, a teacher can determine whether a child is exhibiting some type of deviancy as compared to his or her peers. Time sampling, checklists, rating scales, anecdotal records can be used in assessing a child's behaviors. These observational data can then be used to cross-validate formal testing results. Longitudinal observations provide a more accurate picture of students' behaviors than results based on one testing session.

LANGUAGE DOMINANCE AND LANGUAGE PROFICIENCY
TESTING

Before any formal tests are administered to a LEP child, a determination of the child's language dominance and language proficiency is needed for several reasons. First, to determine the language in which subsequent testing is to be done. Second, to determine whether bilingual professionals are required to assess the child. Third, to determine whether any problem exhibited by the child is due to low academic skills, learning disabilities, or language difficulties.

Language tests must be administered by trained personnel, fluent in the child's native language and familiar with the child's dialectical variety of the language. The language evaluator must be aware that there are regional differences in languages and that judgments must not be made about the specific dialect the child speaks.

A complete language profile on a LEP child should include expressive and receptive language skills as well as the level of proficiency in the native language and in English (oral and written).

If evaluation measures which are commercially available do not provide a complete language profile, informal measures of language assessment can be used. Structured elicitations or samples of spontaneous speech can be utilized for this purpose.

MEDICAL EVALUATIONS

Medical records are valuable sources of information. A child experiencing academic difficulties may not lack intellectual potential but may have a physical problem. Hearing and vision tests are equally important, since problems in visual or auditory acuity cause learning difficulties. A hearing loss caused by recurrent ear infections may affect a child's linguistic development. Medical records are therefore useful in identifying problems which may affect a child's learning process.

HOME ENVIRONMENT DATA

As with medical records, data obtained from home can shed some light on a child's difficulties in school. Living conditions, social, cultural, and religious customs, and family relationships are all important factors in evaluating the total child. Parental interviews can also fill gaps in children's school records. Has the child suffered separation traumas? How long has he or she lived in this country? What language does she or he speak at home? Does she or he experience difficulties in relating to adults? What are parents' educational expectations for the child? Are parents planning on returning to their country? The answers to questions such as these are important in determining whether home factors are influencing school behavior.

DETERMINATION OF LEARNING STYLE

Knowledge of a child's preferred learning modality is an essential component in establishing educational goals. A child's learning style may be culture-related. Certain cultures, for example, value cooperativeness over competitiveness, performance over speed, spiritual satisfaction over material gains. A culturally different child may perform poorly in a testing situation or learning environment based on a totally unfamiliar scale of values. A child may be penalized for working slowly but carefully on a test because this conflicts with the dominant culture's value of speed. Identification of a child's learning style is essential in choosing tests to be administered and in the interpretation of test results. Any evaluation of LEP children must consist of multiple components to appropriately assess the child's performance and potential.

EVALUATING THE EVALUATOR

Once psychologists and teachers are licensed in their field and tenured within an educational system, it is assumed that no further professional evaluations are necessary. Tenured professionals may or may not continue to enhance their specialized skills, and they may or may not choose to incorporate recent educational research findings into their practice. The quality of psychological and educational assessment is rarely evaluated. Assessment reports are not spot checked to determine whether they fulfill the requirements of responsible and professional standards. Therefore, we are frequently exposed to a gamut of evaluation reports which range from excellent to mediocre to shoddy. Evaluators need to be evaluated and held accountable for the interpretations of test results and for the educational recommendations they make. Evaluations must be monitored by competent, knowledgeable supervisors for clarity, precision, appropriateness of test battery, sensitivity to linguistic and cultural differences among the population tested and for the quality and relevance of educational recommendations.

SCHOOL DISTRICTS' ROLE

In addition to establishing monitoring systems for evaluation of assessments, school districts must assume the responsibility of developing and/or purchasing appropriate assessment tools to use in the evaluation of LEP students. Staff training is also necessary to assure appropriate interpretation of test results in linguistically and culturally different children and to heighten the awareness and understanding of evaluators on minority issues in testing. The recruitment of competent, qualified and truly bilingual evaluators must become a priority in local school districts.

TEACHERS' ROLE

Teachers are continuously evaluating children. Informal assessment instruments, developed by teachers, are often used. Formal tests may also be utilized. Since teacher attitudes and expectations may substantially influence a child's performance, it is essential that the sensitive teacher re-evaluate his or her decisions on an on-going basis. Decisions made on ability grouping, referral for special education evaluations, participation in enrichment activities must not be colored by a teacher's negative attitude toward the child's language, culture or social class, nor should these decisions be influenced by knowledge of test scores.

One of the most important roles of any teacher, especially one working with linguistic minority children, is that of a child advocate. Often it is in the hands of the teacher to safeguard the rights of minority children to nonbiased evaluations. If a teacher suspects that a child has been discriminately assessed, there are several avenues she or he can pursue to register a complaint and obtain redress for discriminatory practices. Complaints can be filed, anonymously if so desired, with state and federal agencies or with advocacy centers. It is important that teachers assume an activist position to guarantee the rights of children.

CONCLUSION

Testing has placed an unfair burden on the LEP child. The effects of irresponsible score interpretation and insensitive testing techniques should not be borne by the victims of biased practices. It is time that evaluators and ultimately school districts assume the responsibility of exploring nonbiased evaluation methods for linguistic minorities. It is time that agencies such as the Office for Civil Rights develop a strong monitoring arm to enforce compliance with court decisions and statutes affecting the assessment of language-different children.

This chapter includes a selected list of tests, commercially available, to assist in the assessment process. Never-

theless, we must keep in mind that bias is not only inherently contained in the testing instruments, but is also
evident in assessors' test administration and interpretation
procedure. For this reason, we have included a Guide for Non-
biased Assessment (Northeast Regional Resource Center, 1976)
which should be used by assessors concerned with the biasing
effect of attitudinal factors in the assessment of LEP
children.

GUIDE FOR NONBIASED ASSESSMENT

(Northeast Regional Resource Center, 1976)

This guide prepared by the Region 9 Task Force Group on non-biased assessment, may be used as a resource throughout the assessment process of any referred child but is considered critical for the assessment of the culturally different child. This guide may be duplicated.

REFERRAL

1. Are the parents/guardians aware that a referral has been made for their child, and by whom?

2. Is this child's presenting problem clearly and precisely stated on the referral?

   a. Does the referral include descriptive samples of behavior rather than opinions of the referring agent?

   b. Is there supportive documentation of the problem?

3. Is the referral legitimate?

   a. Does the referring agent have a history of over referral of children from certain cultural groups?

   b. Could irrelevant personal characteristics (e.g. sex or attractiveness) of the child have influenced the decision to refer him/her?

   c. Could the referring agent have misinterpreted this child's actions or expressions due to his lack of understanding of cultural differences between himself and the child?

4. Can the assessment team provide the referring agent with interim recommendations that may eliminate the need for a comprehensive evaluation?

   a. Is it possible that the curriculum being used assumes that this child has developed readiness skills at home that in reality he/she hasn't had the opportunity to develop? If so, can the team assist the teacher in planning a program to give this child the opportunity to develop readiness skills?

b. Can the team provide information on the child's cultural background for the referring agent so that there are fewer misunderstandings between the referring agent and this child and perhaps other children of similar cultural background?

5. Have I informed this child's parents/guardians in their primary language of the referral?

a. Have I explained the reason(s) for the referral?

b. Have I discussed with the parents what next step activities may be involved?
e.g., professional evaluations
use of collected data
design of an individualized educational plan, if necessary

c. Have I discussed due process procedures with the parents?

d. Do I have documented parental permission for the evaluation?

e. Have I asked the parents to actively participate in all phases of the assessment process?

f. Have I informed the parents of their right to examine all relevant records in regard to the identification, evaluation and educational plan of their child?

MEETING THE CHILD

1. What special conditions about this child do I need to consider?

a. What is the child's primary home language?

b. Do I know about the child's home environmental factors?
e.g., familial relationships/placement
social and cultural customs

c. Do I understand this child's culture and language so that I can evoke a level of performance which accurately indicates the child's underlying competencies?

d. Is this child impeded by a handicap other than the referral problem that may result in his not understanding what I am talking about?

2. What special conditions about myself do I need to consider?

   a. How do I feel about this child?

   b. Are my values different from this child's?

   c. Will my attitude unfairly affect this child's performance?

   d. Can I evaluate this child fairly and without prejudice?

   e. If not, would I refer him/her to another assessor if one is available?

3. Have I examined closely all the available existing information and sought additional information concerning this child?

   a. Has the child's academic performance been considered from year to year?

   b. Is there evidence in this child's record that his performance was negatively or positively affected by his classroom placement or teacher?

   c. Are his past test scores consistent with his past class performance?

   d. Am I familiar with past test instruments used to evaluate this child and how well can I rely on his prior test scores?

   e. Have I observed this child in as many environments as possible (individual, large group, small group, play, home)?

   f. Am I making illegitimate assumptions about this child? e.g., do I assume he speaks and reads Spanish simply because he is Puerto Rican?

   g. Have I actively sought additional information on non-school-related variables that may have affected this child's school performance?

4. Does this child understand why he/she is in the assessment situation?

   a. Have I tried to explain at his/her level of understanding what the reasons were for his referral?

   b. Have I given this child the opportunity to freely express his/her perceptions of "the problem"?

   c. Have I discussed with the child what next step activities may be involved?

SELECTION OF APPROACHES FOR ASSESSMENT

1. Have I considered what the best assessment approach is for this child?

    a. Considering the reasons for referral, do I need to utilize behavioral observations, interviews, informal techniques or standardized techniques or a combination of the above?

    b. Have I given as much thought to assessing this child's adaptive behavior as I have to his/her academic school performance?

    c. Are the approaches I am considering consistent with the child's receptive and expressive abilities?

    d. Am I placing an overdependence on one technique and overlooking others that may be more appropriate?

    e. Have I achieved a balance between formal and informal techniques in my selection?

2. If I have selected to use standardized instruments, have I considered all of the ramifications?

    a. Am I testing this child simply because I've always used tests in my assessment procedure?

    b. Am I administering a particular test simply because it is part of THE BATTERY?

    c. Am I administering a test because I have been directed to do so by the Administration?

    d. Does the instrument I've chosen include persons in the standardization sample from this child's cultural group?

    e. Are subgroup scores reported in the manual?

    f. Were there large enough numbers of this child's cultural group in the test sample for me to have any reliance on the norms?

    g. Does the instrument I have selected assume a universal set of experience for all children?

    h. Does the instrument selected employ vocabulary that is colloquial, regional and/or archaic?

    i. Does the instrument selected contain illustrations that are misleading and/or outdated?

    j. Do I understand the theoretical basis of the instrument?

    k. Will this instrument easily assist in delineating a recommended course of action to benefit this child?

l. Have I reviewed current literature regarding this instrument?

m. Have I reviewed current research related to potential cultural influences on test results?

TEST ADMINISTRATION

1. Are there factors (attitude, physical conditions) which support the need to reschedule this child for evaluation at another time?

2. Could the physical environment of the test setting adversely affect this child's performance?

room temperature	poor lighting
noise	furnishings inappropriate
inadequate space	for child's size

3. Am I familiar with the test manual and have I followed its directions?

4. Have I given this child clear directions?

   a. If his/her native language is not English, have I instructed him/her in his/her language?

   b. Am I sure that this child understands my directions?

5. Have I accurately recorded entire responses to test items, even though the child's answers may be incorrect, so that I might later consider them when interpreting his/her test scores?

6. Did I establish and maintain rapport with this child throughout the evaluation session?

SCORING AND INTERPRETATION

1. Have I examined each item missed by this child rather than merely looking at his/her total score?

   a. Is there a pattern to the types of items this child missed?

   b. Are the items missed free of cultural bias?

   c. If I omitted all items missed that are culturally biased, would this child have performed significantly better?

2. Am I aware that I must consider other factors in the interpretation of this child's scores?

   a. Have I considered the effect the child's attitude and/or
      physical condition may have had on his performance?

   b. Have I considered the effect that the child's lack of
      rapport with me may have had on his performance?

   c. Does my interpretation of this child's performance in-
      clude observations?

   d. Do I realize that I should report and interpret scores
      within a range rather than as a number?

3. What confidence do I have in this child's test scores?

   a. Are test scores the most important aspect of this
      child's evaluation?

   b. Will I allow test scores to outweigh my professional
      judgment about this child?

CONSULTATION WITH TEAM MEMBERS AND OTHERS

1. Am I working as an integral member of a multidisciplinary
   team on behalf of this child?

   a. Have I met with the team to share my findings regarding
      this child?

   b. Are other team members' evaluation results in conflict
      with mine?

   c. Can I admit my discipline's limitations and seek assist-
      ance from other team members?

   d. Do I willingly share my competencies and knowledge with
      other team members for the benefit of this child?

   e. Has the team arrived at its conclusions as a result of
      team consensus or was our decision influenced by the per-
      sonality and/or power of an individual team member?

2. Is the multidisciplinary team aware of its limitations?

   a. Are we aware of community resource personnel and agencies
      that might assist us in developing an educational plan
      for this child? Do we utilize such resources before,
      during and after the evaluation?

   b. Do we on the team feel comfortable in including this
      child's parents in our discussions?

ASSESSMENT REPORT

1. Is my report clearly written and free of jargon so that it can be easily understood by this child, his parents, and teachers?

2. Does my report answer the questions asked in the referral?

3. Are the recommendations I have made realistic and practical for the child, school, teacher and parents?

4. Have I provided alternative recommendations?

5. Have I included in my report a description of any problems that I encountered and the effects of such during the assessment process?

INDIVIDUAL EDUCATIONAL PLAN

Are we making this child fit into an established program or are we developing an individualized educational plan appropriate for this child?

1. Have we identified this child's strengths and weaknesses?

2. Have we specified long range goals and immediate objectives for this child?

3. Are we willing to assist the teacher in implementing this child's educational plan?

4. Have we stated when and how this child's progress will be evaluated and by whom?

FOLLOW UP

What are my responsibilities after we have written this child's educational plan?

1. Have I discussed my findings and recommendations with this child's parents and explained their due process rights? Have I given the parents a written copy of this child's educational plan?

2. Have I met with those working with this child to discuss the educational plan and to assist them in implementing its recommendations?

3. Have I discussed my findings and recommendations with this child at his level of understanding?

4. Can I help those working directly with the child to become more familiar with this child's social and cultural background?

5. Have I sought this child's parents' permission for re-
   lease of any confidential materials to other agencies
   and professionals?

6. Will I periodically review this child's educational
   plan in regard to his/her actual progress so that any
   necessary changes can be made?

SOME FINAL THOUGHTS

1. Do I believe in the right to an appropriate education for
   all children?

2. Would I be comfortable if MY child had been involved in
   THIS assessment process?

3. Is there a willingness and desire on my part to actively
   participate in in-service activities that will lead to the
   further development of my personal and professional growth?

SELECTED TEST LIST

Ambert Reading Test (ART). University of Hartford, 200
Bloomfield Ave., West Hartford, CT 06117.

Identifies reading disabilities in Spanish-speaking children.

Ambiguous Verbal Stimulus Test to Measure Language Dominance
in Spanish/English Bilinguals. Motivational Learning Program, 1301 Hamilton Ave., Trenton, NJ 08629.

Identifies language dominance.

Analysis of Readiness Skills: Reading and Mathematics.
Houghton Mifflin, 777 California Ave., Palo Alto, CA 94304.

Identifies children's readiness for reading and mathematics
in Spanish and English.

Attitudinal Inventory of Multicultural Sensitivity. Chess and
Associates, 4500 Campus Dr., Newport Beach, CA 92658

Determines level of student's attitudes toward cultures.
In English and Spanish.

Aural Comprehensive Tests. National Text Book Co., 8529 Niles
Center Rd., Skokie, IL 60076.

Assesses student comprehension in Spanish.

Austin Spanish Articulation Test. Teaching Resources Corp.,
50 Pond Park Rd., Hingham, MA 02043.

Articulation.

Bicultural Test of Non-Verbal Reasoning. Linguametrics,
P.O. Box 454, Corte Madera, CA 94925.

Identification of children whose performance in non-verbal
reasoning is significantly below that of their peers.

Barranquilla Rapid Survey Intelligence Test. The Psychological Corp., 757 Third Ave., New York, NY 10017.

   Measures mental ability in Spanish.

Bilingual Continuous Progress Mathematics. National Educational Laboratory, P.O. Box 1003, Austin, TX 78767.

   Measures children's mathematical skills in Spanish and English.

Bilingual/English As A Second Language Cloze. Bilingual/ English As A Second Language Center, 100 Franklin St., New Holland, PA 17557.

   Determines comprehension level of reading materials in English.

Bilingual Oral Language Test (BOLT). Bilingual Media Productions, P.O. Box 9337, N. Berkeley, CA 94709.

   Oral language skills from simple sentence patterns to more complex syntactical forms of English and Spanish.

Bilingual Science Tests. Curriculum Bureau Board of Education, 131 Livingston St., Brooklyn, NY 11201.

   Measures students' achievement in English and Spanish.

Bilingual Syntax Measure. The Psychological Corp., 757 Third Ave., New York, NY 10017.

   Identification of child's control over basic oral syntactical structures in both Spanish and English.

Boehm Test of Basic Concepts. The Psychological Corp., 304 E. 45th St., New York, NY 10017.

   Identification of children whose overall level of concept mastery is low and who may need special attention in English and Spanish.

Botel Reading Inventory. Bilingual Project, 150 Washington St., Providence, RI 02903.

   Tests oral reading in Portuguese.

California Achievement Tests. CTB/McGraw-Hill, Del Monte Research Park, Monterey, CA 93940.

   Measures achievement in mathematics, reading and language in English and Spanish.

Cantonese I. Bilingual Education Program, Oakland Unified
School District, 1025 Second Ave., Oakland, CA 94606.

Measures language proficiency in Cantonese and English.

Carrow Elicited Language Inventory. Learning Concepts,
2501 N. Lamar Blvd., Austin, TX 78705.

Children's productive control of grammar.

Cartoon Conservation Scales. Linguametrics, P.O. Box 454,
Corte Madera, CA 94925.

Assesses intellectual development of children from diverse
linguistic and ethnic backgrounds.

Chamorro Linguistics Tests. Dept. of Education, Box 1769,
Agana, Guam 96910.

Measures students' receptive language proficiency in
Chamorro.

Chinese Oral Proficiency Test. Bay Area Bilingual Education
League, BABEL Media Center, 1033 Heinz St., Berkeley, CA
94710.

Tests oral comprehension in Chinese.

Chinese Reading and Writing Tests. ESEA Title VII Chinese
Bilingual Program, San Francisco Unified School District,
San Francisco, CA 94101.

Reading and writing.

CIRCO. Addison-Wesley Testing Services, 2725 Sand Hill Road,
Menlo Park, CA 94025.

Receptive language skills, visual discrimination, perceptual
motor coordination and problem solving skills in Spanish.

Columbia Mental Maturity Scale. The Psychological Corp., 757
Third Ave., New York, NY 10017.

Measures children's abilities without requiring verbal responses. In English, Greek and Spanish.

Crane Oral Dominance Test. Motivational Learning Programs,
1301 Hamilton Ave., Trenton, NJ 08629.

Language dominance test in English, Portuguese, Italian
and Spanish.

Cultural Attitudes Scales. Learning Concepts, 2501 N. Lamar
Blvd., Austin, TX 78705.

Measures cultural attitudes and knowledge in English and
Spanish.

Culture Fair Intelligence Tests. Institute for Personality
and Ability Testing, 1602 Coronado Dr., Champaign, IL 61820.

Measures intelligence with techniques which reduce the
cultural, verbal, and educational influencing factors.

Del Rio Language Screening Test. National Educational Laboratory Publishers, P.O. Box 1003, Austin, TX 78767.

Identifies children with deviant language performance.

Developmental Test of Visual Perception. Consulting Psychologists Press, 577 College Ave., Palo Alto, CA 94302.

Visual-perception skills: eye-motor coordination, figure-
ground, constancy of shape, position in space and spatial
relationships.

Developmental Test of Visual Motor Integration. Follett
Publishing Co., Chicago, IL.

Visual-motor integration.

Diagnostic Mathematics Test. Dissemination Center for Bilingual Education, 6504 Tracor Lane, Austin, TX 78721.

Measures student's mastery of mathematics in English.

Dos Amigos Verbal Language Scales. Academic Therapy Publications, P.O. Box 899, San Rafael, CA 94901.

Identifies the dominant language of children, compares the
development of children's English and Spanish, and assesses
functional levels of spoken English and Spanish.

Educational Attitude Survey. Dissemination and Assessment
Center for Bilingual Education, 7703 N. Lamar Blvd., Austin,
TX 78752.

Determines parents' attitudes toward education in Spanish
and English.

Effective Study Test: High School Level. Effective Study
Materials, P.O. Box 603, San Marcos, TX 78666.

Assesses traits related to successful school performance
in Spanish.

Escala de Inteligencia Wechsler. The Psychological Corp., 757 Third Ave., New York, NY 10017.

Assesses children's intellectual abilities in Spanish.

French Reading Test. Bilingual Center, 1100 E. New York Ave., Brooklyn, NY 11203.

Assesses reading achievement in French.

French Test of Reading: Interamerican Series. Guidance Testing Associates, St. Mary's University, San Antonio, TX 78284.

Measures reading achievement in French.

Goodenough-Harris Drawing Test. The Psychological Corp., 757 Third Ave., New York, NY 10017.

Measures mental ability through nonverbal testing technique.

Greek/English Language Dominance Test. Greek/English Bilingual Program, 400 E. Oakwood Ave., Tarpon Springs, FL 33589.

Measures children's dominant language.

Hannah-Gardner Test of Verbal and Nonverbal Language Functioning. Lingua Press, P.O. Box 293, Northridge, CA 91234.

Assesses verbal and nonverbal language skills in English and Spanish.

Hebrew Language Test. National Testing Bureau, American Association for Jewish Education, 114 Fifth Ave., New York, NY 10011.

Measures proficiency, sentence comprehension, vocabulary recognition, and grammar in Hebrew.

Henderson Environmental Learning Process Scale. ETS Test Collection, Educational Testing Service, 1947 Center St., Berkeley, CA 94704.

Measures characteristics of the home environment related to the intellectual and academic performance of young children. In English and Spanish.

Illinois Test of Psycholinguistic Abilities. Department of Special Education, College of Education, University of Arizona, Phoenix, AR 85062.

Assessment of language abilities.

Ilyin Oral Interview Test. Newbury House, 68 Middle Rd.,
Rowley, MA 01969.

To test the ability of secondary and adult students to
communicate with content and structural accuracy.

James Language Dominance Test. Learning Concepts, 2501 N.
Lamar Blvd., Austin, TX 78705.

Assesses language dominance of kindergarten and first
grade Mexican-American children.

Japanese Language Recognition Tests. Asian American Bilingual
Center, 2168 Shattuck Ave., Berkeley, CA 94704.

Measures language proficiency in Japanese for kindergarten
and first grade level students.

Kaufman Assessment Battery for Children (K-ABC). American
Guidance Service, Publishers Building, Circle Pines, MN
55014.

Achievement and intelligence.

Key Math Diagnostic Arithmetic Test. American Guidance Service, Publishers Building, Circle Pines, MN 55014.

Mathematical skills.

Korean Diagnostic Reading Test. Bilingual Education Project,
1426 N. Quincy St., Arlington, VA 22207.

Diagnoses reading difficulties in Korean.

Language Assessment Battery. Houghton Mifflin Co., 777
California Ave., Palo Alto, CA 94304.

To identify children who cannot participate effectively in
English and to determine if those children can better participate in the learning process in Spanish.

Language Assessment Scales Levels I and II. Linguametrics
Group, P.O. Box 454, Corte Madera, CA 94925.

To measure oral proficiency in English and Spanish.

Leamos. Paul S. Amidon Publishers, 1966 Benson Ave., St. Paul,
MN 55116.

Assesses Spanish reading skills.

Learning Potential Assessment Device. University Park Press,
233 E. Redwood St., Baltimore, MD 21203.

Intellectual potential.

Medida Española de Articulacion. San Ysidro School District, 4350 Otay Mesa Road, San Ysidro, CA 92073.

Articulation test.

Meeting Street School Screening Test. Early Recognition Intervention Systems, P.O. Box 1635, Pawtucket, RI.

Perceptual, auditory, and visual-motor skills.

National Bilingual Assessment Battery. National Testing Service, 1905 Chapel Hill Rd., Durham, NC 27707.

Tests reading comprehension and mathematic skills in English and Spanish.

Navajo/English Language Dominance Interview. ETS Test Collection, Educational Testing Service, 1947 Center St., Berkeley, CA 94704.

Rates language use of Navajo children.

Northwestern Syntax Screening Test. Northwestern University Press, 1735 Benson Ave., Evanston, IL 60201.

Screens children with deviant syntactic development in English.

Oral Placement Test for Adults. National Educational Laboratory Publishers, P.O. Box 1003, Austin, TX 78767.

Measures English oral production and aural comprehension proficiencies in adult basic education learners.

Peabody Picture Vocabulary Test. American Guidance Service, Publishers' Building, Circle Pines, MN 55014.

Assesses receptive language.

Peabody Picture Vocabulary Test (Chinese Version). Bilingual Education Program, Los Angeles School District, Los Angeles, CA.

Receptive language.

Pictorial Test of Bilingualism and Language Dominance. Texas Testing Services, 401 Poenisch St., Corpus Christi, TX 78412.

Measures language facility in English and Spanish and can be used to determine language dominance.

Primary Self-Concept Inventory. Learning Concepts, 2501 N.
Lamar Blvd., Austin, TX 78705.

  Evaluates self-concept in English and Spanish.

Prueba de Comprension de la lectura. Calexico Intercultural
Design, P.O. Box 792, Calexico, CA 92231.

  Measures reading comprehension in Spanish.

Prueba de Preparacion para Lectura (Reading Readiness Test).
Allen Co., 4200 Arbutus Ct., Hayward, CA 94542.

  Measures children's ability to listen and follow directions,
  as well as auditory and visual discrimination.

Pupil Record of Educational Behavior (PREB). Teaching Resources, 50 Pond Park Rd., Hingham, MA 02043.

  Auditory/visual perception, receptive and expressive language, fine and gross motor coordination, visual-motor coordination, math skills, reading, Spanish and English.

Quick Language Assessment Inventory. Moreno Educational Co.,
7050 Belle Glade Lane, San Diego, CA 92119.

  Screens children for ESL and bilingual education placement.

Ravens Progressive Matrices. The Psychological Corp., 305 E.
45th St., New York, NY 10017.

  Assesses intellectual capacity through the use of visual
  perception.

Safran Culture-Reduced Intelligence Test. Safran Tests,
19500 S.E. Debora Dr., Boring, OR 97009.

  A culturally-reduced measure of intelligence which uses
  picture puzzles to measure non-verbal reasoning.

Santillana Program Management System Criterion-Referenced
Assessment. Bilingual Educational Services, P.O. Box 669,
S. Pasadena, CA 91030.

  Diagnoses specific reading difficulties and prescribes
  remedial activities for unacquired skills. In Spanish.

School Attitude Tests. Learning Concepts, 2501 N. Lamar Blvd.,
Austin, TX 78705.

  Measures school attitude in Spanish and English.

Screening Test for Auditory Comprehension. Teaching Resources Corp., 50 Pond Park Rd., Hingham, MA 02043.

Assesses receptive language.

Screening Test of Spanish Grammar. Northwestern University Press, 1735 Benson Ave., Evanston, IL 60201.

Assesses language abilities.

Shutt Primary Language Indicator Test. Webster/McGraw-Hill, 1221 Ave. of the Americas, New York, NY 10020.

Identifies children's language proficiency in English and Spanish.

Southwestern Cooperative Educational Laboratory Comparative Language Test: Spanish/English. National Educational Laboratory Publishers, P.O. Box 1003, Austin, TX 78767.

Measures comparative language dominance in students who speak two languages.

Southwestern Cooperative Educational Laboratory Test of Oral Language Proficiency. National Educational Laboratory Publishers, P.O. Box 1003, Austin, TX 78767.

Assesses English language competence in limited English speaking and non-English speaking students.

Southwest Spanish Articulation Test. Academic Tests, Inc., P.O. Box 18613, Austin, TX 78760.

Articulation.

Spanish Accent Auditory Discrimination Test. Peter Proul, Merced County Dept. of Education, 632 W. 13th St., Merced, CA 95340.

Auditory discrimination skills.

Spanish/English Dominance Assessment Test. ETS Test Collection, Educational Testing Service, 1947 Center St., Berkeley, CA 94704.

Measures dominant language.

Spanish/English Language Performance Screening. CTB/McGraw-Hill, Del Monte Research Park, Monterey, CA 93940.

Measures children's dominant language.

Spanish Oral Proficiency Test. Bay Area Bilingual Education
   League, BABEL Media Center, 1033 Heinz St., Berkeley, CA
   94710.

   Tests oral comprehension in Spanish.

Spanish Picture Vocabulary Test. ERIC Document Reproduction
   Service, P.O. Box 190, Arlington, VA 22210.

   Assesses receptive language.

Spanish Reading Criterion-referenced Test (1st-3rd).
   B.A.B.E.L., Inc., 255 E. 14th St., Oakland, CA 94606.

   Reading.

Spanish Reading Criterion-Referenced Test. Bay Area Bilingual
   Education League, BABEL Media Center, 1033 Heinz St.,
   Berkeley, CA 94710.

   Assesses readiness skills, beginning reading skills and
   phonics in Spanish.

Stanford Early School Achievement Test. The Psychological
   Corp., 757 Third Ave., New York, NY 10017.

   Measures reading and mathematics skills in English,
   Spanish, and Navajo.

System for Objective Based Evaluation of Reading: Español.
   Science Research Associates, 259 E. Erie St., Chicago, IL
   60611.

   Measures reading achievement in Spanish.

System of Multicultural Pluralistic Assessment (SOMPA). The
   Psychological Corp., 757 Third Ave., New York, NY 10017.

   A pluralistic special education assessment procedure.

Test for Auditory Comprehension of Language. Learning Concepts, 2501 N. Lamar Blvd., Austin, TX 78705.

   Measures students' receptive language in English and
   Spanish.

Test of Basic Language Competence in English and Spanish.
   Educational Resources Information Center (ERIC), Document
   Reproduction Service, P.O. Box 190, Arlington, VA 22210.

   Measures children's basic competence in language through
   perceptual and motor modes of linguistic and communicative
   phenomena.

Tests of Reading: Interamerican Series. Guidance Testing
Associates, St. Mary's University, One Camino Santa Maria,
San Antonio, TX 78284.

Measures achievement in reading in English and Spanish.

The Non-Motoric Visual Gestalt Test. Himes Printing Co.,
State College, Philadelphia, PA 16801.

Visual perception.

Toronto Tests of Receptive Vocabulary. Academic Test, Inc.,
P.O. Box 18613, Austin, TX 78760.

Receptive language.

Torrance Tests of Creative Thinking. Personnel Press, P.O.
Box 2649, Columbus, OH 43216.

Assesses mental characteristics of creative thinking in
English, French, and Spanish.

REFERENCES

Alvarez, M.D. "Practical Considerations in the Psycho-
    educational Assessment of Minority Children: The Case of
    Bilingual Hispanics." *Proceedings of a Multi-Cultural Col-
    loquium on Non-Biased Pupil Assessment.* Albany: State
    University of New York, June 1977.

Ambert, A.N. "The Identification of Limited English Profi-
    ciency Children with Special Needs." *The Bilingual Journal*,
    1982, 6:17-23.

Ambert, A.N., and N. Dew. *Special Education for Exceptional
    Bilingual Students: A Handbook for Educators.* Milwaukee:
    The University of Wisconsin Midwest National Origin Desegre-
    gation Assistance Center, 1982.

Bachman, L.F., and A.S. Palmer. "The Construct Validation of
    Some Components of Communicative Proficiency." *TESOL Quar-
    terly*, 1982, 16:449-465.

Cartwright, C.A., and G.P. Cartwright. *Developing Observation
    Skills.* New York: McGraw-Hill, 1974.

DeAvila, E.A. *Cartoon Conservation Scales (CCS).* Corte
    Madera, California: Linguametrics Group, 1976, 1980.

DeAvila, E.A., and B. Havassy. *I.Q. Tests and Minority Chil-
    dren.* Austin: Dissemination Center for Bilingual Bicultural
    Education, 1974.

DeAvila, E.A., and S. Paulos. "Group Assessment of Cognitive
    Level by Pictorial Piagetian Tasks." *Journal of Educational
    Measurement*, 1979, 16:167-175.

Federal Register, Washington, DC: U.S. Government Printing
    Office. August 23, 1977.

Feuerstein, R.; R. Miller; Y. Rand; and M.R. Jensen. "Can
    Evolving Techniques Better Measure Cognitive Change?" *The
    Journal of Special Education*, 1981, 15:201-219.

Feuerstein, R.; Y. Rand; and M. Hoffman. *The Dynamic Assess-
    ment of Retarded Performers. The Learning Potential Assess-*

ment *Device: Theory, Instruments and Techniques.* Baltimore: University Park Press, 1979.

Gonzalez, G. "Language, Culture and Exceptional Children." *Exceptional Children*, 1974, 40:565-570.

Kaufman, N.L., and A.S. Kaufman. *The Kaufman Assessment Battery for Children (K-ABC).* Circle Pines, Minnesota: American Guidance Service, 1983.

Massachusetts Advocacy Center. *Double Jeopardy: The Plight of Minority Students in Special Education.* Boston: Task Force on Children Out of School, Inc., 1978.

Mercer, J.R. "Institutionalized Anglocentrism: Labeling Mental Retardates in Ten Schools." In *Race, Change, and Urban Society*, P. Orleans and W. Rusell, Jr. (eds.), Urban Affairs Annual Review, Vol. V. Los Angeles: Sage Publications, 1971.

Mercer, J.R., and J.F. Lewis. *System of Multicultural Pluralistic Assessment (SOMPA).* New York: The Psychological Corporation, 1978.

Northeast Regional Resource Center. *Guide for Non-biased Assessment.* Newark: Northeast Regional Resource Center, 1976.

Oller, J. "Two Mutually Exclusive Hypotheses about Second Language Ability: Factor Analytic Studies of a Variety of Language Tests." ERIC Document Reproduction Services, ED 139267, 1976.

Passow, A.H. "Instrumental Enrichment: Redeveloping Cognitive Structure." *The Educational Forum*, 1980, 54:393-400.

Salvia, J., and J.E. Ysseldyke. *Assessment in Special and Remedial Education.* Boston: Houghton Mifflin, 1978.

Samuda, R.J. *Psychological Testing of American Minorities: Issues and Consequences.* New York: Harper & Row, 1975.

Smith, J. "The Kaufman Assessment Battery for Children: A Major Advance in Intelligence Testing for Educational Intervention." *The Independent Counterpoint*, 1982, 3:1-26.

U.S. Commission on Civil Rights. *Puerto Ricans in the Continental United States: An Uncertain Future.* Washington, DC, October 1976.

Ysseldyke, J.E., and B. Algozzine. *Critical Issues in Special and Remedial Education.* Boston: Houghton Mifflin, 1982.

ANNOTATED BIBLIOGRAPHY

Agrawal, K.C. "The Short Tests of Linguistic Skills and Their
    Calibration." *TESOL Quarterly*, 1979, 13:185-208.

    The "Short Tests of Linguistic Skills" was developed by
the Chicago Board of Education to help teachers determine
language dominance of bilingual children aged 8-13. A
latent trait model, the Rosch model, was used to single out
items that do not fit the construct of fluency in English
or fluency in Spanish. After removing the defective items
the English and Spanish subtests were calibrated. Conver-
sion tables are provided in the index for users of this particular test. The technique is applicable to any other
test, and its effectiveness is evidenced in its singling
out some defective items that remained undetected through
traditional item analysis when the test was first published.
Ability scores produced by this technique should be more
refined and discriminating. The tables will be useful to
those who are currently using this test or intend to use it
in the future for establishing language dominance of Spanish-
English bilingual students.

Alderson, C.J. "The Cloze Procedure and Proficiency in Eng-
    lish as a Foreign Language." *TESOL Quarterly*, 1979, 13:
    219-227.

    This article reports on a series of experiments carried
out on the cloze procedure where the variables of text difficulty, scoring procedure, and deletion frequency were
systematically varied and that variation examined for its
effect on the relationship of the cloze test to measures of
proficiency in English as a foreign language. Previous
assumptions about the cloze procedure tests are questioned,
and it is suggested that cloze tests are not suitable tests
of higher-order language skills but can provide a measure
of lower-order core proficiency. Testers and teachers should
not assume that the procedure will produce automatically
valid tests of proficiency in English as a foreign language.

Alley, G., and C. Foster. "Nondiscriminatory Testing of
   Minority and Exceptional Children." *Focus on Exceptional
   Children*, 1978, 9:1-16.

   The authors examine current approaches to nondiscriminatory
   testing. Evaluation criteria are outlined and procedures
   used in translating and adjusting testing and assessment
   tools are discussed. Nondiscriminatory testing procedures
   for minority children as well as for the severely and pro-
   foundly handicapped are considered. Recommendations for
   testing procedures and future research are made.

Ambert, A., and N. Dew. *Special Education for Exceptional
   Bilingual Students: A Handbook for Educators*. Milwaukee:
   The University of Wisconsin, Midwest National Origin Deseg-
   regation Assistance Center, 1982.

   Examines the inherent biases of traditional assessment
   tools which must be considered when testing minority students and provides procedures which can be adapted to suit
   the specific needs of varied bilingual populations. These
   include formal testing, informal assessment using a standardized procedure, and the use of parents as part of the
   assessment team. Emphasizes the selection of data collection methods which serve to identify and place students,
   as well as have direct programming implications. Techniques
   such as observation, interviews, language proficiency assessment, aptitude and/or intellectual testing, and informal
   procedures are discussed. Resources in testing are provided.

Bachman, L.F., and A.S. Palmer. "The Construct Validation of
   Some Components of Communicative Proficiency." *TESOL Quarterly*, 1982, 16:449-465.

   This study examines the construct validity of some tests
   of components of communicative competence and of a hypothesized model. Three distinct traits--linguistic competence,
   pragmatic competence and sociolinguistic competence--are
   posited as components of communicative competence. A multi-
   trait, multi-method design was used in which each of the
   three hypothesized traits was tested using four methods: an
   oral interview, a writing sample, a multiple choice test,
   and a self-rating. The subjects were 116 adults, non-native
   speakers of English from various language, and language-
   learning backgrounds. Confirmatory factor analysis was used
   to examine the plausibility of several causal models, involving from one to three trait factors. The results indicate
   that the model which best fits the data includes one general
   and two specific trait factors--grammatical/pragmatic compe-

tence and sociolinguistic competence. The relative importance
of the trait and method factors in the various tests used is
also indicated.

Baily, D.B., and G.L. Harbin. "Nondiscriminatory Evaluation."
Exceptional Children, 1980, 46:590-595.

Describes the current status of nondiscriminatory evaluation as well as the research on current attempts to reduce
bias. Discusses some broad considerations that have implications for school systems attempting to meet current legislation and societal mandates for nondiscriminatory evaluation.

Briere, E.J., and F.B. Hinofotis. *Concepts in Language Testing:
Some Recent Studies*. Washington, DC: TESOL, 1979.

A collection of papers developed by researchers currently
active in the area of language testing. Papers include discussion of different aspects of the cloze testing procedure,
analysis of the problems encountered in attempting to measure
levels of language proficiency, and the problems of validation in language testing.

Bureau of School Psychological and Social Services. *Proceedings of a Multicultural Colloquium on Non-Biased Pupil
Assessment*. Albany: State University of New York, June
1977.

Proceedings of a workshop designed to assist school staff
members responsible for the psycho-educational assessment of
non-English dominant students conform to the evaluation procedures required by Public Law 94-142. Topics include: Is
non-biased assessment possible?, non-verbal communication
among Puerto Ricans; the assessment of multi-cultural children utlizing a task analysis approach, and the psychoeducational assessment of Hispanic children.

Buriel, R. "Relationship of Three Field-Dependence Measures
to the Reading and Math Achievement of Anglo-American Children." *Journal of Educational Psychology*, 1978, 70:167-174.

A comparison of Anglo-American and Mexican-American children on three commonly used measures of field dependence:
Portable Rod-and-Frame Test, Children's Embedded Figures
Test, and the Wechsler Intelligence Scale for Children
Block Design Subtest. The purpose of this study was to
determine the consistency of crosscultural differences and
to identify the reliability, inter-correlations, and predictive validity of these measures for both groups of
children.

Butcher, J.N., and R.E. Garcia. "Cross-National Application of Psychological Tests." *Personnel & Guidance Journal*, 1978, 56:472-475.

Discusses problems in adaptation and application of English-language personality inventories for use in other countries. Specific examples of translations into Spanish are given. The article identifies translator problems in the following areas: (1) linguistics and (2) cultural equivalence of items.

Cartwright, C.A., and G.P. Cartwright. *Developing Observation Skills*. New York: McGraw-Hill Book Company, 1974.

Discusses the role observation plays in instructional decision making. The book presents methods of designing and using observation procedures and problems applicable to all observation situations. Deals with specific types of records used for observation: behavior tallying and charting, checklists, rating scales and participation charts, and anec-dotal records.

Center for Bilingual Education, Northwest Regional Educational Laboratory. *Assessment Instruments in Bilingual Education: A Descriptive Catalog of 342 Oral and Written Tests*. Los Angeles: National Dissemination and Assessment Center, 1978.

This catalog contains descriptions of 342 different tests covering 38 languages appropriate for use in bilingual edu-cation programs, from pre-kindergarten to adult education levels. The catalog describes tests in the areas of lan-guage proficiency, language dominance, self-concept, per-sonality, socio-cultural, reading and reading readiness, general achievement, aptitude, interests, school readiness, psychomotor performance, and learning problems.

Correia, L.M. "The Goodenough-Harris Drawing Test and Ethni-city." *Bilingual Journal*, 1980, 5:13-14.

This study tests the hypothesis that non-familiarity with drawing materials and test situations, as well as differences in type of education received, would affect the Goodenough-Harris Drawing Test (Harris, 1963) scores of Portuguese school children. Twenty school children, 10 Portuguese and 10 American, were used in the study to determine the influ-ence of the previously mentioned non-intellective factors on the raw scores obtained on the Goodenough-Harris Draw-a-Man Test. Performance of the American group was significantly higher than that of the Portuguese group.

Cummins, J. "Four Misconceptions about Language Proficiency

in Bilingual Education." *NABE Journal*, 1981, 5:31-44.

This paper identifies four misconceptions about language proficiency which are currently impeding the implementation of effective bilingual education programs. These misconceptions involve: (1) the attribution of deficient language or cognitive skills on the basis of non-standard varieties of L_1 and the consequent attempt to eradicate these stigmatized varieties; (2) the attribution of "English proficiency" to language minority students on the basis of adequate surface structure in "context-embedded" face-to-face communicative situations, with the result that low English academic performance in "context-reduced" communicative situations is attributed to deficient cognitive abilities; (3) the belief that L_1 and L_2 proficiencies are separate rather than manifestations of a common underlying proficiency; (4) the belief that a home-school language switch, or "linguistic mismatch," is the major cause of language minority students' academic failure.

Cummins, J. "Psychological Assessment of Immigrant Children: Logic or Intuition?" *Journal of Multilingual and Multicultural Development*, 1980, 1,2:97-111.

Examination of current assumptions regarding psychological assessment and minority-language children. It is argued that immigrant children tend to acquire fluent surface skills in their second language more rapidly than they develop second language conceptual and literacy skills. Data are presented that show that immigrant children require, on the average, at least five years of residence in the host country to approach native norms in second language conceptual and literacy skills. Failure by psychologists to take account of this developmental process and of the limitations of psychological assessment instruments can result in incorrect diagnoses of immigrant students' academic difficulties and, consequently, in appropriate academic placement. The potential pitfalls in current assessment procedures are illustrated by examples from an ongoing study in which the psychological assessments of over 400 immigrant students are being analyzed, and suggestions are made for developing more appropriate assessment procedures for immigrant and minority language children.

DeAvila, E.A., and S.E. Duncan. "A Few Thoughts about Language Assessment: The *Lau* Decision Reconsidered." *Bilingual Education Paper Series*, Vol. 1, 1978, No. 8.

The authors review the outcome of the *Lau v. Nichols* Supreme Court decision and questions of language assessment which have been raised at the national and district levels. They also discuss 46 currently available language tests in terms of some commonly accepted notions about the structure of language and general questions of language acquisition in relation to development.

DeAvila, E.A., and B. Havassy. "The Testing of Minority Children: A Neo-Piagetian Approach." *Today's Education*, 1974, 63:72-75.

The limitations of standard I.Q. tests for minority children are analyzed. Authors propose an alternative assessment model based on research on neo-Piagetian measures of cognitive development with Mexican-American and other children in four Southwestern states.

DeBlassie, R.R. *Testing Mexican American Youth: A Non-Discriminatory Approach.* Hingham, Massachusetts: Teaching Resources, 1980.

A book for teachers, counselors, school administrators, educational diagnosticians, school psychologists, and private practitioners. The author discusses the bias suffered by Mexican-Americans which have resulted in misdiagnosis, mislabeling, and misclassification in school systems because of the misuses of tests and other assessment data. Discusses concepts dealing with the principles of psychological testing, statistics, test scores, and other relevant factors in using assessment data. Presents procedures and suggestions in using assessment data with Mexican-American youth for instructional, counseling, and administrative purposes. Also provides test users with case studies involving the use of assessment data with culturally different Mexican-American youths.

Duffey, J.B., J. Salvia, J. Tucker, and J. Ysseldyke. "Nonbiased Assessment: A Need for Operationalism." *Exceptional Children*, 1981, 47:427-434.

Discusses current technical history of nonbiased assessment. Reviews definitions of fairness and experts' attempts to alleviate problems associated with bias in assessment. Reviews decisions currently made as a result of the assessment process and examines how decisions are based on inappropriate evaluation which negates the validity of the assessment process. Finally, the utility of many recent efforts to resolve the problems of bias in assessment is questioned, and it is suggested that very basic systematic changes are needed before progress can be made in reducing bias in assessment.

Erickson, J.G., and D.R. Omark, eds. *Communication Assessment of the Bilingual Bicultural Child: Issues and Guidelines.* Baltimore: University Park Press, 1981.

The book includes articles by diverse authors on various aspects of language assessment: issues in syntax and semantics, phonological assessment, discrete point language tests, quasi-integrative approaches, assessing communicative competence, pragmatics, the role of contextual factors, and techniques for observational assessment of communicative abilities. Information is offered on the selection and development of assessment instruments, detailed methods for their evaluation and critiques of language tests currently in use. The appendices include suggestions for interviewing children, rules for calculating the mean length of utterances in morphemes for Spanish, and an annotated bibliography on the communication assessment of bilingual children.

Federal Register, Washington, DC: U.S. Government Printing Office, August 23, 1977. Public Law 97-142.

The Education for All Handicapped Children Act.

Gonzalez, G. "Language, Culture and Exceptional Children." *Exceptional Children*, 1974, 40:565-570.

Discusses the linguistic and cultural bias of I.Q. tests, as well as the role of adaptive behavior and community acceptance in minority groups. Note is made of the difficulty of identifying gifted children who are culturally different.

Henggler, S.W., and J.B. Tavormina. "Stability of Psychological Assessment Measures for Children of Mexican American Migrant Workers." *Hispanic Journal of Behavioral Sciences*, 1979, 1:263-270.

Describes a study which examined one-year stability of scores from several standardized psychological tests on a group of fifteen Mexican-American migrant children. The subjects were administered a battery of six tests and retested one year later. Some stability coefficients were significant, but several measures were not stable.

Hennessy, J.J., and P.R. Merrifield. "Ethnicity and Sex Distinctions in Patterns of Aptitude Factor Scores in a Sample of Urban High School Seniors." *American Educational Research Journal*, 15:385-389.

Analyzes scores of urban high school seniors on three aptitude test factors: verbal, reasoning, and technology. A comparison is made of the patterns and levels of performance by sex and ethnic groups. Blacks, Hispanics, Jews, and gentiles are represented. Results of the study indicate differences between ethnic groups exist on three factors and between male and female on two factors.

Hilliard, A.G., III. "Standardization and Cultural Bias as Impediments to the Scientific Study and Validation of 'Intelligence.'" *Journal of Research and Development in Education*, 1979, 12:47-58.

The author examines standardized I.Q. tests' validity and utility as scientific assessment devices. Discusses the issues of race stereotyping, test norms, content, and cultural and linguistic bias. Identifies problems in predictive value, diagnostic misuse, and statistical analysis of tests.

Hosley, D., and K. Meredith. "Inter and Intra-Test Correlates of the TOEFL." *TESOL Quarterly*, 1979, 13:209-217.

The study provides validity information for the TOEFL by examining some of its inter- and intra-test correlates. Inter-test correlates included: (1) grades in an intensive English program, (2) accumulated scores from objective quizzes administered after each of 15 lessons in a course designed to teach listening comprehension and note-taking skills, and (3) scores on the Comprehensive English Language Test (CELT) with subtests representing structure, listening comprehension, and vocabulary abilities. In addition inter-correlations were done within ability groups to determine if correlation patterns vary according to the academic level of the student. Intra-test correlates consisted of investigations of correlations among subtests within the TOEFL. Factor analysis was used to aid in interpretation of the various correlation structures. The purpose of this study is to initiate a validation study of the content of the TOEFL.

Jensen, A.R. *Bias in Mental Testing*. New York: The Free Press, 1980.

The author examines psychometric methods for detecting bias in mental testing and for administering standardized tests for academic and personnel placement. Discusses the method and purpose of the standard testing formats and their statistical interpretation. Includes a chapter on "culture reduced tests and techniques." Also includes a glossary of more than 40 technical terms.

Kent, J., and R.A. Ruiz. "I.Q. and Reading Scores among Anglo, Black and Chicano Third- and Sixth-Grade School Children." *Hispanic Journal of Behavioral Sciences*, 1979, 1:271-277.

Describes a study which investigated the prediction value of group I.Q. tests for scholastic achievement as measured by reading ability. The subjects were third- and sixth-grade Anglo, Black, and Chicano children of low SES living in the same inner-city area and attending the same parochial school.

Linares-Orama, N., and L.J. Sanders. "Evaluation of Syntax in Three-Year-Old Spanish-Speaking Puerto Rican Children." *Journal of Speech and Hearing Research*, 1977, 20:350-357.

The performance of 30 normal and 30 language-disordered three-year-old Spanish-speaking Puerto Rican children was compared to two measures of linguistic proficiency. They are: the mean length of utterance following a scoring procedure adapted for Spanish-speakers by the primary investigator, and Lee's Developmental Sentence Scoring procedure adapted for Spanish by Toronto. Results indicate that both methods of language assessment are sensitive to age and language status differences within the three-year age range. The authors conclude that these measures can be usefully employed in research investigations to equate subjects on a linguistic basis, and in the clinical evaluation of small differences in the language maturity of preschool Spanish-speaking Puerto Rican children.

Locks, N.A., B.A. Pletcher, and D.F. Reynolds. *Language Assessment Instruments for Limited-English-Speaking Students: A Needs Analysis*. Washington, DC: National Institute of Education, 1978.

A report which provides information on the adequacy of instruments available for assessing the performance of limited-English-speaking students to indicate areas of need. The report includes three sections: A discussion of the priorities for development and dissemination of bilingual assessment instruments for seven language groups, a rating of each instrument, and the survey and review forms developed for use in study.

Longstreth, L.E. "A Comment on 'Race, I.Q., and the Middle Class' by Trotman: Rampant False Conclusions." *Journal of Educational Psychology*, 1978, 70:469-472.

The author questions the validity of Trotman's 1977 study on "Race, I.Q., and the Middle Class." The purpose is to demonstrate that Trotman's findings are in contrast to a position that assigns some role to the genes in accounting for racial differences in intelligence.

Massachusetts Advocacy Center. *Double Jeopardy: The Plight of Minority Students in Special Education*. Boston: Task Force on Children Out of School, Inc., 1977.

A study of Black and Hispanic students in special education programs throughout Massachusetts. Examines the overrepresentation of minorities in the most restrictive special education settings and their underrepresentation in the less restrictive environments.

Mercer, J.R. "Implications of Current Assessment Procedures for Mexican-American Children." *Bilingual Education Paper Series*. Los Angeles: California State University, 1977.

The author examines findings from research conducted between 1963 and 1969 concerning the processes and procedures which appear to be resulting in a disproportionately high rate of Mexican-American children being placed in special education classes in California school systems. She examines the referral process in the public schools, the clinical process in the public schools, the standardized intelligence tests (several tests are considered), pluralistic evaluation of intelligence, identifying sociocultural characteristics correlated with I.Q. for Mexican-American children, developing a sociocultural index for classifying children by family background, and interpreting the meaning of the I.Q. against two normative standards. Data are presented and discussed.

Mercer, J.R. "Institutionalized Anglocentrism: Labeling Mental Retardates in Ten Schools." In *Race, Change, and Urban Society*, ed. P. Orleans and W. Russell, Jr., *Urban Affairs Annual Review*, Vol. V. Los Angeles: Sage Publications, 1971.

Discusses a study conducted in Southern California. The author contends that so-called intelligence tests, as presently used, are "anglocentric," that is, they reflect the standards, values, and experiences of the white, Anglo-Saxon, middle-class person. The results of such tests affect persons from a different cultural background and those from lower socioeconomic status. This eight-year study documents the placement of children in classes for the mentally retarded in the public schools. Criteria for placement in such classes were based on an almost exclusive reliance on I.Q. test scores, utilization of a high cutoff score in order to draw the border line between mental retardates and non-retarded students, and failure to take into account sociocultural factors when inter-

preting I.Q. test results. The study found that four times
as many Mexicans and twice as many Blacks were enrolled in
the classes for the mentally retarded, a disproportionate
number for their population in the state.

Oakland, T. "Predictive Validity of Readiness Tests for
Middle and Lower Socioeconomic Status Anglo, Black, and
Mexican American Children." *Journal of Educational Psycho-
logy*, 1978, 70:574-582.

Identifies the predictive validity of six tests of academic readiness for Anglo, Black, and Mexican-American
first-grade children from middle and lower socioeconomic
status backgrounds. Results of the study indicate that the
readiness measures tend to be more valid for Anglos and
Blacks and tend to have a greater predictive validity for
middle-class than for lower-class children.

Oakland, T. *Psychological and Educational Assessment of
Minority Children.* New York: Brunner/Mazel, Inc., 1977.

Identifies several issues regarding appropriate use of
assessment techniques with minority children and diagnostic
intervention services. Discusses historical and current
issues, legislative action, technology, and a conceptual
model for service delivery. Includes an annotated bibliography of language dominance tests.

Oller, J. "Two Mutually Exclusive Hypotheses about Second
Language Ability: Factor Analytic Studies of a Variety of
Language Tests," Dec. 30, 1976, ERIC Document ED 139267.

Two hypotheses proposed to explain the variance in second-
language tests are investigated. Hypothesis H1 claims that
language skill is separable into components either related
to linguistically defined categories (i.e., listening,
speaking, reading, and writing). Another possibility (H2)
is that second-language ability may be a more unitary factor,
so that once the common variance on a variety of language
tasks is explained, essentially no meaningful unique variance
attributable to separate components will remain. Previous
studies have provided rather convincing support for H2. Data
from 159 Iranian subjects from the University of Tehran, Iran,
who took a cloze test, a dictation and the five subparts of
the test of English as a Foreign Language, also support H2 in
this report. However, when an oral interview task is included,
the picture is less clear. Data from 106 foreign students
(from mixed language backgrounds) at the Center for English
as a Second Language at Southern Illinois University suggest

the possibility of unique variances associated with separate skills.

Oller, J., and K. Perkins. *Language in Education: Testing
the Tests.* Rowley, Mass.: Newbury House, 1978.

Addresses the question of what educational tests are
really assessing, by examining language proficiency as a
possible main factor to successful results on educational
tests. Methods for assessing the validity of such tests
are suggested. The authors also examine the similarities
of what intelligence, achievement, and personality tests
assess and what is measured by language tests. Items from
several widely used standardized tests are examined and
similarities demonstrated. The authors also consider the
importance of global proficiency in English as related to
success on educational tests and how this would be relevant
in a bilingual setting.

Pullenza de Ortiz, P. "Chicano Children and Intelligence."
Aztlan, 1979, 10:69-83.

Discusses problems in the use and interpretation of
standardized I.Q. tests with Chicano children. Linguistic
and cultural factors are discussed as well as various types
of tests and the use of test results in grade retention,
ability grouping, and special education classification.
The author offers possible solutions to the problems of
ability grouping and placement in classes for the mentally
retarded, including teaching students how to take standardized tests and developing specialized measurement instruments.

Reschly, D.J. "WISC-R Factor Structures among Anglos, Blacks,
Chicanos, and Native-American Papagos." *Journal of Consulting and Clinical Psychology*, 1978, 46:417-422.

Compares factor structures of Verbal Comprehension, Perceptual Organization, and Freedom from Distractibility of
the WISC-R for a sample of Anglo, Black, Chicano and Native
American Papago children. Appropriateness of test is investigated as well as the comparability of factor structures
and construct validity evidence for full scale I.Q. and
verbal performance.

Salvia, J., and J.E. Ysseldyke. *Assessment in Special and
Remedial Education.* Boston: Houghton Mifflin Co., 1978.

An introduction to psychoeducational assessment in special
and remedial education. Provides a general overview of and
orientation to assessment, describes assessment as a multi-

faceted process, and introduces basic terminology and concepts in assessment. Discusses assessment of achievement, intelligence, perceptual-motor skills, sensory functioning, language, personality and adaptive behavior, and readiness. Diagnostic testing in reading and mathematics is also discussed.

Samuda, R.J. *Psychological Testing of American Minorities: Issues and Consequences.* New York: Harper and Row, 1975.

    Discusses issues involved in standardized norm-referenced testing of minorities. Analyzes intelligence testing, genetic and environmental theories, and technical problems of measurement. Discusses the effects of environmental factors on performance and educational and social consequences of testing, including criterion-referenced tests. Includes a compendium of tests for minority adolescents and adults.

Toronto, A.S. "Developmental Assessment of Spanish Grammar." *Journal of Speech and Hearing Disorders,* 1976, 41:150-171.

    The Developmental Assessment of Spanish Grammar (DASG) provides a language analysis procedure for Spanish-speaking children similar to the Developmental Sentence Scoring (DSS) procedure in English. The DASG is not an attempted translation of the DSS but was developed independently, taking into consideration the present knowledge of Spanish language acquisition. The purpose of the DASG is to evaluate the language of children with deficient grammatical skills in Spanish and to serve as a model for structuring Spanish-language therapy. Proposed syntactic hierarchies for the following six grammatical categories are presented: indefinite pronouns and noun modifiers, personal pronouns, primary verbs, secondary verbs, conjunctions, and interrogative words. Weighted scores are assigned to groups of structures within the hierarchies and are used to score Spanish sentences children use spontaneously in conversation with an adult. The DASG was standardized on 128 Spanish-speaking children between the ages of 3.0 and 6.11 years. Norms and reliability measures are presented.

Trotman, F.K. "Race, I.Q., and Rampant Mispresentations: A Reply." *Journal of Educational Psychology,* 1978, 70: 478-481.

    Responds to criticisms to an earlier article, "Race, I.Q. and Middle Class" published in 1977. Discusses issues raised by Longstreth in "A Comment on 'Race, I.Q. and the Middle

Class' by Trotman: Rampant False Conclusions" (1978) which
questioned conclusions involving correlations between parental responses to child rearing interviews and measures of
achievement and I.Q. of black and white children. The
author also responds to Wolff's "Utility of Socioeconomic
Status as a Control in Racial Comparisons of I.Q." (1978)
regarding questions about experimenter bias.

Trotman, F.K. "Race, I.Q., and the Middle Class." *Journal of
Educational Psychology*, 1977, 69:266-273.

The purpose of this study is to investigate whether socioeconomic status indicators sufficiently represent those
aspects of the home environment relevant to I.Q. The study
compares 50 black and 50 white middle-class families of
ninth-grade girls. The specific question asked was: "Do
middle class black and white ninth-grade girls experience
similar home environments in those areas related to intelligence test performance?"

Ulibarri, D.M., M.L. Spencer, and G.A. Rivas. "Language Proficiency and Academic Achievement: A Study of Language Proficiency Tests and Their Relationship to School Ratings as
Predictors of Academic Achievement." *NABE Journal*, 1981,
5:47-80.

A study of the comparability of three language assessment
instruments and their relationship to achievement tests.
The purpose of the study was (1) to compare three oral language proficiency tests in terms of their language classification levels and (2) to determine the relationship of the
language categories defined by each test to standardized
achievement test data. The data were collected from Hispanic students in the first, third, and fifth grades in five
school districts in Northern California Bay Area, Central
Valley, Greater Los Angeles, and San Diego. Over 1,100
students were tested in English on the Language Assessment
Scale, Bilingual Syntax Measure, and the Basic Inventory of
Natural Languages.

U.S. Commission on Civil Rights. *Puerto Ricans in the Continental United States: An Uncertain Future*. Washington, DC:
October 1976.

A report discussing the problems of Puerto Ricans in the
mainland. Includes analysis of patterns of migration, problems in education, employment, and income. The report discusses testing and concludes that the use of standardized
achievement tests contributes to the failure of the public

schools to teach Puerto Rican students.

Vasquez, J.A., S.E. Gonzalez, and M.E. Pearson. *Testing and Ethnic Minority Students: An Annotated Bibliography.* Rosslyn, Virginia: National Clearinghouse for Bilingual Education, 1980.

A sampling of the research and literature regarding various aspects of psychological and educational testing of ethnic minority students. The bibliography contains selections that are theoretical, practical, and/or experimental in nature. Annotations provide a brief summary of the content, major findings, and/or issues discussed in each work.

Walters, J. "Language Variation in Assessing Bilingual Children's Communicative Competence." *Bilingual Education Paper Series*, 1979, Vol. 3, No. 3.

The author critically examines four basic assumptions of current procedures in language assessment. It is suggested that if a single domain of language ability is to be assessed, it should be the pragmatic domain. Language variation (i.e., the number of different structures a child can produce or comprehend) as an alternative approach to language assessment is discussed. Data on an experiment using this method are presented.

Willard, R.W. "Competence in Competency Testing?" *Bilingual Journal*, 1978, 3:22-23.

The author discusses the following questions regarding competency testing: What competencies should be measured? When should competencies be measured? Should competencies be measured?

Wolff, J.L. "Utility of Socioeconomic Status as a Control in Racial Comparisons of I.Q." *Journal of Educational Psychology*, 1978, 70:473-477.

The author questions the validity of Trotman's conclusions as stated in "Race, I.Q., and the Middle Class" (1977). The author presents a critique of Trotman's methodology and a critical examination of her results.

Chapter 5

READING

As a visual language, reading shares many of the characteristics and universal aspects of oral language. Like oral
language, reading is a symbolic system with sequential patterns of acquisition or development. It is an important component of language. Language acquisition progresses through a hierarchy of
development in most persons: (1) Listening or receptive oral
language skills; (2) speaking or expressive oral language
skills; (3) reading or receptive visual language skills; and
(4) writing or expressive visual skills (Lerner, 1976; Johnson and Myklebust, 1967). A strong foundation in oral language skills is a prerequisite for the adequate development
of visual language. Reading is a crucial aspect of language development in
our society. An understanding of the language development
process will assist us in comprehending the reading process.
Language development, in all its facets, is of particular concern to bilingual practitioners working with populations who
must develop oral and visual language skills in two languages. This chapter will address issues in reading in bilingual
populations. We will analyze theories of oral and visual lan-
guage acquisition as well as current research on reading in
bilingual education.

LANGUAGE UNIVERSALS

Language is a system of symbols that relates sounds to
meanings; these symbols represent real-life referents. There
is no iconic relationship between the symbol and the referent;
therefore, which symbol stands for which referent is arbitrary.
Language is a species-specific behavior unique to man. Humans
are neurologically equipped for language learning, and we
genetically transmit this language learning ability to our
children. Research findings suggest that children discover
the regularities in the language and proceed to analyze lan-

guage at deeper levels until they are able to produce sentences which parallel adult linguistic constructions. It
appears that imitations or parent's corrections and expansions
of children's speech are not crucial factors in language
acquisition. Research evidence indicates that language is a
rule-governed system, and we must know the rules of combination that govern the language to determine the way we construct
and understand an infinite number of sentences from a finite
number of words. By applying the rules of the grammar, we
have the potential to generate the production of an infinite
number of original sentences. Studies performed on aphasics
and split-brain patients indicate that language is a function
of the left hemisphere of the brain (Lenneberg, 1964 and 1967).

All normal developing children acquire the language spoken
by the community in which they live. A Vietnamese child raised
in the United States by English-speaking parents will learn to
speak English with the same facility as other English-speaking
children within that community.

The science of linguistics initially propounded a struc-
turalist theory where emphasis was placed on the structure of
language, parts of speech, and sentence types. The focus of
applied linguistics was on pairing of sentences, correctness
of grammar, and standard production of language.

Noam Chomsky (1957) revolutionized existing linguistic
theory when he proposed that the ability to acquire language
is innate and genetically transmitted. As with previous linguistic studies, Chomsky's work concentrates on the syntactic
development of language, but the emphasis is shifted to the
cognitive intent of the message rather than the exterior production of the message. Chomsky identifies two parallel levels
of language formulation: deep structure and surface structure.
Deep structure refers to the cognitive formulation of a linguistic rule applied to a semantic concept. Surface structure
refers to the sentences produced which express a concept according to phonological rules. It is at the deep structure
level that an awareness and resolution of a sentence's ambiguity are resolved when ambiguity appears in surface structure.
For example, the headline

                    SQUAD HELPS DOG BITE VICTIM

is ambiguous from the surface structure. It is at the deep
structure level that meaning is resolved. Chomsky further
argues that deep structure meaning has cognitive priority over
surface structure. One remembers the details of a discussion
more easily than the exact words, so the listener does not
attend to every phoneme, word, or sentence of a conversation
but rather uses the features of the language to cue into meaning. In Chomsky's linguistic model the child is not a passsive

learner of language structures but is an active formulator and processor of language. The theoretical framework of syntax acquisition which Chomsky contributed to linguistic theory is now called psycholinguistics. In the past twenty-five years research in psycholinguistics as it relates to both first and second language acquisition has been extensive (Dulay and Burt, 1974; Ervin-Tripp, 1973).

READING UNIVERSALS

Goodman (1969, 1972, 1973, 1976) applies psycholinguistic theory to the reading process. Goodman maintains that the same linguistic processing strategies developed by the child in the acquisition of oral language are applied to the written text in the acquisition of literacy.

In the Goodman model, the relationship that exists in visual/graphic language is one where surface structure/written text is an expression of deep structure/meaning. This relationship is comparable to oral language where surface structure/phonology is the expression of deep structure/meaning. The reading process is not one of decoding to oral language and then reading to deep structure. Instead, the reader decodes graphic symbols directly into deep structure. Goodman points out that beginning readers may decode written texts to oral language as some beginning second language learners may initially translate from the native language before speaking the second language. But while the beginning reader may initially process graphic input into oral input, the efficient reader uses a minimal amount of cues in determining the meaning of a text. Reading is a psycholinguistic guessing game in which minimal language cues are selected from the visual input on the basis of the reader's expectations. As these cues are processed, the reader confirms, rejects, or refines meaning as the reading progresses. According to Goodman, efficient reading consists of selecting the fewest cues necessary to make guesses about meaning that are correct the first time, rather than a complete perception and identification of all elements in the reading process.

Goodman considers that the reader simultaneously uses three interdependent cue systems in determining meaning: graphic, syntactic, and semantic. The graphic cue system refers to the information acquired visually, that is, the grapheme/morphonemic relationship of surface structure to deep structure. The syntactic system enables the reader to recognize and predict grammatical structures and apply appropriate concepts to the structures. The semantic system is the set of cognitive ex-

periences the reader brings into the reading process and allows
the formulation of meaning. Both oral and written language
are processed through a method of sampling the linguistic
features, predicting structures, testing against existing
semantic concepts, and confirming or rejecting the prediction.
According to Goodman, the reading process will be similar for
all languages with variations to accommodate the specific
characteristics of the orthography used and the grammatical
structures of the language.

The psycholinguistic reading model is a processing or
acquisition model rather than an instructional model. As oral
language is acquired through exposure to language, literacy is
acquired through exposure to graphic materials. Goodman (1976)
lists several implications of his model for reading instruction:

1. Where should reading instruction begin? Not with
   letters or sounds but with the whole real relevant
   natural language we think.
2. What is the hierarchy of skills that should be taught
   in reading instruction? We think there is none. In
   fact, in learning to read as in learning to talk,
   one must use all skills at the same time.
3. Why do some people fail to learn to read? Not because of their weaknesses but because we've failed
   to build on their strengths as competent language
   users.
4. What should we do for deficient readers? Build their
   confidence in their ability to predict meaning and
   language. *
5. Can anyone learn to read? Yes, we say. Anyone who
   can learn oral language can learn to read and
   write. (pp. 22-23)

The psycholinguistic reading model proposes that decoding
graphic print to oral language is a process of decoding from
surface structure to surface structure. Therefore, it is not
safe to assume that mastery of oral reading skills implies
mastery of meaning. Comprehension is the principal objective
of reading, and the efficient reader may make miscues without
affecting comprehension. Deep structure meaning has priority
over surface structure expression, and there may be cases of
readers who process visual information for understanding at a
level higher than that which he or she can express in oral
reading.

Lopez (1977) replicated Goodman's psycholinguistic model
of the reading process with seventy-five Spanish speakers in
Texas. The researcher found that young Spanish-speaking
readers, like young English readers, use contextual cues and

their knowledge of sound and symbol relationships in the pi
diction of sentence content in reading.

READING AND BILINGUAL EDUCATION

Reading appears to be a universal process. Learning to
read, like learning to speak, should not require much effort,
since children seem to make quick associations between the
visual symbols and meaning. The studies and reading models discussed so far have
focused on the reading process in children who learn to read
in their native language in monolingual settings. However,
this is not the case for all children. Children who speak a
minority language may experience learning situations in which
reading occurs in a language other than their own. They may
also be placed in bilingual education settings where two languages are utilized as instructional mediums.
    This section will explore the theoretical implications of
bilingualism in pluralistic societies. An analysis of studies
performed on reading in bilingual education programs follows
in an effort to explore the issue of which language should be
used to introduce reading in bilingual settings.

THEORETICAL FOUNDATIONS

Cummins (1979) provides a theoretical framework to describe the different outcomes of bilingual education in multicultural societies. He cites several studies which suggest
that early childhood exposure to two languages can accelerate
aspects of cognitive growth beyond that achieved by monolingual
children. He notes that in these studies bilingualism had the
characteristic of additive bilingualism. That is, competency
in the second language was achieved with no threat of the second language replacing the native language. By contrast, he
cites studies which indicate low-level academic skills in bilingual children when compared to monolingual peers. In these
cases bilingualism was subtractive. Subtractive bilingualism
is a condition in which a child's native language is gradually
replaced by a more dominant second language. Additive bilingualism is associated with immersion programs. Subtractive
bilingualism is associated with submersion programs.
    To account for the different outcomes of immersion and
submersion programs within a theoretical framework, Cummins
formulates three hypotheses: the threshold hypothesis, the
two-threshold hypothesis, and the developmental interdependence
hypothesis.

old hypothesis proposes that the development
tterns of bilingual skills produces different
emic consequences.

re may be threshold levels of linguistic com-
e which bilingual children must attain both in
to avoid cognitive deficits and to allow the
tially beneficial aspects of becoming bilingual
to _ fluence cognitive growth. (p. 229)

In the two-threshold hypothesis, Cummins suggests that
the child fails to attain the lower threshold; although he
may appear to be orally fluent in one or both languages, he
may actually be performing at less than native-like capacity.
Thus the child will have difficulty in reading-comprehension
skills. Presumably, at the lower threshold level, the child
has sufficient cognitive-linguistic control of one language
that cognitive development is equal to that of monolingual
children. Once the child has attained the higher-threshold
level, he is able to integrate concepts in both languages so
as to accelerate cognitive growth.

The developmental interdependence hypothesis states that

the type of competence developed in L^2 is partially a
function of the competence developed in L^1 at the time
when intensive exposure to L^2 begins. (p. 224)

Cummins suggests that for the children whose knowledge of
the native language is well advanced, language medium of instruction may be irrelevant. However, vernacular education
for minority-language children may be more successful than
instruction in the majority language because the children's
linguistic knowledge may not be sufficiently developed prior
to entry into school. Due to the children's preschool exposure
to two languages in a manner which promotes unintegrated concept development, these children may be more dependent on the
school than on the environment to provide the prerequisites
for the acquisition of reading skills necessary for academic
achievement.

Cummins lists three native language competencies that may
influence success in acquiring literacy skills:

1. vocabulary-concept knowledge: the child must have a
referent for each word decoded.

2. metalinguistic insights: print must be meaningful to
the child.

3. facility in processing decontextualized (non-inter-
personal) language.

Development of these skills is facilitated by providing
reading materials for the child and through reading to the
child.

Cummins concludes that effective program planning and evaluation must consider child input and process variables and the degree to which these variables interact with educational treatment. Cummins (1981) also hypothesizes that a child's basic interpersonal communicative skills (BICS) in the native language and in the second language can be differentiated from the cognitive/academic language proficiency (CALP) required for the development of literacy. The native language and the second-language CALPs are interdependent and the product of a common underlying proficiency (CUP). However, inadequate exposure to both languages and/or lack of motivation to learn the second language may weaken the relationship. The native language and the second language BICS are not strongly related to academic progress as may be said of CALP. Educational programs which base entrance and exit criteria on measures of oral language proficiency only are using measures of little predictive value in determining academic success. He argues that measures of native language literacy skills (L_1 CALP) are a more effective measure.

The underlying rationale of bilingual education is based on a CUP model of language proficiency which assumes that less exposure to English and more exposure to the native language will produce greater proficiency in English. English-only programs assume a separate underlying proficiency (SUP) in language. In this model, greater exposure to English leads to greater proficiency in English. Cummins argues that none of the empirical research supports the SUP model. Bilingual programs which are transitional in nature begin with a CUP model but switch to a SUP model which is a logical contradiction of educational philosophy. Children in transitional programs are expected to make sufficiently rapid progress so as to compete equally with their monolingual English-speaking peers after a period of two or three years. Most studies indicate that the full benefit of bilingual education may not be realized until the fifth or sixth year of instruction. Even at this level of bilingual education, it would seem that if an additive form of bilingualism is achieved, there is little reason to revert to a monolingual (SUP) program. Given that an additive form of bilingualism may enrich cognitive linguistic skills beyond that achieved by monolingual children, and given that oral proficiency in the second language is an inadequate measure of cognitive skills required in abstracting meaning from printed texts, a skill vital for academic success, Cummins concludes that the concept of a transitional bilingual program which involves measures of oral fluency only as exit-entrance criteria is inadequate and philosophically unsound for many minority students.

RESEARCH

Educational programs for the achievement of literacy for minority-language children may be grouped into three basic classifications: bilingual/maintenance, bilingual/transitional, and second language only. The goal of a bilingual/maintenance program is biliteracy. Oral language and literacy skills are developed and maintained in the native and second languages. The goal of a bilingual/transitional program is the achievement of literacy in the second language. While reading in the native language may be introduced, this skill is not maintained once reading in the second language begins. The goal of a second-language-only program is literacy in the second language. In this program design, the child's native language is not used at any time. Reading in the second language is initiated once the child demonstrates oral language proficiency in that language.

An examination of the outcome effectiveness of these educational treatments in the development of reading skills raises several issues which make the research data difficult to interpret. First, while it is generally assumed that oral competence in a language precedes the acquisition of initial reading skills, the level of oral competence necessary is not specified.

Second, when educational goals for minority language children have been directed toward the achievement of literacy in the majority language, vernacular competencies in oral language and reading often remain unassessed. The developmental relationship between native-language abilities and second-language abilities is unclear. However, there does exist an empirical trend to assess vernacular skills in minority-language children receiving initial educational instruction in a second language considered to be of equal or lesser status than the majority language.

Finally, the sociopolitical and economic goals of a society often form the underpinnings of educational policy. How an educational outcome is to be achieved can have a wide range of interpretation from community to community. Brisk (1981) discusses the recent influx of East Asians, Haitians, and Cubans to the United States. She states that while U.S. schools may be prepared to provide for the needs of native Spanish-speakers, they are ill prepared for children whose languages are Creole, Mon, Laotian, or Cambodian. Nor can U.S. educators agree on an educational policy for these children. It would seem that many societal-cultural-experiential factors may interact to promote or compromise minority-language children's efficient use of their existing linguistic foundations in the development of bilingual skills.

With these considerations in mind, this section will discuss and summarize studies performed on reading in bilingual settings.

Chu-Chang (1981) investigated the dependency relation between oral language and reading in bilingual children. She reviewed the literature in related areas of study which include: studies of oral language and reading in monolingual speakers of English, models of reading processes, phonological recoding as an intermediary process in reading, research in reading instruction for bilingual children, and studies discussing the cognitive processes involved in dual language processing.

Chu-Chang reports that in investigations which study the relationship between oral language and reading in monolingual English speakers there are as many studies showing no correlation between these two variables as there were which show significant correlation. She concludes that correlational studies do not imply a causal relationship; therefore, these studies cannot effectively answer the question of whether learning to read is dependent on oral language.

In the research on phonological recoding as an intermediary process in reading, Chu-Chang found evidence to suggest that phonological mediation in the reading process occurs for users of languages of both an alphabetic nature and a non-alphabetic nature. Phonological recoding is described as a strategy for holding words in memory while processing the sequence of stimuli in a sentence. This phonological recoding may occur at the articulatory level, but in reading might also be in the form of auditory images.

In her review of research on reading instruction for bilingual children, Chu-Chang discusses empirical studies on the issue of which language should be used to introduce initial reading instruction.

Chu-Chang also reviews cognitive studies which explore whether the bilingual brain functions differently from the monolingual brain. She describes three types of bilingualism: compound bilingualism, coordinate bilingualism, and subordinate bilingualism. The compound bilingual is one who has acquired both languages simultaneously and both languages are viewed as neurologically and conceptually organized as one system. The coordinate bilingual is one who has learned the second language after the first language has been established. These two languages are organized as separate systems. Compound bilingualism and coordinate bilingualism cannot be easily separated because linguistic systems may share common features that would not be stored separately. Also, for both monolinguals and bilinguals, the input and processing of concepts may be linguistic and non-linguistic. The subordinate bilingual processes the second language via the first language.

Based on a review of the literature, Chu-Chang presents a model of the reading process for monolingual speakers versus bilingual speakers. Her model incorporates the Goodman psycholinguistic model (1970) and the Laberge and Samuel (1974) information processing model. The Laberge and Samuel model is comprised of three memory systems which hold different representations of the input string. These representations include a visual memory system, a phonological memory system, and a semantic memory system. These systems function to map words and word groups into meaning. As word identification skills increase, mapping skills become increasingly automatic, and the reader is able to devote more attention to processing the meaning of the message. Chu-Chang states that bilinguals cannot be assumed to process language in the same way as monolinguals. Her bilingual reading model allows for the storage of the three types of bilingual systems labeled as the one storage bilingual system (compound), the two storage bilingual system (coordinate), and the translation bilingual system (subordinate).

Chu-Chang concludes that an oral language repertoire is the most important factor in the development of reading skills. She indicates that initial reading instruction for minority-language children in the United States should be in the native language, and that these children should be given intensive preparation in oral English prior to the introduction of reading in that language.

It is rare to find a study on the teaching of reading to bilingual children which does not refer to Modiano's 1967 study. This investigation was conducted in the Chiapas highlands of Mexico. Its purpose was to compare the effectiveness of two educational approaches used in the teaching of reading in the national language, Spanish, to children whose native languages were of Mayan origin (Tzotzil or Tzeltal). The first approach was used by federal and state schools in which all reading instruction was in Spanish. Rote learning and memorization were stressed in the classroom. Teachers in these schools had professional training and they spoke Spanish as their mother tongue. None of the teachers could speak the languages of the populations they served.

The second educational approach, used by the schools of the National Indian Institute, was a bilingual method in which prior to initial reading instruction in Spanish, the children were taught to read in their mother tongue and were taught some oral Spanish vocabulary. A phonetics approach was emphasized. Teachers in these schools were native Indians who spoke the local languages of the community they served. These teachers averaged six years of formal education. Most had only a fair command of the Spanish language.

Modiano used two principal measures to determine which educational approach led to greater reading comprehension in Spanish. The first measure was the proportion of students selected by their teachers as being able to understand what they read in Spanish. The second measure was a test of reading comprehension in Spanish. The test was developed especially for the study, and it was based on materials that reflected the cultural experiences of the children tested. Modiano reports that both measures indicated significantly greater reading comprehension in Spanish for children taught by native speakers in bilingual schools than for those children instructed in Spanish only by native Spanish speakers.

Modiano concludes that children learn to read the national language more efficiently when they are first taught reading in their mother tongue. She further concludes that the teacher's ability to communicate with the children is more important than the teacher's educational training or knowledge of the target language in successful teaching of reading.

Mes-Prat and Edwards (1981) investigated English and French word perception and the use of orthographic structure in the reading skills of English-speaking students enrolled in grades three and six of a French immersion program. In this study, phonological and orthographic regularity are seen as important factors of word perception. It is hypothesized that the bilingually schooled child who begins reading in one language will already have some experience with abstracting spelling pattern units. When immersion children, schooled in French, begin to read in English, their native language, spelling patterns shared by the two languages may be more readily identified than those spelling patterns typical of English. Results of this study indicate that students are aware of the regularities of their two languages and have strong expectations about permissible letter strings. The authors conclude that, for related languages, the orthographic constraints of word perception do not present a problem in the transfer of reading skills. The study concludes that when the immersion child who has begun initial reading instruction in the second language begins reading in the vernacular, he is not beginning at the same level of instruction as the monolingual child, but at a more advanced level.

Rosier and Farella (1976) discuss results of reading test scores on the Stanford Achievement Test administered to fourth- and fifth-grade Navajo students enrolled in a bilingual education program. The fourth-grade students had received continuous bilingual education since entering school under a Title VII program. They were the first group in the school to have done so. Literacy was first achieved in Navajo (from K through 2). The fifth-grade group entered school under a

Title I program. These children received reading readiness
instruction in Navajo but were in a monolingual English program until third grade. In the fourth and fifth grades, they
received some content area instruction in Navajo, and in the
fifth grade they were reintroduced to literacy in Navajo.

Reading achievement scores of the fourth- and fifth-grade
1975 group are compared with scores of fourth- and fifth-grade
1972 Rock Point students who had received no bilingual instruction. Scores of the continuous bilingual education group are
compared with scores of the interrupted bilingual education
group. The Rock Point fifth-grade average is compared to the
combined average of fifth grades in eight Navajo Area Bureau
of Indian Affairs (BIA) schools. Finally, the rate of growth
for Rock Point's grades two through five in 1972 and 1975 are
compared to those for the BIA's grades two through five for
the same year. All these comparisons are discussed in relation to national norms.

When a comparison was made between Rock Point fourth-
grade reading achievement scores of 1972 and those of 1975,
both groups scored below the national norms. However, the
deficit for the 1975 scores was seven months less than the
1972 scores. When fifth-grade scores for the same years were
compared, the results were similar. The difference in total
reading averages between the two groups was 1.1 years.

When the fourth-grade continuous bilingual instruction
group scores were compared to scores of fifth-grade interrupted bilingual instruction, the continuous bilingual group
averaged total reading scores which were eight months higher
than the interrupted bilingual group. The continuous bilingual
group score was six months below the national norms. When Rock
Point fifth-grade student achievement scores were compared to
the fifth-grade scores of children in eight BIA schools, the
difference in the total reading average between the two groups
was 1.6 years. The Rock Point fifth graders were .5 years
below the national norms.

Growth rates for the eight BIA schools and for Rock Point
grades two through five, for the years 1972 through 1975, were
calculated and compared. The growth rate was calculated by
subtracting the average score of the lowest grade tested from
that of the highest grade tested. The difference was divided
by the national norm rate for the same interval. Growth rate
for the BIA schools was .5 per annum. At this rate of growth,
BIA students could never hope to achieve national norms.
Growth rate for the Rock Point students, both groups combined,
was 1.03. Results of this study indicate that the effects of
continuous bilingual instruction may be cumulative, and students who learned to read in Navajo appear to obtain progres-
sively higher scores than those who did not.

As described by Troike (1978), Skutnabb-Kangas and Toukamaa (1976) found that Finnish children who migrated to Sweden
at the preschool and primary level age fell well below the
norms of Swedish children in Swedish-language skills. However,
Finnish children who had begun their education in Finland in
their native language and who were 10 to 12 years old were
more apt to meet Swedish-language norms. Moreover, these
children's language skills excel those of Finnish children
born in Sweden.

This study suggests that a solid foundation must be
achieved in the mother tongue before instruction in the second
language begins. If instruction in the second language begins
before strong native language skills are achieved, a state of
semilingualism may occur in which, though children exhibit a
superficial fluency in the second language, they may lack
semantic, syntactic, morphological linguistic skills necessary
to function efficiently in the second language.

As a result of the Swedish study, Finnish children receive initial instruction in the vernacular until grade three.
This is followed by continued instruction in Swedish (the
national language). By grade six, Finnish children approach
Swedish national norms in both languages.

The St. Lambert experiment (Lambert and Tucker, 1972) is
a longitudinal study of the impact of elementary schooling
provided to English-speaking monolingual children through the
medium of French. This program developed as a result of
parental concerns that traditional English-Canadian programs
which introduced French-as-a-Foreign Language were not effective in teaching native-like functional skills in that language. The St. Lambert program is described as a French immersion program. An immersion program is one in which all
children begin the program with little or no knowledge of the
target language which is the language of the school (Swain,
1979). This type of program differs from a submersion model.
In submersion programs, children who do not know the school
language are placed in the classroom with children who are
native speakers. The teacher often is unfamiliar with the
child's language and culture. The children's difficulty in
the classroom is often considered to be related to limited
academic ability rather than limited proficiency in the second
language.

In the St. Lambert study French-speaking children were
placed in a school where the language was English. The purpose of the study was to determine the effects of second-
language immersion on native language cognitive/linguistic/
academic skills, to determine the degree of second language
proficiency attained when compared to monolingual speakers of
the second language, and to determine the emotional and intel-

lectual effects on children involved in this type of program.

Two experimental groups were used, a pilot class and a follow-up class which began kindergarten the following year. Two monolingual English-speaking classes and a monolingual French-speaking class were used as control groups. There were approximately 30 children in each class to agree with a general number of students per class in the Canadian school system. The children, who were all from middle-class families, were matched for socioeconomic status and for home background.

For both experimental groups, instruction in kindergarten and first grade was entirely in French. Children were initially free to speak their native language in the classroom. The teacher, a native French speaker, would translate the children's comments into French for the class and then would respond to the children in French. By grade two, 60 percent of instruction was presented in French and taught by native French speakers. The remaining 40 percent of instruction was in English and taught by native English speakers. English-language instruction included two daily thirty-five-minute programs in English language arts and instruction in physical education, music, art, and library.

Evaluation measurements used in this study included achievement tests in English and French, non-verbal intelligence tests, listening comprehension, story-telling, phoneme discrimination, creativity, self-concept, and attitude toward the program.

At the end of grade four evaluation results indicate that learning through the weaker language did not interfere with academic achievement. Both the experimental group and the control groups were generally at the same level of achievement. They were slightly lower than both the English and French control group in story telling.

Engle (1975) reports that in a follow-up study children were retested in the sixth grade. Their performance was equal to English speakers who had received instruction only in English. Though the original study indicates that the children did not acquire native-like facility in the French language, the achievement test scores fell within the 50th percentile of the Montreal norms. Engle also reports that the children were satisfied with the program and wanted to learn more French. These children rejected the idea of returning to an English-only program.

Perhaps the results that prove to be the most interesting and the most challenging to explain are the results of English-language competence tested at the end of grade two. In tests of reading skills, spelling, and vocabulary in English, the experimental group, who had been receiving minimum training in English language arts, performed at a level comparable to English control classes. The one exception to this was on a test of reading comprehension of sentences and paragraphs. In this instance, the experimental group performed equally well as English Control II, but scored reliably lower than English Control I. Nonetheless, the experimental group scores fall within the 80th percentile of national norms. Lambert and Tucker suggest that cognitive and linguistic maturational processes may influence readiness for acquisition of reading skills. Delaying the introduction of reading in the native language for a year may facilitate the teaching of reading in this type of program. It is interesting to note that at the end of grade one, the experimental group, having received no instruction in reading in English, still attained scores within the 15th percentile of national norms.

Lambert and Tucker also hypothesize that in this educational setting the child becomes a skilled mental translator. This skill may facilitate the ability to compare and contrast the two language systems. The child may process the information received in one language into the other language or the processing may be simultaneous in both languages. English conceptual knowledge is used to interpret information gained in the new language. This contrasting of related languages leads to a deeper awareness of the native language.

The Ottawa Study (Barik and Swain, 1975) is a replication of the St. Lambert Experiment conducted with Ottawa children from kindergarten through grade two. It primarily differs from the St. Lambert study in its inclusion of a large number of classes throughout the school system. Three successive groups are involved: those enrolled in the 1970-71 school year, the 1971-72 school year, and the 1973-74 school year.

The purpose of the study was to evaluate whether learning in the second language produced any detrimental effects on cognitive skills and academic achievement and to compare a French immersion program to a French-as-a-second language (FSL) program in terms of proficiency achieved in that language. The comparison groups were English students receiving one period of instruction per day in English. The children in both groups were from middle- and upper-middle-class backgrounds.

Evaluation measurements included achievement tests in English and French, a mental ability test, a prereading test battery, and a French comprehension test.

Results of this study indicate that by the end of kindergarten both the control and comparison groups were ready for school work in grade one. By the end of grade one immersion students lag behind the comparison group in English reading. However, there is some indication that transfer of reading skills has occurred without formal instruction in English.

By the end of Grade 2, children had received an hour of

English language instruction per day and had caught up with
their peers in English language skills. Although immersion
students do not achieve native-like proficiency in French by
the end of grade 2, they do achieve considerably more than the
comparison group receiving 20 to 40 minutes of instruction in
French per day. Both groups perform equally well in mathematics and show the same levels of cognitive development. The
authors conclude that their findings are consistent with those
of the St. Lambert experiment.

The authors caution that before an immersion program is
established, the social status of the target language must be
considered. Lambert and Tucker (1972) suggest that bilingual
education for minority-language children may need to be programmed differently than bilingual education for majority-
language children (which is the case in the Canadian studies).
They recommend that instructional priority be given to the
language most likely to be neglected. For minority-language
groups they offer various options: half-day instruction in
the native language and half-day instruction in the second
language at the prekindergarten and kindergarten levels;
have been achieved, then introducing instruction in the second
language; and a bilingual program with dual educational structures in each language.

Cohen (1974) evaluates the first two years of the Culver
City Spanish immersion program for kindergarten and first-
grade monolingual English-speaking children in California.
This program was modeled after the St. Lambert Experiment.
The experimental group is composed of a pilot group and a
follow-up group. In grade one, six Spanish dominant or monolingual Spanish-speaking children were added to the pilot
group.

Findings from this project indicate that English-speaking
children were able to successfully complete an all-Spanish
curriculum at the kindergarten and first-grade level, with
no retardation of oral English skills when their skills were
compared with that of a control group of children not receiving
instruction in a second language. When compared to a control
group on a reading readiness test in English at the end of the
kindergarten year, the pilot group scored significantly lower
than the control group. The grade one pilot group was introduced to Spanish reading in November of the school year. Because of parental concerns regarding the development of English reading skills, English reading was introduced in January
of the same school year. Thus, Spanish and English reading instruction were presented concurrently. Cohen states that prior
to introduction to reading in English, no English interference
was observed in the oral reading of Spanish. However, once
English reading began, children started to use English pronun-

ciation in their oral production of Spanish.

By the end of grade one, the pilot immersion group was
equal to the first-grade comparison group in English reading
skills. When the reading skills of the pilot group were compared to Spanish-speaking children receiving a regular Spanish
school curriculum in Ecuador, no significant differences were
found between the two groups. Both the Culver City and Ecuadorian groups were matched for socioeconomic status (they be-
longed to middle-class families) and amount of exposure to
Spanish reading instruction. But the Ecuadorian children did
not have the familiarity with the testing format which the
Culver City children had.

Among immersion students, Spanish reading ability was
highly correlated with English reading ability. Children who
were good readers in Spanish were good readers in English.
The pilot immersion class received one hour more of instruction
per day than other school children, since they received one
hour of reading instruction in Spanish and one hour of reading
instruction in English daily.

In 1973 the Milingimbi School, serving as aboriginal community in the Northern Territory of Australia, began the
gradual phase-in of a bilingual education program in English
and Gupapuyngu to replace its previous program of instruction
in English only (Gale, et al., 1981). The program was initially
introduced in the preschool and first grade and continued to
advance by one grade level each year until the phase-in was
completed in the seventh year. Thus, the children who began
their education in English only continued their education in
English to the completion of their educational program.

By 1976, years five, six and seven were English-only
classes; all lower years were bilingual classes. From 1976
through 1979, all year 5, 6 and 7 classes were administered
the same achievement tests. By 1979 the program was completely
bilingual. This report compares the academic achievement
scores from years 1976 through 1979 of bilingual program children in years 5, 6 and 7 with the English-only children in
years 5, 6 and 7.

In the bilingual model used in this school, the preschool year curriculum was presented in the vernacular with
some oral English. In the infant year, reading in the vernacular was introduced. In the primary year, the curriculum was
approximately 50 percent in the Aboriginal language taught by
a trained or untrained Aboriginal teacher. Fifty percent of
instruction was in English taught by a trained non-Aboriginal
teacher. Literacy in English began in year 5 or 6 depending
on students' abilities in vernacular reading, oral reading,
and reading of informal English.

Measures for this study were taken in the areas of oral

English, English reading, English composition, and arithmetic.
Because the students in the bilingual program were compared
to students in the English-only program, they were not tested
for achievement in the vernacular. Reading tests administered
were the Dolch Sight Words Test, the Schonell Reading Age
Test and the Cloze Test.

In year 5 the English-only group scored significantly
better on the Dolch Sight Words Tests than those in the bilingual group. In year 6 the bilingual group scores were
better, and in year 7 the children in bilingual classes were
performing better than the English-only children in seven out
of ten measures of academic achievement.

In the bilingual program, children developed writing
skills in their native language as soon as they began to read
it (approximately two or three years after starting school).
The authors state that many of the children in the bilingual
classes were good writers at the end of Year 3. Furthermore,
the researchers found that the children had no difficulty
transferring their vernacular written expression skills to
English. The bilingual children tested had become literate
in both English and their first language.

Results of the Milingimbi School study indicate that the
children in bilingual programs are not only learning to read
and write in their own language, but they are also achieving
better academic results in oral English, reading, English composition, and mathematics than they were under the former
monolingual education system.

Although there does not appear to be a definite consensus
of the appropriate introduction of literacy skills in minority-
language populations, several important statements can be
gleaned from a review of the research on bilingual literacy.
First, it appears that teaching minority-language children to
read in the native language before introducing literacy skills
in the majority language is more successful than teaching them
to read initially in the majority language. Second, oral language training in the second language is a prerequisite to
successful second-language literacy. Third, the successful
cases of initial second-language literacy have occurred in
immersion programs where majority-language children are taught
to read in a minority language. It appears that the relative
status of the child's native language to the second language
is important. Fourth, some of the studies analyzed have observed spontaneous transfer of reading skills from one language
to another without formal instruction in the reading of the
second language.

The transferability of reading skills from one language
to another is an important issue in bilingual education. A
number of researchers have observed this transfer to occur

automatically. Let us look at this phenomenon more closely.

TRANSFER OF READING SKILLS

Vygotsky (1962) maintained that there were two types of knowledge: spontaneous knowledge which referred to familiar, everyday concepts and scientific knowledge which encompassed formal, school-learned concepts. As a result of his research Vygotsky found that young children would commit more errors when attempting to incorporate spontaneous concepts into familiar everyday situations than when incorporating scientific concepts into technical situations in sentence completion exercises.

The children would complete the following sentences with the words *although* and *because*:

"The boy fell off his bicycle because...."
"The girl cannot yet read, although...."
"Planned economy is possible in the USSR because...."
"If a ball rolls off a table, it will fall downwards because...."

The children were given similar problems dealing with either scientific or familiar material and their solutions compared. This included making up stories from sequential pictures which showed the beginning, continuation, and end of an action.

Vygotsky found that scientific concepts were mastered and understood earlier than the spontaneous ones. Children made more mistakes when completing sentences which dealt with familiar situations than when the sentences referred to scientific concepts. For example, the children would say: "The boy fell off his bicycle because he was taken to the hospital"; but "If a ball rolls off a table, it will fall downwards because of the force of gravitation."

Vygotsky argues that scientific concepts are mastered earlier because the teacher has explained, questioned, corrected, and elicited explanations from the child, thus bringing these concepts into consciousness. The child, by knowing the concepts, can use and work with them independently.

Spontaneous concepts, on the other hand, are not acquired through deliberate instruction. Children are not aware of these concepts and do not use them correctly until they have become conscious. But Vygotsky argues that once a number of scientific concepts are mastered, the awareness of their development spreads to everyday concepts. Eventually children are able to solve problems involving everyday concepts with the same accuracy as scientific concepts. By the age of 10,

the child uses both scientific and spontaneous concepts in-
telligently.

Vygotsky applies his transfer of skills theory to learning
a second language.

> Success in learning a second language is contingent on
> a certain degree of maturity in the native language.
> The child can transfer to the new language the system
> of meanings he already possesses in his own. (p. 110)

Vygotsky goes on to state that when new systems are formed
which are similar to earlier ones, such as written language,
foreign language, and verbal thought, a transfer or shift occurs
in which the later system repeats the course of the earlier one.
It is, therefore, suggested that learning one task will affect
learning another. In language learning there is an interrelationship which can be strengthened and capitalized upon.

The St. Lambert Experiment described earlier in this
chapter is an example of transfer of skills in language learning. To review, in this study a group of Canadian English-
speaking students were placed in a French immersion program
where children were not drilled in the traditional foreign language teaching technique but were immersed in a French milieu
where the second language was learned through daily interaction
with native-speaking teachers. In kindergarten, for example,
French language skills were developed through story-telling,
songs, and art group projects. In subsequent grades, the children were exposed to the normal curriculum of the Montreal
school system; all material and instruction was in French with
no formal language instruction being provided.

An interesting finding in the St. Lambert experiment was
that English-speaking children, taught in French, transferred
the reading and computation skills learned in French to English
without being instructed in these skills in English. The children, having mastered concepts in a language, were able to
transfer these concepts into another language. The Ottawa study
also found that a spontaneous transfer of reading occurs from
one language to another.

In a study performed with Arabic students learning English-
as-a-second-language (Al-Rufai, 1976), it was also found that
reading skills are transferable from one language to another.
Al-Rufai argues that the transfer can only occur when the languages are used with ease by the readers.

> The reader must know the language he is reading before
> he is able to read for meaning. It follows that if his
> reading skills have been developed, through efficient
> guidance and sufficient training, there is a strong in-
> dication that they will be transferred to the reading
> act of the other language known. (p. 239)

The researcher concludes that success in teaching the reading of a foreign language can best be achieved through the teaching of reading skills in the mother tongue.

The research we have reviewed suggests that a transfer of reading skills occurs automatically when a child has achieved oral command of two languages and reading mastery in one of the languages. It appears then that oral language competence will beneficially affect other aspects of linguistic development including reading.

METHODS

The research presented in this discussion of the appropriate language for introduction of literacy in a bilingual setting suggests that children best process reading in the language they speak. It seems that for minority-language children, literacy in the native language should precede literacy in the second or majority language.

The development of native language literacy for minority-language children may be hindered by practical realities, however. The native language may have no written tradition. The minority culture may not value literacy as a goal for all its members. The most obvious restraints in implementing a reading program in the vernacular are lack of qualified teaching personnel and lack of available written materials in the vernacular language. The discussion of literacy methods which follows focuses on Spanish. Spanish has a historical tradition of usage in the United States where the Spanish language is spoken by 11.1 million residents. Therefore, the majority of children in bilingual programs come from Spanish-speaking backgrounds. These factors have facilitated the development of instructional materials and texts in reading instruction for Spanish-dominant children. Appendix A includes material resources available for other language groups.

Thonis (1976) and Pena and Verner (1981) describe traditional methodology in initial reading instruction in Spanish. These instructional approaches include the phonetic method, the global method, and the eclectic method which is a combination of the other two approaches.

The phonetic method is a synthetic approach which moves from the specific to the general. It includes four basic approaches: alphabetic, syllabic, phonic, and onomatopoeic.

In the alphabetic approach, the vowels are learned first and then the consonants. Through a plan based on repetition, vowels and consonants are expanded into syllables, words, phrases, and sentences. Another alphabetic approach involves teaching the names of the letters first, then the forms, fol-

lowed by their sounds. Again, the letters are combined to
form syllables which are then expanded into words.

In the syllabic method, the primary unit is the syllable.
The vowel, as the stable basic language unit, is introduced
in the initial position of a syllabized word, usually accompanied by its pictorial representation.

In the phonic method, the sound of the letter is taught
rather than the name of the letter. The focus of the phonic
method is on the acquisition of word recognition skills rather
than on meaning.

In the onomatopoeic method, the sound of the letter is
introduced in association with an environmental sound. For
example, the letter *u* is associated with the sound of a train
whistle. Only twenty letters may be introduced in this manner.

The global method is considered an analytical method
which moves from the general to the specific. In this method,
the basic introductory unit is the word, the phrase, the sentence, or the story. Once the basic unit has been taught, it
is broken down into the smaller components. This method utilizes vocabulary words that are highly meaningful to the child.
Although the teacher may provide the story for the child, a
language experience approach is also an example of the global
method at the story level. The teacher and the students create
a story based on a common experience shared by the class. The
teacher writes the story on the board for the children. The
children analyze the story together and break it down into its
structural components, that is, sentences, words, syllables,
and letters.

The eclectic method includes both synthetic and analytic
components. For example, after the vowels have been taught,
a simple sentence is introduced. The sentence is broken down
into words, the words are reduced to syllables, and the syllables into their letter components. The process is then presented in reverse. The children recombine the letters into
syllables and create new words from these syllables, and these
words are then used to create a new sentence.

The effectiveness of these methods will depend both on
the skills of the teachers applying them and the developmental
level of the child learning through them.

One of the goals of bilingual education is the achievement
of language competence in English. Therefore, English-as-a-
second-language (ESL) programs are essential components of bilingual education models. Ebel (1980) has discussed the trend
of expanded emphasis on the teaching of reading in ESL programs. In the 1940s the United States ESL population served
was characterized by young adults already literate in the vernacular, so the focus of ESL programs was on the development
of listening and conversational skills. Since the needs of

today's ESL population encompass all educational levels,
ability in the teaching of initial reading skills has gained
increasing importance in the repertoire of competencies the
ESL teacher brings to the classroom. In her evaluation of
teacher training texts for ESL teachers, Ebel found only four
publications which adequately meet her criteria for preparation in this area.

1. Techniques and Procedures in Second Language
   Teaching *(Decaney, 1967)*

Unlike the other three books, which concentrate primarily
on the teaching of reading skills, this text presents chapters
on the teaching of oral and written language, spelling, and
reading. Methods of testing knowledge of the second language
are discussed. The chapter on reading addresses the differences between learning to read in the vernacular and learning
to read in the second language. Illustrated discussions of
activities for developing reading readiness and beginning
skills in reading are presented. The strength of this text
lies in the many practical exercises presented to the teacher
for classroom use in the development of children's English
language skills.

2. Reading and the Bilingual Child *(Ching, 1976)*

This slim volume may best serve as a supplementary text.
It discusses the introduction of reading both to the non-
standard English speaker and the non-native speaker of English.
Teaching strategies for reading instruction include development of motivation and self-concept, and emphasis is placed on
the development of listening and speaking skills. A discussion
of formal reading instruction includes the language experience
approach as well as those basal readers available as teaching
materials. The author concludes that once listening and speaking skills are adequately developed in the target language,
teaching reading to the bilingual child is no different than
teaching reading to the monolingual child.

3. The Reading Process: The Teacher and the Learner
   (Zintz, 1975)

The teaching of reading to the bilingual child and the
inner city child is discussed as a unit on linguistics and
reading. It is emphasized that many beginning reading series
used by school systems fail to reflect the cultural and preschool experiences of children from minority cultures. From
this point of view, the advantages and disadvantages of the

Miami Linguistic Readers are discussed and the series is recommended for teaching of beginning reading in English to native Spanish-speaking children.

Also stressed is the development of good oral language skills prior to the teaching of reading in English. The teaching of initial reading in the vernacular is advocated, and a list of sources for available reading materials in Spanish is provided.

4. Teaching English to Non-English Speakers
   (Thonis, 1977)

Based on theoretical and practical considerations, this book compares and contrasts the prerequisite skills a child must possess to achieve meaningful decoding of printed material presented both in the vernacular and in a second language. Thonis provides a checklist of considerations for the selection of effective teaching materials to be used with non-native English speakers. Content area reading in both languages is discussed. She briefly reviews the strengths and weaknesses of several assessment tools currently used in the evaluation of the non-native speakers' verbal and nonverbal skills.

Among the writers in the area of reading instruction for bilingual children, Thonis is exceptional in her consistent view of the teacher as facilitator who builds upon the skills and experience that the child, as an active learner, brings into the classroom.

The ESL literature reviewed which focuses on the teaching of English reading skills consistently stresses that reading in the second language should not be introduced until the child demonstrates an adequate oral command of the target language. There is also agreement that the child's native language and culture be given positive recognition in the learning environment.

ESL literature on teaching methodology does not adequately assess to what extent native language skills influence the acquisition of second-language literacy skills. While oral language competency in the second language is considered a prerequisite to the acquisition of second-language reading skills, the level of oral linguistic competency needed prior to initial reading instruction is not adequately defined. Similarly, bilingual literature on literacy in minority-language children often does not assess native-language oral proficiency and literacy skills. When the developmental relationship between knowledge of the native language and the second language is unknown, it is unclear how one discusses the question of how and when to transfer reading skills from one language to another.

Cohen (1980) has developed a program to facilitate the transfer of reading skills from the native language to the second language. He recommends accurate identification of the child's dominant language through use of a cognitively oriented dominance test, the Language Assessment Umpire (LAU). A team teaching approach is recommended in which the dominant language teacher and the ESL teacher coordinate the teaching of similar structural concepts shared by the two languages in a method which compares and contrasts the two structures. He presents fifteen comparative English/Spanish structures, such as the pronoun position of possessive adjectives and demonstrative adjectives; and twenty-four contrastive English/ Spanish structures such as the "in front of" noun position of adjective base form versus the Spanish position of the adjective following the noun. Cohen suggests a hierarchal development of those syntactic concepts. Once the linguistic structure can be read meaningfully in the dominant language, it may be taught in the second language. This may be taught on a skill-by-skill basis or a skill cluster basis. In this approach, reading skills are taught concurrently in both languages. Cohen states that this method is preferable to establishing all basic reading skills in the native language prior to introduction of reading in the second language. He suggests that concurrent presentation in both languages reinforces the concept in the native language. He offers no research data to support the effectiveness of his program.

While Cohen's program for transfer of reading skills may be effective for some children, this theory does not appear to be based on any educational research which supports the teaching of reading skills in both languages concurrently in order to promote transfer of those skills. Although Cohen's position may be valid, this is difficult to assess because he provides no supportive data.

The issue of appropriate assessment of children's expressive English language skills was addressed by Gonzalez (1981). Gonzalez proposes a descriptive method for analyzing bilingual children's expressive language skills in English at the syntactic and semantic level of production. This analysis of oral language skills is then compared with the structural level of the reading material being presented in English. Gonzalez suggests that reading failure may occur when the linguistic demands of the text exceed the child's oral control of the language. The child's expressive use of language, then, is a good indicator of the appropriate linguistic level from which the child will be able to successfully decode reading texts with meaning.

From a theoretical viewpoint it must be noted that a descriptive analysis method, as proposed by Gonzalez, does not take into account that a child's receptive language skills may be better developed than expressive language skills. It is possible that the child may comprehend written material that is beyond the level of his or her spontaneous oral production. This model also does not take into account the differences between the highly contextualized, personally salient nature of oral language as compared to the decontextualized, abstract nature of written language. Thus, the child's oral competence in the second language may not accurately reflect the child's cognitive ability to meaningfully decode written material in the second language.

One would like to see this method expanded to include, when possible, a comparison of the child's oral control of the semantic and syntactic structures in both the native language and the target language, as well as some indication of the child's native language literacy skills.

Past, et al. (1980), present a descriptive report of a successful reading program for kindergarten Spanish-speaking children which appears not to compromise the children's native language abilities. The program was implemented in Austin, Texas, and is based on the theory that children from lower socioeconomic levels are often limited in preschool reading readiness experiences which promote successful reading in school. The program provides a classroom environment rich in printed language in Spanish and English. Reading is introduced in the child's dominant language by an individualized system which stresses the presentation of words of personal salience to the child. This program incorporates the use of individual word codes, individual and group reading lessons, child-developed storybooks, and phonics. Parent participation in language activities is encouraged both at home and in the classroom. The authors report that the receiving first-grade teachers of these children were satisfied with the performance of the students. This performance represents an improvement over the performance of children who had not been in the program.

While this is only a descriptive study of one classroom, it does suggest that the focus of methodology should probably be on developing the existing skills children bring to the educational environment.

CONCLUSION

The literature on reading in bilingual settings indicates that in minority language populations, such as those in the United States, biliteracy is more effectively acquired when reading is introduced initially in the native language followed by reading in the second language. Reading in the second language should be introduced when the child has achieved mastery of oral language skills in the second language.

Successful initial reading acquisition in the second language has occurred in North American immersion programs where the native language of the children is a majority language, respected and considered prestigious. It has been found that the relative status of children's native language with regard to the second language is an important factor in achievement of second-language skills.

Transfer of reading skills from one language to another appears to occur automatically without formal instruction. It seems that once children have learned to read in a language, they transfer these skills to the other language they are exposed to spontaneously. It is not clear how this transfer occurs nor what teachers can do in bilingual classrooms to promote this transfer.

What researchers have consistently found is that oral language skills have an important influence on the successful development of literacy skills.

REFERENCES

Al-Rufai, H. "Ability Transfer and the Teaching of Reading."
   English Language Teaching Journal, 1976, 30:236-241.

Barik, H.C., and M. Swain. "Three-Year Evaluation of a Large-
   Scale Early Grade French Immersion Program: The Ottawa Study."
   Language Learning, 1975, 25:1.

Brisk, M.E. "Language Policies in American Education." *Boston
   University Journal of Education*, 1981, 163:3-15.

Ching, D. *Reading and the Bilingual Child*. Newark, Del.:
   International Reading Association, 1976.

Chomsky, N. *Syntactic Structures*. The Hague: Mouton, 1957.

Chu-Chang, M. "The Dependency Relation Between Oral Language
   and Reading in Bilingual Children." *Boston University Journal of Education*, 1981, 163:30-55.

Cohen, A.D. "The Culver City Spanish Immersion Program: The
   First Two Years." *Modern Language Journal*, 1974, 58:95-103.

Cohen, B. *Issues Related to Transferring Reading Skills from
   Spanish to English*. Los Angeles, California: National Dissemination and Assessment Center, 1980.

Cummins, J. "Empirical and Theoretical Underpinnings of Bilingual Education." *Journal of Education*, 1981, 163:16-49.

Cummins, J. "Linguistic Interdependence and the Educational
   Development of Bilingual Children." *Review of Educational
   Research*, 1979, 49:222-251.

Decanay, F.R. *Techniques and Procedures in Second Language
   Teaching*. Dobbs Ferry, NY: Oceana Publications, 1967.

deVilliers, J.G., and P.A. deVilliers. *Language Acquisition*.
   Cambridge, Massachusetts: Harvard University Press, 1978.

Dulay, H., and M.K. Burt. "National Sequences in Child Second
   Language Acquisition." *Language Learning*, 1974, 24:37-53.

Ebel, C.W. "An Update: Teaching Reading to Students of English as a Second Language." *The Reading Teacher*, 1980, 33:403-407.

Engle, P.J. "Language Medium in Early School Years for Minority Language Groups." *Review of Educational Research*, 1975, 45:283-325.

Ervin-Tripp, S.M. *Language Acquisition and Communicative Choice*. Stanford: Stanford University Press, 1973.

Gale, K., D. Mclay, M. Christie, and S. Harris. "Academic Achievement in the Milingimbi Bilingual Education Program." *TESOL Quarterly*, 1981, 15:297-314.

Gonzalez, P.E. "Beginning English Reading for ESL Students." *The Reading Teacher*, 1981, 35:154-162.

Goodman, K.S. "Analysis of Reading Miscues: Applied Psycholinguistics." *Reading Research Quarterly*, 1969, 5:9-30.

Goodman, K.S. *Miscue Analysis: Application to Reading Instruction*. Urbana, Ill.: National Council of Teachers of English, 1973.

Goodman, K.S. "Reading: A Psycholinguistic Guessing Game." In H. Singer and R.B. Ruddell (eds.), *New Horizons in Reading*. Newark, Del.: International Reading Association, 1976.

Goodman, K.S. "The Reading Process: Theory and Practice." In R.E. Hodges and E.H. Rudorf (eds.), *Language and Learning to Read: What Teachers Should Know about Language*. Boston: Houghton Mifflin, 1972.

Johnson, D., and H. Myklebust. *Learning Disabilities: Educational Principles and Practices*. New York: Grune and Stratton, 1967.

Laberge, D., and S.J. Samuel. "Toward a Theory of Automatic Information Processing in Reading." *Cognitive Psychology*, 1974, 6:293-323.

Lambert, W.E., and G.R. Tucker. *Bilingual Education of Children: The St. Lambert Experiment*. Rowley, MA: Newbury House, 1972.

Lenneberg, E.H., ed. *New Directions in the Study of Language*. Cambridge, Massachusetts: M.I.T. Press, 1964.

Lenneberg, E.H. *Biological Foundations of Language*. New York: Wiley, 1967.

Lerner, J.W. *Children with Learning Disabilities*. Boston: Houghton Mifflin Company, 1976.

Lopez, S.H. "Children's Use of Contextual Clues in Reading

Spanish." *The Reading Teacher*, 1977, 30:735-740.

Macintosh, H.K., ed. *Children and Oral Language*. Joint publication of the Association for Childhood Education International Association for Supervision and Curriculum Development, International Reading Association, National Council of Teachers of English, 1964.

Mes-prat, M., and H.P. Edwards. "Elementary French Immersion: Children's Use of Orthographic Structure for Reading." *The Canadian Modern Language Review*, 1981, 37:682-693.

Modiano, N. "National or Mother Language in Beginning Reading: A Comparative Study." *Research in the Teaching of English*, 1968, 1:32-43.

Past, K.C., A. Past, and I.B. Guzman. "A Bilingual Kindergarten Immersed in Print." *The Reading Teacher*, 1980, 33: 907-913.

Pena, S.C., and Z. Verner. "Developing Reading Skills in Spanish." *Research, Materials and Practice*, 1981, 64: 425-432.

Rosier, P., and M. Farella. "Bilingual Education at Rock Point: Some Early Results." *TESOL Quarterly*, 1976, 10: 379-388.

Skutnabb-Kangas, T., and P. Toukamaa. *Teaching Migrant Children's Mother Tongue and Learning the Language of the Host Country in the Context of the Socio-Cultural Situation of the Migrant Family*. Helsinki: Finnish National Commission for UNESCO, 1976.

Swain, M. "Bilingual Education: Research and Its Implications." In C.A. Yorio, K. Perkins, and J. Schachter (eds.). *On TESOL '79: The Learner in Focus*. Washington, D.C.: TESOL, 1979.

Thonis, E.W. *Literacy for America's Spanish Speaking Children*. Newark, Del.: International Reading Association, Inc., 1976.

Thonis, E.W. *Teaching Reading to Non-English Speakers*. New York: Collier-Macmillan, 1977.

Troike, R.C. *Research Evidence for the Effectiveness of Bilingual Education*. Washington, DC: National Clearinghouse for Bilingual Education, 1978.

Vygotsky, L.S. *Thought and Language*. Cambridge, MA: M.I.T. Press, 1962.

Zintz, M.V. *The Reading Process: The Teacher and the Learner*. Dubuque, Iowa: William C. Brown, 1975.

ANNOTATED BIBLIOGRAPHY

Al-Rufai, H. "Ability to Transfer and the Teaching of Reading." *English Language Teaching Journal*, 1976, 30:236-241.

Describes a statistically based investigation performed with Arabic students learning English as a second language. Demonstrates the transfer of reading skills and habits from L_2 to L_1 and vice versa and suggests a feasible way to increase facility in reading a foreign language.

Arnold, R.D. "San Antonio Language Research Project." 1956-66, ERIC Document Reproduction Service No. E.D. 022528.

Three groups of disadvantaged Mexican-American children were tested to determine changes in reading achievement between second and third grade. During the school year, an oral-aural English group of 102 children were given intensive English-language instruction while an oral-aural Spanish group of 67 children were given intensive Spanish-language instruction. A control group of 115 children did not receive intensive language instruction. In the Spring and again in the Fall the three groups were tested with (1) the Metropolitan Achievement Tests, (2) Tests of Reading, Inter-American Series, and (3) Prueba de Lectura, Serie Inter-americana. Mean difference scores were determined for each group. The oral-aural Spanish group showed significant gains on the vocabulary subtest and on total score on the Test of Reading. They showed a significant loss on the speed subtest of the Prueba de Lectura. The oral-aural English group showed no significant changes. The paper was introduced at the International Reading Association Conference, Boston, MA, April 24-27, 1968.

Becker, A. "Teaching Reading in English to Portuguese Speakers: A Background for Teachers." In Macedo, D.P. (ed.). *Issues in Portuguese Bilingual Education*. Cambridge, Massachusetts: National Assessment and Dissemination Center for Bilingual/ Bicultural Education, 1980.

The author analyzes the complex problems involved in teaching non-literate Portuguese children to read in English.
She discusses different beginning reading methods and suggests that there is no one right method of beginning reading;
therefore, it is essential that teachers acquaint themselves
with the options available and adapt them to the individual
needs of the children. Learning styles, strengths, and limitations of instructional methods are important factors to
consider in selecting an appropriate reading method.

Ching, D. *Reading and the Bilingual Child.* Newark, Dela-
    ware: International Reading Association, 1976.

Describes the special educational needs of bilingual children and reviews and summarizes research on teaching English
as a second language. The author also provides a description
of teaching approaches used to meet the reading needs of bilingual children. Practical ideas are given on the development of reading skills, motivation and self-concept, auditory
discrimination, vocabulary and concepts, oral language, and
formal reading instruction.

Christian, C.C. "Social and Psychological Implications of Bi-
    lingual Literacy." In Simoes, A., ed. *The Bilingual Child.*
    San Francisco: Academic Press, 1976.

The author discusses the effects of self-concept on literacy
and problems resulting from acquisition of a written language
different from the home language. The author argues that a
transition from family use of a minority language to literacy
exclusively in the school language can never be fully satis-
factory. An education which effects this transition attempts
to change rather than develop a child's identity through
literacy. Literacy is used as an assimilation tool. Early
and continuing bilingual literacy, on the other hand, can
benefit the child psychologically and socially.

Chu-Chang, M. "The Dependency Relation Between Oral Language
    and Reading in Children." *Boston University Journal of
    Education*, 1981, 163:30-55.

Issues related to the topic of the dependence relation between oral language and reading in bilingual children are
discussed. The literature reviewed includes studies of oral
language and reading in monolingual speakers, models of reading processes, phonological recording as an intermediary process in reading, studies on reading instruction for bilingual
children, and the processing of dual languages by bilingual
speakers. A model of monolingual versus bilingual reading

is developed based on the review of the literature. An experimental study by the author verifying the model is presented. Implications of this model for reading instruction
for bilingual children and future research are raised.

Coballes Vega, C. "Sociolinguistics and the Teaching of Read-
ing to Bilingual Children." In Trueba, H.T., and Barnett-
Mizrahi, C., eds., *Bilingual Multicultural Education and the
Professional.* Rowley, Massachusetts: Newbury House, 1979.

This article discusses four issues in bilingual reading:
(1) extralinguistic and linguistic factors affecting reading
performance, (2) relevance of sociolinguistics to the teaching of reading, (3) language diversity among Spanish-speakers,
(4) potential research areas in bilingual literacy.

Cohen, A. "The Culver City Spanish Immersion Program: The First
Two Years." *Modern Language Journal,* 1974, 58:95-103.

Reports results of a Spanish immersion program for kindergarten and first-grade monolingual English-speaking children
at the Linwood Howe School in Culver City, California. This
program was modeled after the St. Lambert French immersion
project developed in Montreal, Canada, for monolingual English-
speaking Canadian children. Findings from the Culver City
project indicate that English-speaking children were able to
successfully complete an all-Spanish curriculum at the kindergarten and first-grade level with no retardation of oral
English skills when these skills were compared with that of
a control group of children not receiving instruction in a
second language. When compared to a control group on a test
of reading readiness in English at the end of the kindergarten
year, the pilot immersion group scored significantly lower
than the control group. By the end of grade one, the pilot
immersion group was equal to the first-grade comparison group
in English reading skills. The pilot immersion class received one hour more of schooling per day as they received
two hours of reading instruction per day, one hour in Spanish
and one hour in English. The study reports that children who
were good readers in Spanish were good readers in English.

Cohen, B. *Issues Related to Transferring Reading Skills from
Spanish to English.* Los Angeles, CA: National Dissemination
and Assessment Center, 1980.

A method to transfer reading skills from the dominant language to the second language is discussed. The author recommends accurate identification of the child's dominant language
and a team teaching approach between the dominant language

teacher and the English-as-a-Second-Language teacher which
coordinates the teaching of similar structural concepts in
the two languages. Once the linguistic structure can be
used meaningfully in the dominant language, it may be taught
in the second language. A sequence of twenty-six syntactic
patterns of Spanish and English are compared and presented
for instructional use.

Cohen, S.A., and S. Rodriquez. "Experimental Results That
Question the Ramirez-Castaneda Model for Teaching Reading to
First Grade Mexican Americans." *The Reading Teacher*, 1980,
34:12-18.

The authors argue that direct instruction to precise competency-based behavioral objectives is more effective in the
teaching of reading to Mexican-American children than a
curriculum designed on a Mexican socio-cultural model as
presented by Ramirez and Castaneda in a 1974 study. The
authors suggest that the field dependent learning style
described in the Ramirez-Castaneda research as unique to
Mexican-American children is better explained as related to
socioeconomic level rather than ethnocultural background.
The contention is made that ethnocultural characteristics do
not adequately explain the large incidence of underachieve-
ment among this population. A study, using 150 first-grade
Mexican-American students as subjects, compares the effectiveness of both teaching models. Although results of the Cohen-
Rodriquez project support the greater effectiveness of direct reading instruction to precise competencies, the authors
point out the limitations of the study and caution against
over-generalization of the results.

Cribano, W. "Helping the Student of Low Language Ability."
Hispania, 1977, 60:508-510.

The author considers traditional classroom programs designed to teach Spanish to English speakers and suggests
that these approaches are not the best for learners, specifically those of lesser language ability. He describes a
preliminary program which he designed and instructed for
such students preceding the regular beginner's course.
Program emphasis is reading comprehension, which fosters
knowledge of the essentials of basic grammar, and therefore
improves comprehension. Results of the course are presented,
and the need for further development of such preliminary
courses is suggested.

Cummins, J. "Empirical and Theoretical Underpinnings of Bilingual Education." *Boston University Journal of Education*,
1981, 163:16-29.

Empirical research on the consequences of bilingual education for minority-language children is reviewed, and a theoretical model is constructed to account for the research
findings. It is argued that Cognitive/Academic Language
Proficiency (CALP) becomes differentiated and can be empirically distinguished from Basic Interpersonal Communication
Skills (BICS) in L_1 and L_2 and that L_1 and L_2 CALP are interdependent. The implications of these positions are examined
for using L_1 in the home, for the logic of entry and exit
criteria and for language assessment practices in bilingual
education.

Cummins, J. "Linguistic Interdependence and the Educational
Development of Bilingual Children." *Review of Educational
Research*, 1979, 49:222-251.

The central thesis of this paper is that a cognitively and
academically beneficial form of bilingualism can be achieved
only on the basis of an adequately developed first language
(L_1) skills. Two hypotheses are formulated and combined to
arrive at this position. The "developmental interdependence"
hypothesis proposes that the development of competence in a
second language (L_2) is partially a function of the type of
competence already developed in L_1 at the time when exposure
to L_2 begins. The "threshold" hypothesis proposes that there
may be threshold levels of linguistic competence which a bilingual child must attain, both in order to avoid cognitive
disadvantages and to allow the potentially beneficial aspects of
bilingualism to influence his cognitive and academic functioning. These hypotheses are integrated into a model of
bilingual education in which educational outcomes are explained as a function of the interaction between background,
child input, and educational treatment factors. It is suggested that many evaluations of bilingual education programs
have produced uninterpretable data because they failed to
incorporate the possibility of these interactions into their
research designs.

Cziko, G.Z. "The Effects of Language Sequencing on the Development of Bilingual Reading Skills." *Canadian Modern Language
Review*, 1976, 32:534-539.

A study is reported evaluating the effects on the development of bilingual reading skills of a second language/native
language sequence of reading instruction as opposed to a
native language/second language sequence in elementary grade
French immersion programs.

Decanay, F.R. *Techniques and Procedures in Second Language Teaching.* Dobbs Ferry, N.Y.: Oceana Publications, 1967.

A training text for teachers of English language, this book presents chapters on the teaching of oral and written language, spelling, and reading. Testing knowledge of the second language is discussed. The chapter on reading addresses the differences between learning to read in the vernacular and learning to read in a second language. Illustrated discussions of activities for developing readiness and beginning reading skills are presented. Many practical exercises are presented to the teacher for classroom use in the development of English language skills.

Deemer, H.B. *The Transfer of Reading Skills from First to Second Language: The Report of an Experiment with Spanish Speakers Learning English.* 1978. ERIC Document No. 172532.

Certain aspects of the reading process have suggested that second language reading skills are determined to some extent by native language reading skills. Some of this research is reviewed here and an experiment is described in which the reading skills in Spanish and in English of three groups of Spanish speakers learning English are compared. It is shown that the highest English proficiency group had a strong significant correlation between reading skills in the two languages, the middle group had a slight correlation and the beginners had no correlation. It is concluded that reading for meaning is a skill which is non-language specific and so is transferred to a foreign language that is being learned.

deVilliers, J.G., and P.A. deVilliers. *Language Acquisition.* Cambridge, MA: Harvard University Press, 1978.

This text includes a discussion of language development, beginning with sounds made at birth and continuing through the acquisition of complex language expression. Chapters discuss such topics as early and late grammar, processes, and constraints. Also included is a chapter concerning language in developmentally disabled children.

Ebel, C.W. "An Update: Teaching Reading to Students of English as a Second Language." *The Reading Teacher*, 1980, 33: 403-407.

Discusses the implications of historical trends in teaching reading to English-as-a-second-language (ESL) students. As the ESL student population continues to expand to include students of all educational levels, reading gains increasing relevance in the ESL program. An analysis of teacher training texts in reading reveals few books which provide information on the teaching of reading to non-native English speakers. The author suggests that the knowledge of the reading specialist and the ESL specialist has not been adequately shared in developing training programs and texts for teachers of reading to ESL students.

Engle, P.L. "Language Medium in Early School Years for Minority Language Groups." *Review of Educational Research*, 1975, 45:283-325.

Reviews and discusses the empirical research to 1975 on the debate regarding the efficacy of teaching in the vernacular versus teaching in the national language. The author concludes that the debate is not yet settled. Researchers have not adequately compared the effects of teaching via the direct method and via the native language approach. A summary is presented of those confounding factors that must be controlled in future research.

Ervin-Tripp, S.M. *Language Acquisition and Communicative Choice.* Stanford, CA: Stanford University Press, 1973.

This book provides a collection of essays by the well-known sociolinguist. Addressed are such topics as bilingualism, language acquisition, and sociolinguistics.

Feeley, J.T. "Bilingual Instruction: Puerto Rico and the Mainland." *Reading Teacher*, 1977, 30:741-744.

The author compares and contrasts bilingual reading programs for Spanish-speaking children in the United States with two programs in Puerto Rico. Programs observed are described, including mention of location, socioeconomic conditions, and an outline of the classroom activities which are part of the reading lessons, as well as the overall emphasis the program places on English acquisition.

Gale, K., D. McClay, C. Michael, and S. Harris. "Academic Achievement in the Milingimbi Bilingual Education Program." *TESOL Quarterly*, 1981, 15:297-314.

In 1973, the Milingimbi School, serving an Aboriginal community in the Northern Territory of Australia, began the gradual phase-in of a bilingual education program in English and Gupapuyngu to replace its previous program of all-English instruction. The program was initially introduced in the Preschool and Year 1 and continued to advance by one grade level each year until the phase-in was completed at year 7. This report compares the academic achievement scores

of students in the bilingual program for years 5, 6, and 7
to students in the all-English program for the same academic
years. The authors report that by year 7 the children in
the bilingual classes were performing better than the English-only children in seven out of ten measures of academic
achievement.

Golub, L. "Evaluation, Design and Implementation of a Bilingual
Education Program, Grades 1-12, Spanish/English." *Education
and Urban Society*, 1978, 10:363-382.

Examines a bilingual education program evaluation conducted
in a Pennsylvania school district. The 200 children considered are Puerto Rican students placed in bilingual education programs. The author states that "the evaluation design
provides for a formative, systematic, evaluation design which
is intended to provide baseline data to be used for the formulation of guidelines for program planning, modification,
and improvement in years to come" (p. 365). Included in the
presentation are: the purpose of the evaluation, evaluation
design, and data collection procedures and instructional
variables tested in Spanish and English. A summary and
recommendations based on the evaluation are included.

Gonzalez, P.C. "Beginning English Reading for ESL Students."
The Reading Teacher, 1981, 35:154-162.

This article uses a descriptive method of analyzing a
child's expressive language in English at the syntactic and
semantic level for comparison with the structural level of
reading materials presented in that language. The author
suggests that the child's expressive use of the language is
a good indicator of the linguistic level at which the child
will be able to successfully decode reading texts with meaning.

Goodman, K., Y. Goodman, and B. Flores. *Reading in the Bilingual Classroom: Literacy and Biliteracy*. Rosslyn, VA:
National Clearninghouse for Bilingual Education, 1979.

Presented are considerations influencing the development
of literacy in multilingual nations. The authors suggest
that the language of United States federal policies regarding
the education of linguistic minorities implies a view of
language deficiency in these groups which, in turn, adversely
affects how literacy programs are developed. Three common
assumptions dominating bilingual literacy programs are chal-
lenged: (1) the need for oral proficiency in the language
to be read, (2) a "regular" grapheme-phoneme correspondence
in a language makes that language easier to read, (3) read-

ing is a response to print with speech. A psycholinguistic view of reading as a receptive process is emphasized. A comprehension-centered curriculum for literacy is advocated as is a positive teacher attitude toward children and their language.

Gudschinsky, S. "Mother Tongue Literacy and Second Language Learning." In W.F. Mackey and T. Anderson (eds.), *Bilingualism in Early Childhood*. Rowley, MA: Newbury House, 1977.

Presents a discussion of several bilingual education programs which have been established by the Summer Institute of Linguistics. Program sequence and stages of curriculum development are discussed. Rationale for the benefits of bilingual instruction are presented and explained.

Hatch, E. "Research in Reading a Second Language." *Journal of Reading Behavior*, 1974, 1:53-61.

The author describes the research in second language in attempting to answer three questions: (1) Should initial reading be introduced in the native language or in the language of instruction? (2) What factors complicate reading in a second language? (3) How should research findings on reading a second language be applied in the classroom? Research related to these issues is presented and reviewed.

Kolers, P.A. "Reading and Talking Bilingually." *American Journal of Psychology*, 1966, 79:357-376.

Provides a discussion of several experiments designed to examine the ability of bilingual subjects to recall word meanings. Subjects were tested in the areas of comprehension of material presented in several linguistic forms, reading aloud, code-switching and the effects of practice on recall. Errors are tallied, presented and analyzed. The author concludes from his results that "the equivalence for comprehension of the form of the text, the occurrence of unique kinds of errors in reading and the problems of memory-search in generation were taken as evidence that the encoding and decoding of language are not symmetrical operations. The kinds of errors made in reading aloud demonstrate that reading cannot be described accurately only in terms of graphemephoneme translations" (p. 376).

Lambert, W.E., and G.R. Tucker. *Bilingual Education of Children: The St. Lambert Experiment*. Rowley, MA: Newbury House, 1972.

Provides an in-depth discussion of the St. Lambert Experiment, a total immersion bilingual program in which children from English-speaking homes in St. Lambert, a suburb of Montreal, were placed in school programs which provided instruction in French only. Parent input and support for this program were very strong. Discussion of the program includes a description of the classes in action, parent and pupil views toward the program, and academic standings of the children at the end of the pilot program and follow-up classes of grades 1 through 4.

Lopez, S.H. "Children's Use of Contextual Clues in Reading Spanish." *The Reading Teacher*, 1977, 30:735-740.

Children's use of contextual clues in reading process, as it relates to beginning literacy in Spanish, is investigated based on previous research done with young English readers. The Goodman research design is replicated in Spanish with 75 Mexican-American second- and third-grade children in Eagle Pass, Texas, all of whom had received initial literacy instruction in Spanish. The author of the present study concludes that young Spanish-speaking readers, like young English readers, use contextual clues to predict meaning, as well as their knowledge of sound and symbol relationships, in the predication of sentence content in reading. Based on the data, instructional implications are offered for the teaching of reading to Spanish-speaking children.

Markey, W.F., and T.A. Anderson, eds. *Bilingualism in Early Childhood*. Rowley, MA: Newbury House Publishers, 1977.

Many of the pioneer writers who have had an impact on current understanding of the nature and development of child bilingualism from a theoretical, linguistic, sociological, psychological, and pedagogical viewpoint are represented in this collection of papers from a conference on Child Language held in Chicago, Illinois, in 1971.

Mes-prat, M., and H.P. Edwards. "Elementary French Immersion Children's Use of Orthographic Structure for Reading." *The Canadian Modern Language Review*, 1981, 37:682-693.

This study of grades three and six English-speaking students enrolled in a French immersion program examines two aspects of the reading process: English and French word perception and the use of orthographic structure. Phonological and orthographic regularity are discussed as important factors of word perception. It is hypothesized that the bilingually schooled child, who begins reading in one language, will already have some experience with abstracting spelling pattern units. When immersion children schooled in French begin to read in their native language, English, spelling patterns shared by the two languages may be more readily identified than thos spelling patterns typical of English. Results indicate that students are aware of the regularities of their two languages and have strong expectations about permissible letter strings. This research indicates that orthographic constraints of word perception do not present a problem in the transfer of reading skills.

Modiano, N. "National or Mother Language in Beginning Reading: A Comparative Study." *Research in the Teaching of English*, 1968, 1:32-43.

This article discusses a study conducted by the author in 1967, in the Chiapas highlands of Mexico, to determine the effectiveness of two approaches to the teaching of reading in the national language, Spanish, to children whose native languages of Mayan origin were Tzotzel or Tzeltal. One approach was that of the federal and state schools in which all reading instruction was given in Spanish. Teachers in these schools had professional training and spoke Spanish as their mother tongue. None of them could speak the local languages of the Indian populations they served. The second approach was that used by the schools of the National Indian Institute. This was a bilingual method in which, prior to reading instruction in Spanish, children were taught to read in their mother tongue and were taught some oral Spanish vocabulary. Teachers from these schools were native Indians who spoke the local language. Most had only fair command of Spanish. To determine which approach led to greater reading comprehension in Spanish, two principal measures were used. The first measure was the proportion of students selected by their teachers as able to understand what they read in Spanish. The second measure was a test of reading comprehension in Spanish developed especially for the study and based on materials that reflected the cultural experiences of the children being tested. Both measures indicated significantly greater reading comprehension for children taught by native teachers in the bilingual schools. The author concludes that children learn to read the national language more efficiently when they are first taught reading in the mother tongue and that the teacher's ability to communicate with students is more important than language or instructional method in successful teaching of reading.

O'Brien, C.A. *Teaching the Language-Different Child to Read*. Columbus, Ohio: Charles E. Merrill Publishing Co., 1973.

A discussion of the effects of differences in cultural backgrounds on school achievement is followed by an analysis of the implications of linguistic research on reading. The author then provides a contrastive analysis of Spanish and English and black dialect and English. A description of appropriate reading approaches for the linguistically-different child is offered with specific techniques which can be used by the classroom teacher to develop literacy skills.

Olsen, B.H. "Teaching Reading to Bilingual Students." *Journal of Reading*, 1977, 20:346-349.

The author discusses the existence of bilingual/bicultural education programs and their effectiveness. Several programs are discussed, and their teaching strategies examined.

Past, K.C., A. Past, and I.B. Guzman. "A Bilingual Kindergarten Immersed in Print." *The Reading Teacher*, 33:907-913.

This article describes a successful reading program developed for kindergarten children in a bilingual open classroom that provides a classroom environment rich in printed language. Reading is introduced in the dominant language by an individualized system which stresses the presentation of words of personal salience to the child. The program incorporates the use of individual word cards, individual and group reading lessons, child-developed storybooks and phonics. Parent participation is encouraged both at home and in the classroom.

Pena, S.C., and Z. Verner. "Developing Reading Skills in Spanish: Research, Materials, and Practice." *Hispania*, 1984, 64:425-432.

This article reviews the current research on the impact of native language instruction and second language instruction in bilingual education programs. Approaches to the teaching of reading in the second language and materials for teaching reading in Spanish are described. When to effectively transfer reading skills from Spanish to English is still a critical question. The authors list several factors for consideration in data intake design for programs in teaching reading to non-English speaking and limited-English-speaking learners.

Ramirez, A.G., and R.L. Politzer. "The Acquisition of English and the Maintenance of Spanish in a Bilingual Education Program." *TESOL Quarterly*, 9:113-124.

Spanish and English versions of a 38-item grammar test were
administered to 40 Spanish-surnamed pupils, equally divided
by six at grade levels K, one, three, and five in a bilingual
education program. The test was a revision of part of an
earlier test for oral proficiency in Spanish and English.
Test subjects were also questioned about language use and
preference. The relationships between reported language use
and test results appeared to indicate that Spanish proficiency
was determined by use of the language at home. English proficiency showed some relationship to use with the peer group.
There were no significant correlations between the English
and Spanish version scores and only very slight relationships among the factors influencing them. Achievement in
English thus appeared to be unrelated to the maintenance of
Spanish for bilingual children.

Ramirez, M., and A. Castaneda. *Cultural Democracy, Bi-Cogni-
tive Development and Education.* New York, NY: Academic
Press, 1974.

This book discusses how American society can promote and
sustain its diversity and be sensitive to individual differences through educational pluralism. Two focal concepts
are discussed: bicultural identity, including the ability to
function completely in two cultures, and bicognitive development. A philosophy of education built on the ideas of "cultural democracy" is formulated. "This philosophy serves as
the foundation for a new educational policy designed to help
children of diverse backgrounds to learn effectively" (pp.
xi-xii).

Rosier, P., and M. Farella. "Bilingual Education at Rock
Point: Some Early Results." *TESOL Quarterly*, 1976, 10:
379-388.

This paper discusses the results of test scores in total
reading on the Stanford Achievement Test given to fourth and
fifth grade Navajo students enrolled in a bilingual education
program at Rock Point. Fourth-grade students in this study,
who had received their education under a Title VII program,
had received continuous bilingual education since entering
school. Literacy was first achieved in Navajo (from K
through 2). The fifth grade group entered school under a
Title I program. These children received reading readiness
instruction in Navajo but were in a monolingual English program until third grade. In the fourth and fifth grades they
received some content area instruction in the Navajo language

and in the fifth grade they were reintroduced to literacy in Navajo. Bilingual students at Rock Point received significantly higher total reading scores in the fourth and fifth grades than Navajo students in other Indian Bureau Schools who had received no bilingual instruction and were taught in English. The assumption of the Rock Point program is that children learn to read only once, and they learn best in the language they speak. The essential concepts of reading are transferable to the second language.

Seitz, V. *Social Class and Ethnic Group Differences in Learning to Read.* Newark, Delaware: International Reading Association, 1977.

An overview of the changing nature of reading both as a process and as a developmental phenomenon with particular reference to the linguistic minority child of low socioeconomic status. The author focuses on group differences in academic achievement in reading rather than on individual differences. Seitz discusses the interaction of academic expectations of child and society based on linguistic and social differences.

Spolsky, B. *The Language Education of Minority Children.* Rowley, MA: Newbury House Publishers, 1978.

"The purpose of this book is to provide a discussion of contemporary concerns in the language education of minority children in the United States" (p. 8). A collection of readings pertaining to this topic is divided into three sections: multilingualism in the United States, bilingualism, and bilingual education and language education in practice.

Thonis, E.W. *Literacy for America's Spanish Speaking Children.* Newark, Delaware: International Reading Association, Inc., 1976.

Reviews the strengths and weaknesses of traditional methods of reading instruction currently used in both the United States and in Spanish-speaking countries. Discusses the preliterate, literate, and functionally illiterate Spanish-speaking child in relation to the initial reading experience within the classroom. Addresses the variables involved in choosing an appropriate reading program for the child. Suggests that an appropriate program will consider a child's developmental stage as well as a child's linguistic and cultural experience.

Thonis, E.W. *Teaching Reading to Non-English Speakers.* New

York: Collier-Macmillan, 1977.

Thonis states, "Print is a visual system superimposed upon auditory language." Based on theoretical and practical considerations, this book compares and contrasts the prerequisite skills a child must possess to achieve meaningful decoding of printed material presented both in the vernacular and in a second language. Provides a checklist of considerations for the selection of effective teaching materials to be used with non-native English speakers. Content area reading in both languages is discussed. Briefly reviews the strengths and weaknesses of several assessment tools currently used in the elevation of the non-native speakers' verbal and non-verbal skills.

Troike, R.C. *Research Evidence for the Effectiveness of Bilingual Education*. Washington, DC: National Clearinghouse for Bilingual Education, 1978.

Provides evidence from 12 programs attesting to the effectiveness of bilingual education. The conclusion is reached that a quality bilingual education program can be effective in meeting the goals of equal educational opportunity for minority language children. Research on Finnish immigrants in Sweden is cited to show the effect of social and cultural subordination in producing subtractive bilingualism unless strong language instruction is provided through age ten.

Vygotsky, L.S. *Thought and Language*. Cambridge, MA: M.I.T. Press, 1962.

This book closely examines the interrelation of thought and language. The purpose of the author's work is summarized as (1) providing experimental evidence that meanings of words undergo evolution during childhood, and defining the basic steps in that evolution; (2) uncovering the singular way in which the child's "scientific" concepts develop, compared with his spontaneous concepts, and formulating the laws governing their development; (3) demonstrating the specific psychological nature and linguistic function of written speech in its relation to thinking; and (4) clarifying, by way of experiments, the nature of inner speech and its relation to thought. The author discusses transfer of learning and language skills (p. xx).

Williams, J.P. "Learning to Read: A Review of Theories and Models." *Reading Research Quarterly*, 1973, 8:121-146.

A comprehensive review of theories and models of reading acquisition is presented and discussed. Five categories of reading models are outlined as taxonomic, psychometric, psychological, linguistic, and transactional.

Zintz, M.V. *The Reading Process: The Teacher and the Learner.* Dubuque, Iowa: William C. Brown, 1975.

The author describes this textbook as designed for the diagnostic teaching of reading. The section entitled "Linguistics and Reading" deals with the teaching of reading to the bilingual child and to the inner-city child. It is emphasized that many beginning reading series used by school systems fail to reflect the cultural and preschool experiences of both these groups. The advantages and disadvantages of the Miami Linguistic Readers are discussed and this series is recommended for the teaching of beginning reading in English to native Spanish-speaking children. Also stressed is the development of good oral skills in a language prior to the teaching of reading in that language. Teaching initial reading in the vernacular is advocated, and a list of sources for reading materials in Spanish is provided.

Chapter 6

BILINGUAL SPECIAL EDUCATION

Bilingual special education is a rapidly developing field.
Both the educational needs of all limited English proficiency
students and the individual special educational needs of exceptional students have been increasingly recognized by educators and lawmakers during the past decade. Today the educational challenges posed by LEP exceptional students are beginning to be addressed. However, close relationships between
programs for handicapped children and children of limited
English proficiency have deep historical roots in American
education.

Provision of special programs in U.S. public schools came
with compulsory school attendance laws. Between the mid-1800's
and early 1900's, individual states enacted these laws partly
to promote the acculturation of children from disparate ethnic,
cultural and language backgrounds and to prepare citizens for
participation in a democratic society. Compulsory education
laws were also aimed at removing immigrant children, a cheap
source of labor, from the competitive job market and keeping
them off the streets (Hofstadter, 1975).

Coinciding with compulsory education came the establishment of the first special programs for children who posed instructional and behavioral problems for schools. The programs
were variously called "ungraded schools," "streamers," or
"backward" classes. These programs were first established in
large, industrial cities, and many of the students placed in
them were immigrant children who had difficulties in school
primarily due to lack of proficiency in English.

The programs became dumping grounds for children who could
not be handled in regular classes. In many school districts
non-English speaking children who could not compete with their
peers in regular grades were frequently placed in "backward"
classes. This was not because it was the right place for them,
but because it furnished an easy means of disposing of students
who, through no fault of their own, were unsatisfactory members
of the regular grade (Miller, 1961).

The national origins and dominant languages of immigrant

students have changed between the late nineteenth and early
twentieth centuries. Yet it is only within recent years that
conditions in American schools for LEP and for handicapped
students have begun to substantially change from dumping
grounds to effective programs. Court litigation and legislation have both reflected and promoted changes in educational
policies affecting programming for these two groups and for
the LEP handicapped child.

Yet, there is no consensus on the appropriate treatment
of exceptional children of limited English proficiency in public school settings. Numerous questions are being asked by
educators: Does limited-English proficiency, itself, constitute
a handicap? How are LEP handicapped children identified? How
do we determine whether a LEP child's learning problems stem
from limited English proficiency, learning impairments or program deficits? Are LEP handicapped children the bilingual
department's responsibility or that of the schools' special
education departments? Is the acquisition of two languages a
realistic expectation for LEP handicapped children? How are
decisions made concerning the most appropriate language of
instruction?

Major, complex issues are involved in educational planning
for the LEP exceptional child. Prior to a child's referral,
evaluation, and placement, the issue of appropriate identification must be addressed. The identification of LEP handicapped
children may be extremely problematic. Educators are faced
with the danger both of "false positive" and of "false negative"
identification of LEP students as exceptional. That is, there
is concern that children, both non-handicapped and LEP, are
inappropriately identified, labeled, and subsequently placed in
special programs along with concern that all LEP children who
do present educational exceptionalities are identified and provided appropriate special education programs.

Historically and currently many LEP children have been
placed in special education programs, not because they presented
clearly established learning impairments (Mercer, 1973; Tucker,
1980; Zabel, 1980), but due to their inability to meet school
expectations for functioning in English. Others have been
placed in special classes due to differences in language dialect and/or cultural differences. For example, the Massachusetts Advocacy Center (1978) reports that Hispanics and blacks
are disproportionately placed in the more restrictive special
education programs compared to whites. In recent years, a number of class action suits have been filed against school districts to remedy this situation. The litigation has resulted
in major changes in the identification and placement procedures
involving LEP students (Ambert and Dew, 1982).

This chapter will discuss the legal rights of LEP handi-

capped children to special education services in their dominant language. An analysis of the special education process
will follow with particular emphasis placed on the implications of the process for language minority students. Identification, assessment, parental involvement, individual educational programs, program options, and bilingual special education program implementation guidelines will also be discussed.

SOURCES OF LEGAL RIGHTS

Federal legislative support for bilingual special education is found in the text and in the administrative and court
interpretations of sections 601 (Title VI) of the 1964 Civil
Rights Act (42 U.S.C. 2000d), Section 504 of the 1973 Vocational Rehabilitation Act (29 U.S.C. 784), Section 204 of the
1974 Equal Education Opportunities Act (20 U.S.C. 1703(f))
and, most specifically, in Public Law 94-142, the Education
of All Handicapped Children Act of 1975. In addition to
federal legislation some states have enacted special education
statutes, implementation guidelines and regulations, which
provide support for bilingual services to LEP handicapped
children.(Ambert and Dew, 1982).

Review of federal legislation

1. *1964 Civil Rights Act*: This was the first major piece
of federal legislation requiring that school districts receiving federal funding ensure non-discrimination on the basis of
race, color or national origin. Later interpretations of the
Act by the United States Office of Civil Rights (e.g., OCR's
May 25, 1970 Memorandum, 35 Fed. Reg. 11595) led to the requirement that such school districts had the obligation to provide specialized instruction to LEP students and to guarantee
that non-discriminatory testing mechanisms were utilized in
evaluations.

2. *Vocational Rehabilitation Act of 1973*: Following the
trend of civil rights legislation, Congress enacted the Vocational Rehabilitation Act to guarantee the civil rights of
handicapped individuals. Section 504 of this Act declares:

> No otherwise qualified handicapped individual in the
> United States shall, solely by reason of his handicap,
> be excluded from participation in, be denied the bene-
> fits of, or be subjected to discrimination under any
> program or activity receiving federal financial assist-
> ance.

Section 504, like Title VI of the Civil Rights Act, requires that school districts receiving federal assistance ensure access of handicapped students to public education. It also allows the Office for Civil Rights to conduct compliance reviews of school districts receiving federal funds, often requiring that they design an educational plan to correct civil rights violations.

The U.S. Office of Civil Rights has also drafted regulations for implementation of the Rehabilitation Act of 1973, which direct educational agencies in their placement of handicapped persons:

> A recipient [of federal funds] shall provide educational services to each qualified handicapped person who resides in the recipient's jurisdiction, regardless of the nature or severity of the person's handicap, in the most normal setting possible and may not remove a handicapped person from, or place such a person in a setting other than, the regular educational environment except when the nature or severity of the person's handicap is such that education in regular classes with the use of supplementary aids and services is demonstrated by the recipient not to be in the best interest of such person. (U.S. Federal Register, 41(96), 1976)

3. *Equal Educational Opportunities Act of 1974*: By the time of the enactment of the EEO Act of 1974, Congress had become aware of the need for national education policy that would express its concern with equity in education and the major educational reform movements affecting the country. One of these movements was the quest for bilingual education by language minority groups. In 1968 Congress had enacted Title VII of the Elementary and Secondary Education Act, 20 U.S.C. 880b et seq., also known as the Bilingual Education Act, where Congress declared its support and appropriated funds for demonstration projects in the field of bilingual education.

By 1974 a significant number of states had also enacted bilingual legislation, federal courts had ordered the establishment of bilingual programs, and the United States Supreme Court had confirmed the authority of the government's Office for Civil Rights to enforce civil rights mandates. The Equal Educational Opportunities Act includes the codification into law of the guarantee of equal education rights for language minority students and of legal principles declared by the Supreme Court in the landmark case *Lau v. Nichols*, 414 U.S. 563 (1974) (discussed in Chapter 2).

In perhaps its strongest statement against discriminatory treatment by the public schools, Section 1701 (1) of the Equal Educational Opportunities Act states:

> All children enrolled in public schools are entitled to
> equal educational opportunity without regard to race,
> color, sex, or national origin....

Of particular relevance for language minorities, section 1703
of the Act also states:

> No state shall deny equal educational opportunity to an
> individual on account of his or her race, color, sex,
> or national origin, by the failure of an educational
> agency to take appropriate action to overcome language
> barriers that impede equal participation by its students
> in its instructional programs.

Under this section, even school districts not receiving federal
funds are obligated to provide adequate educational services to
any *individual* eligible for participation in its programs.

4. *Education of All Handicapped Children Act of 1975*: This
Act, also known as Public Law 94-142, is the major federal
legislation mandating education for handicapped children.
Several of the judicial principles emerging from court proceedings of the 1960s and 1970s, such as the right to education,
individualized programming, least restrictive alternative, and
due process requirements including parent involvement, are included in this legislation, along with considerable federal
funding to support implementation at the state and local level
(Ambert and Dew, 1982).

It declares that every handicapped child between the ages
of 3 and 21 has a right to a free and appropriate education.
Furthermore, programs available to non-handicapped children
must also be available to the handicapped. These programs include, but are not limited to, vocational education, bilingual
education, music, art, and extracurricular activities.

P.L. 94-142 also guarantees the rights of handicapped
children to an education designed to meet their specific individual needs. For this purpose, local education agencies must
evaluate all handicapped children in their jurisdictions using
non-discriminatory procedures. Testing must be done in the
child's native language conducted by qualified professionals
with tests that are valid for their intended purpose. Following such evaluation, local schools must develop and implement
an Individualized Education Program (IEP), which must be revised annually, for each child in need of special education.

P.L. 94-142 defines handicapped children as mentally retarded, hard-of-hearing, deaf, orthopedically impaired, other
health impaired, speech impaired, visually handicapped, seriously emotionally disturbed, or children with specific learning
disabilities who, because of their disability, require special
education services.

The law mandates the placement of handicapped students in the least restrictive environment. That is, to the extent possible and appropriate, handicapped children are to be educated with children who are not handicapped. Handicapped children should be removed or segregated from the regular educational environment only when the severity of the handicap is such that services cannot be provided satisfactorily in a regular classroom setting.

P.L. 94-142 also guarantees due process procedures, requiring parental notification, evaluation in the dominant language, and parental involvement and approval in the development of their child's individual educational program.

In summary, the Education Act for All Handicapped Children Act of 1975 establishes:

- The right to procedural due process to protect individuals from erroneous classification, capricious labeling, and denial of equal education.

- Protection against biased testing procedures.

- Placement in an educational setting that is the least restrictive environment.

- A free and appropriate education designed to meet the specific individual needs of handicapped students.

- Equal access to programs available to non-handicapped children.

Case law

Parallel to legislative enactments is a focus on the courts as a forum for the establishment and clarification of educational rights of the handicapped. During the 1970's a significant number of cases were litigated in state and federal courts that helped define the process by which handicapped students were to be identified and evaluated for program placement. Often, the courts proscribed the usage of discriminatory testing of students which led to misplacements in programs for the handicapped. Later in the decade, the focus of the litigation switched to the adequacy of programs available for those rightfully eligible for services.

Litigation has been crucial to the establishment of rights for language minority handicapped children. Since *Diana v. State Board of Education* to *Jose P. v. Ambach*, the rights of these students have been expanded to require the consideration of linguistic and cultural factors in their evaluation for placement and in the actual provision of instruction. Pending litigation in *Diana* and in *Parents in Action on Special Education (PASE), et al. v. Hannon, et al.* may be settled along new grounds in light of the impact that legislation such as the Equal Educational Opportunities Act of 1974 and P.L. 94-142

have had on educational policy and practice during the last
few years.

An overview of key litigation may help in a better understanding of the issues before the courts (Ambert and Dew,
1982).

Arreola v. Board of Education (1968). The plaintiffs demanded that before the decision to place a child was made, the
parents were to be notified and given a formal opportunity to
challenge placement. An injunction was also granted to pro-
hibit the continuation of these special classes unless a hearing was provided before placement.

Diana v. Board of Education (1970). This suit was filed
in Federal court on behalf of nine Mexican-American children
from Spanish-speaking homes. All had been placed in classes
for the mentally retarded following diagnoses based upon the
results of tests which relied on verbal English skills and
ignored the children's own native language skills. The court
found that the inherent cultural bias of the tests discriminated against the Mexican-American plaintiffs. The case was
settled out of court with stipulated agreements on testing
procedures and requirements for re-evaluating Mexican-American
children in classes for the retarded.

Covarrubias v. San Diego Unified School District (1971).
Covarrubias resembles the *Diana* and *Arreola* cases with three
basic differences: (1) twelve of the plaintiffs were black and
five were Mexican-American; (2) the plaintiffs sought punitive
damages in the amount of $400,000 for the period they spent in
special education classes; and (3) plaintiffs sought to have
the influence of the social/cultural environments recognized
in determining a student's learning ability. The case was
settled out of court with stipulated agreements involving re-
evaluation and assignment based on appropriate tests. The court
also granted parents the right to be provided information in
their native language. On the matter of punitive damages, each
plaintiff was awarded one dollar.

Larry P. v. Riles (1972). This class action suit was filed
in the federal district court of northern California on behalf
of six black children who claimed that San Francisco's special
education assignment policy was racially biased causing black
children to be inappropriately segregated into classes for the
mentally retarded. The plaintiffs requested that the court require the defendants to: (1) use more culturally relevant evaluation instruments; (2) re-evaluate black children presently in
classes for the mentally retarded; (3) correct disparities in

racial representation in classes for the mentally retarded;
and (4) employ sufficient numbers of black and other minority
psychologists.

In its judgment, the court ordered a moratorium on the
use of any standardized intelligence test in the identification of black children as educable mentally retarded or for
their placement in such classes, without securing prior approval of the court.

Guadalupe Organization v. Tempe (1978). To act on the
disproportionate representation of Yaqui Indian and Mexican-
American children in classes for the mentally retarded was
the charge of this Arizona case. In Tempe, placement occurred
on the basis of IQ tests given in English and not the children's
native language. The case was settled out of court with stipulations regarding (1) re-evaluation of the children in
classes for the mentally retarded; (2) testing in the primary
language; and (3) informed parental consent for placement.

Lora v. The Board of Education, City of New York (1978).
Alleged lack of adequate facilities in the public schools resulting in racially and ethnically segregated special day
schools for emotionally disturbed students that were more restrictive than appropriate was the basis for the *Lora* lawsuit.
The court found that black and Hispanic students were disproportionately assigned to these special day schools and held
that the students were discriminated against on the basis of
race in violation of the Fourteenth Amendment and the Civil
Rights Act of 1964. The special day schools were also judged
to be inadequate and the plaintiffs found to have suffered
inadequate treatment in the referral, evaluation, and due
process procedures.

Jose P. v. Ambach (1979) and *Dyrcia S. v. Board of
Education* (1979). Two class action suits filed on behalf
of handicapped children between the ages of five and twenty-
one who had been deprived of a free appropriate education in New York had implications for culturally and linguistically diverse children. Plaintiffs alleged that the Board
of Education failed to provide evaluation and prompt placement
in appropriate educational programs.

The court ordered the New York City school system to (1)
identify children with special education needs; (2) develop
appropriate evaluation procedures with adequate staff, facilities, and nondiscriminatory bilingual testing techniques; (3)
establish appropriate programs in the least restrictive environment, including a continuum of services for both high and
low incidence disabilities and bilingual programs for each

level of the continuum; and (4) develop a handbook, in both
English and Spanish, which describes due process and parental
and student rights under the law.

Summarizing, the litigation supports the contention that
minority students, and specifically ethnic language group children, are entitled to specialized treatment which takes into
consideration culture and linguistic background. Consequently,
the cumulative of legislative policy and the litigation
strongly suggest that a bilingual education model is applicable to the provision of services to LEP handicapped students.

It is clear that LEP handicapped children have a right to
special educational services in their dominant language. This
constitutes an "appropriate" education according to legislation and case law.

IDENTIFICATION

School districts are legally responsible for the provision
of special education services to LEP handicapped students in
their dominant language. In attempting to offer appropriate
services to these children, the first difficulty to emerge is
the proper identification of children who, in addition to
having special education needs, are also of limited English
proficiency.

Initial identification of LEP handicapped children poses
serious concerns. LEP children have been placed in special
education classrooms, not because they experienced a learning
impairment, but due to their inability to function in English.
Others have been placed in special programs due to dialectical
and/or cultural differences. On the other hand, there are LEP
children with learning problems who do not receive the special
services they require because it is believed that their learning problems stem from a limitation in English proficiency.
In order to appropriately identify LEP children with handicaps,
it is necessary to consider the unique linguistic, cultural
and socioeconomic factors which affect their learning and may
affect special education identification, referral, and placement decisions (Ambert, 1982).

The rate of English language acquisition, native language
influence, and varying levels of English language proficiency,
as well as regional differences in the language spoken by the
child, can create difficulties in determining whether a LEP
child has learning problems. In addition to linguistic factors,
the influence of cultural differences must be taken into account in the identification of LEP children with special needs.
Cultural differences play a role in how others, namely teachers,
psychologists and school officials may understand and interpret

the behavior of the child from a different cultural background. Many LEP children come from poor backgrounds. Socioeconomic differences can create misunderstandings between children and teachers. Consequently, teachers may penalize children for factors unrelated to academic performance, factors related to socioeconomic background (Rist, 1970). Language, culture and socioeconomic status affect the identification of LEP children as educationally handicapped. It is essential that these factors be considered in the special education process.

ASSESSMENT

As discussed in Chapter 4, special education assessment misapplication creates, to a great extent, the overrepresentation of minority children in special education programs. Although Public Law 94-142 mandates nondiscriminatory evaluation and despite the numerous class action suits filed and won on discriminatory assessment practices, biased assessment continues to plague the special education assessment of LEP children. Tests normed and standardized on white middle-class populations continue to be administered to linguistic minority children. LEP children are frequently tested in English or with translated versions of tests that do not erase the cultural bias inherent in the tests. LEP students are often tested by persons with rudimentary knowledge of the child's language and/or culture. Under these circumstances we find that assessment results of LEP students are frequently invalid and interpretations inaccurate. Many of the problems in the assessment of linguistic minorities remain in practice.

Ambert and Dew (1982) examine promising procedures in the appropriate special education assessment of LEP populations. It is recommended that a pre-referral process precede any referral of a LEP child for a special education assessment. The pre-referral process should include the appropriate identification of children who are experiencing learning difficulties (already discussed in the previous section), data collection, and modification of the regular classroom.

Data collection

The data collected prior to referring a child should include student variables, such as sensory functioning, general health data, language performance data, sociocultural background information, cognitive development information, academic achievement data, and learning style information. Teacher variables should also be analyzed, such as teaching style, personality, expectations, interaction patterns, values, professional competence, language facility, socioeconomic status, and ethnicity. The relationship between teacher variables and student performance has been clearly established by research (Rist, 1970; Rosenthal and Jacobson, 1968; Ross and Salvia, 1975) which indicates that teachers' attitudes and expectations have a strong influence on children's performance. Children who are well-dressed, well-groomed, more fluent in standard English and "cuter," for example, are apt to be evaluated more positively than children who are poorly clothed, untidy, limited in standard English, and unattractive. Teacher expectations influence the performance of their students so strongly that students will live up to or down to those expectations (Rosenthal and Jacobson, 1968).

The data compiled in the pre-referral process should also include curricular variables which can affect a child's performance. These include inappropriate curriculum design, lack of materials developed for LEP students' specific needs, class size and overall quality of the instructional program.

Modification

Before a child is referred for a special education evaluation, attempts must be made to remedy the child's learning difficulties in the regular classroom. An important step in the pre-referral process is the modification of the regular program to assist a child with special problems. Often a slight change within the regular classroom may remedy a child's difficulty and eliminate the need for a special education evaluation or placement. For example, a child who cannot copy from the chalkboard may have a problem with visual acuity, visual perception, or visual motor coordination, to name a few possibilities. The teacher can eliminate possibilities by sitting the child closer to the board (and referring him or her for an eye examination) and observing the effect of this change on the child's performance. If, in fact, the problem was one of limited visual acuity, the situation may be resolved by eye glasses.

The pre-referral process involves the appropriate identification of children with learning problems, taking into consideration the linguistic, cultural, and socioeconomic status factors which affect a child's performance; the collection of appropriate data on student, teacher, and curricular variables; and the modification of the regular classroom. If the pre-referral process information reveals that a LEP child cannot receive an appropriate education for his or her educational needs in the regular classroom, parents should be notified and a special education referral should be considered.

Parent involvement

Once the possibility of a special education referral and assessment is established, parents need to become involved in the special education process. The importance of parent involvement in each phase of planning and programming for handicapped LEP children has been increasingly recognized (Marion, 1980).

Public Law 94-142 guarantees procedural safeguards for handicapped children and their parents or guardians regarding the provision of special education services. Some of these have particular relevance for LEP children. The due process safeguards required by P.L. 94-142 include:

(A) Prior notice to parents in their native language before special educational diagnoses are performed.

(B) Prior notice in parent's native language and parental consent before any change in the child's program. The notification must fully inform parents of their rights and those of their child and include a description of the special education process.

(C) Opportunity for parents to examine all relevant records pertaining to the identification, evaluation, and educational placement of the handicapped child.

(D) The right to obtain independent evaluations of their children.

(E) Opportunity to present complaints on matters pertaining to the special education process.

(F) The right to attend all meetings in which their child's education is discussed and to approve or reject the IEP developed for the child. In these meetings, all documents should be translated into the parents' native language and interpreters should be available.

(G) The right to appeal educational decisions made through impartial due process hearings conducted by the state educational agency. In these, parents may be represented by counsel, present evidence, and have the right to appeal the decision.

It is to the advantage of the school district to go beyond the minimal legal requirements. Parents can provide invaluable information and insights about their children to educators. Parents are knowledgeable about their children's culture and language, as well as their individual differences. They can assist in a better understanding of their children's strengths and weaknesses which will in turn help to better address their educational needs.

Parents have the capacity to assist at another level. They can be a great asset in the development, monitoring, and

evaluation of the overall bilingual special education program.
As a resource, parents have been grossly underutilized. Attitudes of both educators and parents have contributed to this
situation. Teachers and other school personnel have sometimes
not recognized the value of working with parents, have resented
the additional responsibility, or have simply been unaware of
means of accomplishing effective parent-school interaction.
Parents, especially of LEP students, may be distrustful of
schools where their children have not been accepted or learned
acceptably. Some feel intimidated by the "expertise" of educators and their own "inadequacies" in education and language
proficiency. However, teachers are becoming increasingly aware
of the need to work with parents, and parents are becoming more
informed of their rights and obligations.

The assessment procedure for special educational purposes
must include observation data, interviews, review of records,
as well as formal and informal testing in the child's dominant
language and in the second language (to determine language
proficiency). Chapter 4 contains a broader discussion on the
assessment of LEP students. Parents have the right to obtain
an independent assessment, at no cost to them, if they are not
satisfied with the school district's assessment procedures.

Once the assessment process is completed and it is determined that a student requires special education placement, an
individual educational program is developed.

INDIVIDUAL EDUCATIONAL PROGRAMS

Public Law 94-142 requires that school districts develop
an individualized education program (IEP) for every child enrolled in a special program. The program developed and implemented for a handicapped child must address the special educational needs of that child rather than a group or class of
children. Assurances must be made that parental involvement
occurs in the IEP process.

The IEP is developed by a team or committee including: a
representative of the educational agency, other than the child's
teacher, who is qualified to supervise special education (this
is often the school principal or the director of special education); the child's teacher or teachers; one or both of the
child's parents; the child when appropriate; other individuals
at the request of the agency or the parents (these individuals
might include a speech therapist, physical therapist, social
worker, bilingual teacher, or counselor); and a member of the
evaluation team, usually a school psychologist.

The IEP is composed of several sections, which provide
accurate descriptions of the child's current performance and

the progress expected in one school year. The first section includes the child's present level of performance. This section describes the student's strengths and weaknesses as identified by the evaluation data. The federal interpretation guidelines suggest that

1. The statement should accurately describe the effect of the child's performance in any area of education that is affected, including academic areas (reading, math, communications, etc.) and non-academic areas (daily life activities, mobility, etc.). Labels such as "mentally retarded" or "deaf" may not be used as a substitute for the description of present levels of educational performance.
2. The statement should be presented in objective measurable terms to the extent possible. Data from the child's evaluation is used for this purpose. Test scores that are pertinent to the child's diagnosis may be included, where appropriate, although the scores should be self-explanatory (i.e., they can be interpreted by all participants without the use of manuals or any other aids), or an explanation should be included. Test results used should reflect the impact of the handicap on the child's performance.
3. There should be a direct relationship between the present levels of educational performance and the other components of the IEP. If the statement describes a problem with the child's reading and points to a deficiency in a specific reading skill, this problem should be addressed under both the goals and objectives, and the specific special education and related services to be provided to the child. (Federal Register, 1981, pp. 5469-5470)

The second section of the IEP contains the annual goals which are statements that indicate the progress expected for that student during the school year. These statements should arise directly from the present level of performance statement.

Short-term objectives, the third component of the IEP, are:

> measurable, intermediate steps between handicapped child's present levels of educational performance and the annual goals that are established for the child. The objectives (a) are developed based on a logical breakdown of the major components of the annual goals, and (b) can serve as "milestones" for indicating progress toward meeting the goals. (Federal Register, 1981, p. 5470)

IEP objectives, like objectives in an instructional plan, are used to "(1) describe what the child is expected to accomplish in a particular area within some specified period of time and

(2) to determine the extent to which the child is progressing toward those accomplishments" (Federal Register, 1981, p. 5470).
In addition, the IEP must include appropriate objective evaluation criteria and schedules to determine on at least an annual basis whether the short-term instructional objectives are being achieved (Federal Register, 1977, p. 42491).
The IEP document must also include a list of related services needed to provide the child with an appropriate education. P.L. 94-142 defines related services as:

transportation and such developmental, corrective, and other appropriate supportive services as are required to assist a handicapped child to benefit from special education, and includes speech pathology and audiology, psychological services, physical and occupational therapy, recreation, early identification and assessment of disabilities in children, counseling services, and medical services for diagnostic or evaluation purposes. The term also includes school health services, social work services in schools, and parent counseling and training. (Federal Register, 1977, p. 42479)

For handicapped children of limited English proficiency, this component provides the assurances that services provided will be linguistically and/or culturally appropriate. If a child requires instruction in his or her native language, bilingual materials, or other such support services, the school must provide these services or must contract for such services through other school districts, private agencies, public agencies, or individuals. Contracting the services must be at no expense to the parents if the services have been determined to be essential to the provision of an "appropriate" education. Under the law, no longer can the school system fail to provide linguistically/culturally different students appropriate services because of the lack of personnel, resources, or the costs involved. The school must seek the required services and pay for them (Ortiz, undated).
The IEP must also include a statement indicating the extent to which the child will participate in the regular classroom and a statement of the projected date for initiation and anticipated duration of services.
Through careful interpretation of testing and observation by a multidisciplinary team, appropriate IEPs can be developed. Strengths can be utilized to develop successful remediation techniques to deal with the child's areas of disability. If a child has a strong visual modality, for example, this information can be useful in deciding upon an effective reading method, and to ensure that the child receives sufficient visual rein-

forcement for orally presented materials.

For handicapped children of limited English proficiency to receive an appropriate education, instruction must be provided in a language the child understands. The IEP must, therefore, include the language of instruction. If a Spanish-dominant language disordered child, for example, receives speech therapy services in English, this does not constitute an appropriate education, nor are the child's individual needs being met.

IEPs must be translated into parents' dominant language and approved by parents before implementation.

The Individualized Instruction Program is a statement of a child's specific learning problems, how these problems will be remediated, for how long, and what criteria will be used to decide whether the child's needs were met. Based on a handicapped child's individual needs, a decision is made as to the most appropriate program option.

PROGRAM OPTIONS

Once the LEP handicapped child is assessed and an IEP developed and approved by the parent, a decision on program placement is made depending on the specific needs of the child. Public Law 94-142 requires that handicapped children receive a free appropriate education in the least restrictive educational environment. That is, to the extent possible, children with handicaps must be educated with children who are not handicapped. The degree of participation in the regular program will depend on the unique needs of each child. Some children will benefit from more participation in regular classrooms than others. Services for handicapped children will range from full-time placement in the regular classroom to full-time placement in special education programs.

From the least restrictive to the most restrictive, special education placement options are:

- Regular classroom placement with consultation services, materials and equipment provided for the teacher by special education specialists.
- Regular classroom placement with direct support services provided to the child. These support services include speech and language therapy, physical therapy, psychological therapy, etc.
- Regular classroom placement with partial placement in a resource room where the child will receive special instruction.
- A special educational program which is substantially

separate from the regular school program (self-contained). The students are placed in these programs during most of the day. Integration or mainstreaming in the regular program, if feasible, can be attained during lunch, physical education, music, and art.

- Placement in a private day school program, if the school system does not have a program which will be appropriate for the student's particular needs.
- Placement in a residential school program when the child's educational needs require that she or he live at a separate school.

Other special educational options include:

- Home or hospital program for children whose illnesses may prevent them from attending school for an extended period of time. A home or hospital tutor is sent to provide services.
- Parent-child instruction. An after-school program in which the child and his or her parent(s) work together to achieve determined educational goals.
- A diagnostic program for children whose learning problems are not clear. Placement in a diagnostic setting has a limited time span, and the purpose is to observe the child more closely to decide on an appropriate placement.
- Special vocational programs for youngsters between the ages of 16 and 21.

Most handicapped children can be appropriately served in the regular classroom with support services provided either to the regular teachers or to the students on a part-time basis. More severely handicapped children, on the other hand, will require more restrictive special education placements.

Program options for LEP students should take into consideration their linguistic and cultural backgrounds, offering services that are appropriate to their special educational needs in a language they can understand and through instructional media and materials that are culturally relevant.

BILINGUAL SPECIAL EDUCATION PROGRAM IMPLEMENTATION

Legislation and case law have affirmed LEP children's rights to special educational services in their dominant language. School districts are responsible for the provision of an appropriate education to LEP handicapped students. Bilingual special education programs, with qualified bilingual

personnel, fulfill the need to provide LEP handicapped children with remediation of their special educational needs in a language they can understand, while they acquire the English-language skills needed to survive in this society.
In teaching exceptional children we must capitalize on their strengths to help them learn more effectively. LEP children with handicaps have acquired important language skills in their native language which must be utilized as effective mediums of instruction. Teaching LEP handicapped children in the native language will not impede their acquisition of English. Recent research indicates that LEP children with handicaps can transfer skills from one language to another as non-handicapped children do (Ambert, 1980).
Bilingual special education programs address the needs of LEP handicapped children to non-biased assessments and placements in appropriate educational settings which remediate their learning problems through use of the native language. In addition, bilingual special education placements ease the transition from one language to another in children who would otherwise develop confusion between the languages to which they are exposed.
A frequent concern of program administrators is the locus of responsibility for LEP handicapped children. Should the bilingual department assume responsibility for these students or is the special education department responsible? Evidently both departments are responsible for the provision of appropriate special education services to LEP handicapped children. Both departments must work together in effectively coordinating the services required for the appropriate education of these children. The bilingual department may identify LEP handicapped children in bilingual programs, establish language dominance and proficiency testing procedures, and assist in the integration of the LEP handicapped child in regular bilingual programs. The special education department may provide assessment procedures by professionals who are fluent in the children's languages and familiar with the children's cultures. They may also be responsible for the provision of special education services to LEP handicapped children.
In order to implement an effective bilingual special education program, systematic planning and development needs to take place by the departments in charge of educating LEP handicapped children. To assist in the planning, developing and implementation of such a program, the following guidelines are suggested.

*Bilingual special education program implementation
guidelines*

1. Conduct a needs assessment in the local school district.
   Send questionnaires to all schools requesting information
   on:
   (a) The number of LEP students in the school requiring
       special education services.
   (b) A breakdown of LEP students with special needs by
       dominant language.
   (c) The number of LEP students with handicaps identified
       but not referred for special education evaluation.
   (d) The number of LEP students referred but not yet
       evaluated.
   (e) Dates of referral of above students.
   (f) Number of LEP students evaluated and awaiting placement.
   (g) Number of LEP students with handicaps receiving ser-
       vices from monolingual English-speaking specialists.
   (h) Types of services received by the above, such as speech
       therapy, placement in self-contained classes, etc.
   (i) Number of bilingual teachers interested in training
       leading toward certification in special education.
   (j) Breakdown of above teachers by languages spoken and
       areas of expertise.
2. Appoint a bilingual special education task force to assist
   in formulating program objectives. Members of the task
   force should include parents of LEP handicapped children,
   a bilingual teacher, a special education teacher, represen-
   tatives from the bilingual and special education departments' administration, a bilingual school psychologist and
   a bilingual special education teacher.
3. With data from the needs assessment and with the task force's
   input, prepare a bilingual special education plan to include: non-discriminatory assessments procedures, parental
   notification and involvement, IEP and program development,
   mainstreaming, and follow-up services as they relate to
   LEP handicapped children.
   (a) A clear statement of program objectives including lines
       of responsibility.
   (b) Staffing requirements for appropriate provision of ser-
       vices for LEP handicapped children in the district.
   (c) Recruitment efforts to hire bilingual special education
       specialists.
   (d) In-service training models for bilingual and monolingual
       regular classroom teachers on the appropriate identifi-
       cation of LEP handicapped children and classroom modi-
       fication techniques.
   (e) Coordination with local colleges and universities for

training bilingual personnel in special education.

(f) Establish official and consistent coordination between Bilingual Department and Special Education Department personnel.

(g) The plan should include short-term objectives to deal with the immediate needs of LEP handicapped children, and long-term objectives to institutionalize the bilingual special education program within the school district.

(h) Timelines for plan implementation.

Once a comprehensive bilingual special education plan is developed, implementation can take place under the process depicted in Table 2 (see facing page).

CONCLUSION

Since implementation of Public Law 94-142 (Education for All Handicapped Children Act of 1975) educators have wrestled with the myriad issues involved in providing an appropriate education to children who not only experience learning problems but also are of limited English proficiency. In the special education process, from proper identification to appropriate provision of services, LEP children with handicaps bear the burden of the problems plaguing bilingual special education programs. Discriminatory assessment procedures, lack of qualified bilingual special education teachers, provision of special services in English to children who do not understand the language, violations of due process, lack of instructional materials, and the inability of many school districts to plan and implement programs which service the special needs of this population are some of the difficulties faced. As a result, LEP handicapped children may not receive the appropriate education to which they are entitled by law.

Although the problems faced by school districts in attempting to remedy this situation seem complex, it is possible to implement appropriate bilingual special education programs. School systems throughout the country have developed innovative, imaginative ways to do this from Boston Public Schools' bilingual special education programs in seven languages to the Valley View School in Coachella, California, which offers a psycholinguistic learning disabilities program for Spanish-speaking students.

We need bilingual teachers certified in special education, bilingual psychologists, bilingual speech and language therapists, materials in bilingual special education, nondiscriminatory assessment procedures. We require, most of all, the com-

Table 2

BILINGUAL SPECIAL EDUCATION PROGRAM DEVELOPMENT PROCESS

1. *Identify LEP handicapped children* through contacts with bilingual and monolingual regular classroom teachers. →

2. *Identify bilingual teachers* interested in special education training and placement. Recruit bilingual specialists.

3. *Contact institutions of higher education* on training possibilities for special education. Facilitate placement of bilingual teachers in special education certification programs. →

4. *Assess LEP children* to determine disability. If there are no bilingual specialists in the school district, contract with a consultant. →

5. *Develop IEPs for LEP children* with handicaps. Determine placement needs. →

6. *Place bilingual teachers* in bilingual special education classrooms. Continued placement contingent upon teachers' participation in special education certification program. Request waiver from state Department of Special Education for uncertified teachers.

7. *Place LEP exceptional children in appropriate bilingual special education programs.* →

8. *Establish in-service training* for bilingual special education teachers.

Throughout the process bilingual education department staff provide technical assistance on parental notification, translation of documents, informed consent, language dominance and proficiency testing, parental participations in IEP development, suggested materials in languages other than English, mainstreaming LEP children in regular bilingual classrooms.

mitment of school districts to provide a "free and appropriate"
education to all handicapped children including those of
limited English proficiency.

REFERENCES

Ambert, A.N. "The Identification of LEP Children with Special Needs." *Bilingual Journal*, 1982, 6:17-22.

Ambert, A.N. "Language Disorders and Bilingualism: A Case Study." Unpublished paper, Harvard University Graduate School of Education, 1979.

Ambert, A.N., and Dew, N. *Special Education for Exceptional Bilingual Students: A Handbook for Educators*. Milwaukee: The University of Wisconsin Midwest National Origin Desegregation Assistance Center, 1982.

Arreola v. Board of Education, No. 160 577, Superior Court, Orange County, California, 1968.

Covarrubias v. San Diego Unified School District, No. 70-394-T, S.D. Cal., 1971.

Diana v. State Board of Education, No. 3-70 37 RFP, District Court of Northern California, 1970. Appeal, 7th Circuit, Case No. 80-2266.

Dyrcia S. v. Board of Education, 79 Civ. 270, New York, 1979.

Guadalupe Organization, Inc. v. Tempe Elementary School District No. 3, et al., U.S. District Court of Arizona, 587 F. 2d 1022, 1978.

Hofstadter, R. *Social Darwinism in American Thought*. San Francisco: Jossey-Bass, 1975.

Jose P. v. Ambach, 79-C-270, New York, 1979.

Larry P. v. Riles, 343 F. Supp. 1306, 502 F 2d 963, 1972.

Lora v. the Board of Education, City of New York, 4560-1, Supp. 1211, 1978.

Marion, R.L. "Communicating with Parents of Culturally Diverse Exceptional Children." *Exceptional Children*, 1980, 46: 616-623.

Massachusetts Advocacy Center. *Double Jeopardy: The Plight of*

Minority Students in Special Education. Boston: Task Force on Children Out of School, Inc., 1978.

Mercer, J.R. *Labeling the Mentally Retarded*. Berkeley: University of California Press, 1973.

Miller, M. *The School and the Immigrant*. Cleveland: Survey Committee of the Cleveland Foundation, 1961.

Ortiz, A. *Development and Implementation of Individual Education Programs for Exceptional Bilingual Children*. Austin: University of Texas, undated.

Parents in Action on Special Education (PASE), et al. v. Hannon, et al., Appeal 7th Circuit, Case No. 80-2676.

Rist, R.C. "Student Social Class and Teacher Expectations: The Self-Fulfilling Prophecy in Ghetto Education." *Harvard Educational Journal*, 1970, 40:411-451.

Rosenthal, R., and Jacobson, L. *Pygmalion in the Classroom*. New York: Holt, Rinehart and Winston, 1968.

Ross, M.B., and J. Salvia. "Attractiveness as a Biasing Factor in Teacher Judgments." *American Journal of Mental Deficiency*, 1975, 80:96-98.

Tucker, J.A. "Ethnic Proportions in Classes for the Learning Disabled: Issues in Non-Biased Assessment." *Journal of Special Education*, 1980, 14:93-105.

Zabel, R.H. "Identification and Referral Procedures: Linguistic and Cultural Considerations." Paper presented at the Bilingual Special Education Conference, Evanston, Ill., National College of Education, May 1980.

ANNOTATED BIBLIOGRAPHY

Abudarham, S.   "The Role of the Speech Therapist in the Assessment of Language-Learning Potential and Proficiency of Children with Dual Language Systems or Backgrounds." *Journal of
Multilingual and Multicultural Development*, 1980, 1:187-206.

Discusses the need to differentiate between first language
learning problems and second language learning problems for
subsequent planning of appropriate delivery of services. An
assessment format is offered to enable the assessor to estimate a child's vocabulary level in either of his or her two
languages.

Almanza, H.P., and W.J. Mosley.   "Curriculum Adaptations and
Modifications for Culturally Diverse Handicapped Children."
Exceptional Children, 1980, 46:608-614.

The authors maintain that although racial and ethnic differences in children can affect learning, instructional activities for minority exceptional children have been implemented
with little or no regard for the effects of race, ethnicity,
or culture on learning. To meet the curricular needs of exceptional minority children, individual traits, learning
styles, and values must be taken into account when developing
curricula. Many minority children use a relational/impulsive
learning style instead of the analytical/reflective style
favored in the school setting. This creates a major problem
for minority children who attempt to attack learning tasks
using a style which will not be adequate for the school setting. A major objective for curriculum development must be
to provide instruction that will allow exceptional minority
children to use analytical and reflective approaches in the
learning process.

Ambert, A.N.   "The Identification of Limited-English Proficiency
Children with Special Needs." *Bilingual Journal*, 1982, 6:
17-23.

Issues in the appropriate identification of LEP children are

discussed. The author analyzes language, culture, and socioeconomic status as important factors affecting special education identification. Offers an identification process model
which involves observation, testing, and regular classroom
modification. A list of tests which can be used by the bilingual teacher is provided.

Ambert, A.N. "Tengo un 'migo quichito: Language Disorders in
  Spanish-Speaking Children." Paper presented at the Council
  of Exceptional Children Conference on Culturally Diverse Exceptional Children, New Orleans, 1981.

  The author describes language development of Spanish-
  speaking children, the characteristics of Spanish-speaking
  language disordered children, and specific strategies for
  remediating linguistic disabilities. A discussion of the
  impact of second language acquisition and literacy is also
  provided.

Ambert, A.N., and N. Dew. *Special Education for Exceptional
  Bilingual Students: A Handbook for Educators*. Milwaukee:
  University of Wisconsin Midwest National Origin Desegregation
  Assistance Center, 1982.

  A handbook which discusses the following issues in bilingual
  special education: sources of legal rights, categories of
  exceptionality, assessment, parental involvement, and program
  options. The authors offer a model for program development
  for exceptional bilingual learners. The model includes a
  needs assessment program formulation and program evaluation
  process.

Ambert, A.N., J. Greenberg, and S. Pereira. *Manual for the
  Identification of Limited-English-Proficiency Children with
  Special Needs*. Boston: Bilingual Multicultural Special Educa-
  tion Project, 1978.

  A manual developed to assist teachers in identifying students
  of limited-English-proficiency who may have special educational
  needs. It focuses on the areas of language, informal observation, testing, and learning problems.

Ayala-Vazquez, N. "Bilingual Special Education: Ahora." In
  LaFontaine, H., and L. Golubchick (eds.). *Bilingual Education*.
  Wayne, New Jersey: Avery Publishing, 1978.

  An overview of the evaluation of the equal educational opportunity movement as it relates to the minority child with handicaps. Competencies needed to work with bilingual exceptional
  children and the problems in testing bilingual children are
  discussed.

Baca, L., and Bransford, J. *An Appropriate Education for Handicapped Children of Limited English Proficiency.* Reston, Virginia: Council for Exceptional Children, 1982.

Review research and the legal background of bilingual and bilingual special education.

Ballard, J. *Public Law 94-142 and Section 504: Understanding What They Are and Are Not.* Reston, VA: Council for Exceptional Children, 1978.

A thorough analysis of the Education for All Handicapped Children Act and Section 504 of the Vocational Rehabilitation Act.

Barresi, J.G. "Educating Handicapped Migrants: Issues and Options." *Exceptional Children,* 1982, 48:473-488.

Discussion of the problems in the identification and delivery of services to handicapped migrant students. The author presents a potential corrective policy option which could guarantee the educational rights and protections of handicapped migrant children.

Benavides, A. "The Exceptional Hispanic: Nobody's Stepchild." Paper presented at the Midwest Conference on the Education of Hispanics, Chicago, 1980.

The author discusses legal implications for the education of handicapped limited-English proficiency children and the denial of appropriate educational service to the population.

Bergin, V. *Special Education Needs in Bilingual Programs.* Rosslyn, VA: National Clearinghouse for Bilingual Education, 1980.

Offers a historical review of bilingual special education practices, discusses parent and community support, teacher training models and program implementation models for bilingual special education.

Bransford, J., L. Baca, and K. Lane (eds.). *Cultural Diversity and the Exceptional Child.* Reston, VA: Council for Exceptional Children, 1973.

The articles included address concerns about the education of the culturally and/or linguistically different minority-group child. The authors describe cultural and linguistic differences that exist among Spanish-speaking, black, Indian, and Asian-American ethnic groups.

Bruck, M. "The Suitability of Early French Immersion Programs for the Language Disabled Child." ERIC Reproduction Document No. ED 153-460, 1978.

A report on a longitudinal project in which children with and without language problems were identified in French immersion and English kindergartens in Ottawa. The study investigates the desirability of immersion programs for children with language disabilities. The author concludes that enrollment in French immersion programs has no detrimental effect for English-speaking children with language problems.

Bryen, D.N. "Special Education and the Linguistically Different Child." *Exceptional Children*, 1974, 40:589-599.

Explores discriminatory interclass grouping, assessment, and special class placement of the culturally different child focusing on the linguistic factors which affect minority children's performance. Educational alternatives are analyzed to deal with linguistic divergence in the schools.

Bryen, D.N. "Speech-Sound Discrimination Ability on Linguistically Unbiased Test." *Exceptional Children*, 1976, 42: 195-201.

Speech-sound discrimination was assessed using a bilingual perspective with 32 black, 32 white, and 32 Puerto Rican first- and second-grade children from a low socioeconomic background. Three parallel forms of speech sound discrimination tests (standard English, black English, and Spanish) were administered to all subjects. Results indicate that each language group did best on the discrimination form that most closely approximated the phonological structure of its language. Also, there were no significant differences in speech-sound discrimination ability among the three groups when performance across all language forms was considered. Results have implications on traditional testing practices which have been thought to lead to placing a disproportionate number of black and Spanish-speaking children in special classes.

Canino, I.A., and G. Canino. "Impact of Stress on the Puerto Rican Family: Treatment Considerations." *American Journal of Orthopsychiatry*, 1980, 50:535-541.

The impact of stress due to migration and poverty on family structure of the low-income Puerto Rican family is discussed.

Treatment pitfalls and effective therapeutic techniques are illustrated by a clinical case presentation.

Cole, L.T., and T. Snope. "Resource Guide to Multicultural Tests and Materials," 1981, ASHA, 639-644.

A report on tests, clinical materials, public information pamphlets, bibliographies, books, and other items designed specifically for service to speakers whose dominant language is not English. Includes materials for Spanish and Chinese speakers.

Condon, E.C., J.Y. Peters, and C. Sueiro-Ross. *Special Education and the Hispanic Child: Cultural Perspectives.* Philadelphia: Teacher Corps Mid-Atlantic Network, Temple University, 1979.

An overview of the educational problems and needs of Spanish-speaking children, focusing on the problems of identification, assessment, evaluation, and placement of exceptional Spanish-speaking students. The authors describe the linguistic and cultural variables which affect the education process with respect to Spanish-speaking children and provide guidelines for meeting the specialized needs of exceptional Spanish speakers.

DeBlassie, R.R. *Testing Mexican American Youth. A Nondiscriminatory Approach to Assessment.* Hingham, MA: Teaching Resources, 1980.

The author synthesizes the research literature on testing Mexican-American youth; describes principles of psychological testing, statistics, test scores and other factors in using assessment data; presents procedures and suggestions in using assessment data with Mexican-American youth for instructional, counseling, and administration purposes; and provides case studies involving the use of assessment data with culturally different Mexican-Americans.

Deuchar, M. "Diglossia and British Sign Language." In *Working Papers in Sociolinguistics.* Southwest Educational Laboratory, 1978, Vol. 46.

Describes bilingual speech communities in which the two languages of the community are related and have separate functions, one of the languages is usually more prestigious than the other. The author applies the concept of diglossia to the British deaf-signing community.

"Exceptional Children Conference Papers: Early Childhood Educa-

tion Council for Exceptional Children." Papers presented at
the Annual International CEC Convention, Dallas, Texas,
April 22-27, 1973. ERIC Document No. ED 078631.

   Five conference papers on a bilingual kindergarten program,
language assessment and development, a nursery school program for retarded children, instructional materials for handicapped children, and a comparison study on social status for
bilingual exceptional children, respectively. The bilingual
kindergarten program is described as a total learning system
with three major components: staff development materials
(teacher manuals and filmstrips), the instructional model
(sensory, motor, and language skills training in 12 units),
and parent involvement. Suggested for children's language
assessments are standardized scales, informational observations, and reports from persons close to the child. Remediation techniques are offered for an ongoing program. A free
nursery school program is suggested for mentally handicapped
children, ages 3 to 7 years, who are developing a positive
self-concept and motor, self-help, language, sensory, and
cognitive skills through art activities and creative movement.
Approximately 23 teachers made instructional materials for
training parents of preschool handicapped children. Materials
are presented in a format which gives the name of toy, time
to make material, skill to be developed, materials needed,
procedure, use, and space for trial evaluations. Results of
a study using sociometric techniques to compare 20 bilingual
French-English subjects with 42 primarily English-speaking
subjects, 8-15 years old, in a special class in New Brunswick,
indicate that the status among peers of the bilingual subjects
did not differ significantly from the status of the English-
speaking subjects.

Feuerstein, R. *The Dynamic Assessment of Retarded Performers:
The Learning Potential Assessment Device.* Baltimore: University Park Press, 1980.

   Description of a nondiscriminatory assessment technique
which assesses how much an individual's level of intellectual
functioning can be modified with what amount of investment in
teaching effort.

Gallegos, R.L., A.Y. Garner, and R.C. Rodriguez. "The Exceptional Bilingual Child." *Bilingual Journal*, 1980, 5:15-18.

   Addresses two issues in bilingual special education: (1)
minority children's improper assessment and inappropriate
placement in low ability groups or special education classes;
and (2) the inappropriate services offered to handicapped

minority children. The authors explore some alternatives which may enhance and facilitate the growth of handicapped minority children in educational settings.

Gavillan-Torres, E. "Answering the Needs of Hispanic Handicapped Children: Facts and Issues." *Cutting Edge*, 1980, 1:5.

Offers facts on the number of Hispanic handicapped children, the educational needs of these children, and the objectives for bilingual-bicultural special education.

Gonzalez, G. "Language, Culture and Exceptional Children." *Exceptional Children*, 1974, 40:565-569.

An overview of language is given followed by an analysis of the linguistic and cultural biases of IQ tests.

Greenlee, M. "Specifying the Needs of a 'Bilingual' Developmentally Disabled Population: Issues and Case Studies." *Bilingual Education Paper Series*. Los Angeles: National Dissemination and Assessment Center, 1981.

Examines the issues involved in the assessment and educational programming for linguistically different children who experience developmental disabilities. A review of the literature in Spanish/English developmental bilingualism is given, followed by illustrations of individual linguistic abilities in three "bilingual" children with developmental problems.

Harber, J.R. "The Bilingual Child with Learning Problems." ERIC Reproduction Service Document No. ED 143149, 1976.

Reviews research on the bilingual child with learning problems. The author notes that a disproportionately large number of non-English-speaking children are placed in special education classes for the educable mentally retarded and that this group is underrepresented in classes for the learning disabled. It is suggested that appropriate tools for evaluation of bilingual children be developed and used and that specific remedial programs be planned for each child.

Hilliard, A.G. "Cultural Diversity and Special Education." *Exceptional Children*, 1980, 46:584-588.

Discusses the successes and failures of special education within the realm of cultural diversity.

Hunter, B. "Policy Issues in Special Education for Migrant Students." *Exceptional Children*, 1982, 48:469-472.

A discussion of four general issues in migrant students'
educational problems: access to services, availability of
services, appropriateness of services, and continuity of
services. The importance of changing educational policies
in order to offer services to migrants is discussed. The
author analyzes the statutes of six states which serve migrant students and concludes that statutes in these
states do not preclude interstate cooperation to solve the
problems of educating migrant handicapped students.

Jones, R.L. (ed.). *Mainstreaming and the Minority Child*.
Minneapolis: Leadership Training Institute for Special Education, 1976.

Provided are 16 author-contributed papers dealing with
theoretical questions and practical concerns on the effect
of mainstreaming the minority child. The text is divided
into five parts: overview and perspectives, educational
assessment for mainstream placement, curriculum issues and
teaching strategies, evaluation and research, and case study
and summary propositions.

Langdon, H. "Assessment and Intervention Strategies for the
Bilingual Language Disordered Student." Paper presented at
the Council of Exceptional Children Conference on Culturally
Diverse Exceptional Children, New Orleans, 1981.

The author compares first and second language acquisition
patterns, discusses the formal and informal instruments
available to assess first and second language skills of bilingual students, defines a language disorder in bilingual
populations, and discusses intervention techniques to remediate
language problems in bilingual students.

Marion, R.L. "Communicating with Parents of Culturally Diverse
Exceptional Children." *Exceptional Children*, 1980, 46:
616-623.

Discusses parental reactions to similarities and differences
between the two categories of gifted and handicapped, the
relationship between professionals, and parents of culturally
diverse students. Describes parental concerns in the identification and testing of culturally diverse gifted and handicapped students. The author offers suggestions for communicating with parents.

Martinez, H. (ed.). *Special Education and the Hispanic Child*.
Proceedings from the Second Annual Colloquium on Hispanic
Issues. New York: ERIC Clearinghouse on Urban Education,
Teachers College, Columbia University, 1981.

Includes papers on the right of Hispanic children to bilingual special education, the assessment of bilingual Hispanics, teacher training, and Puerto Rican mothers' cultural attitudes toward children's problems.

McConnell, R.B. "Individualized Bilingual Instruction: A Validated Program Model Effective with Bilingual Handicapped Children." Paper presented at the Council for Exceptional Children Conference on the Exceptional Bilingual Child, New Orleans, 1981.

Describes a program developed for teaching academic areas in Spanish and English to low performing children. Test data are presented on a large number of children which was accumulated over a seven-year period showing the difference in performance by high and low ability Spanish-speaking children after periods of one, two, and three or more years in the program.

McGrath, G.D. "Investigation of Mental Retardation in Relation to Bilingual and Subcultural Factors." Arizona State University, undated.

The purpose of this study was to investigate the difference between true mental deficiency and pseudomental deficiency due to language, cultural, and socioeconomic limitations. The factors were studied by the method of repeated tests over a three-year span in an adapted but relatively constant learning situation. Mental achievement, language tests, and sociological study of the children's environments were used as criteria. The subjects were 188 recent immigrant Mexican and Indian children in special classes for bilingual children. Mental retardation is incorrectly diagnosed among some bilingual children, often as the result of many factors, including socioeconomic and family backgrounds, among others. Typical school programs are not adequately designed to meet the needs or bring out the full potential of these bilingual children who have high mental abilities as demonstrated by the fact that they have developed some facility in two languages. More studies are recommended, and the necessity of continued work in the field is suggested.

National Clearinghouse for Bilingual Education. *Bilingual Special Education Packet*. Rosslyn, VA: National Clearinghouse for Bilingual Education, undated.

An information packet which contains articles, information on funding agencies, teacher training programs, materials publishers, bibliographies and bibliographic searches in bilingual special education.

Nondiscriminatory Testing: A Selective Bibliography. Council
for Exceptional Children, Reston, VA, 1976.

An annotated bibliography on nondiscriminatory testing
contains approximately 79 abstracts and associated indexing
information for documents or journal articles published between 1962–1975 and selected from the computer files of the
Council for Exceptional Children's Information Services and
the Education Resources Information Center (ERIC). It is
explained that the titles were chosen in response to user
requests and analysis of current trends in the field. The
bibliography is divided into the following sections: assessment factors related to the test taker; visually handicapped,
hearing impaired children with physical limitations; children
with verbal response limitations; minority group children in
general; black children; Spanish-speaking children; assessment factors related to the test giver and assessment factors
related to the test. Abstracts include bibliographic data
identification or order number, publication date, author,
title source or publisher, and availability, descriptors including the subject matter covered, and a summary of the
documents' contents. Also provided are instructions for
using the bibliography, a list of journals from which articles
were abstracted, and an order form for ordering microfiche
or paper copies of the documents through the ERIC Document
Reproduction Service.

Plata, M., and S.L. Santos. "Bilingual Special Education: A
Challenge for the Future." *Teaching Exceptional Children*,
1981, 14:97–100.

A discussion of legal issues in bilingual special education.
The authors present examples of program models to meet the
needs of bilingual handicapped pupils and offer a list of
agencies which supply prepackaged inservice training material,
technical assistance, and disseminate information on bilingual special education. Includes a self-study questionnaire
to be used by local education agencies to assess whether they
are fulfilling the legal and educational requirements of LEP
handicapped children.

Pyecha, J.N., and L.A. Ward. "A Study of the Implementation of
Public Law 94–142 for Handicapped Migrant Children." *Exceptional Children*, 1982, 48:490–495.

Description of a telephone survey conducted by the Research
Triangle Institute to determine the extent to which a sample
of 153 handicapped migrant children were identified as being
handicapped and had IEP's developed by schools in which they

were enrolled. The survey was also used to determine the
extent to which IEP's and other related information were
transmitted and utilized by staff. Findings indicate that
(a) the schools in which students were enrolled were incon-
sistent in identifying students as needing special education
and preparing IEP's for them; (b) IEP's were developed less
frequently for the most mobile than for the less mobile
migrant students; (c) only a small percentage of the students
had IEP's developed; and (d) IEP's and related information
were rarely transmitted between schools.

Ramirez, B.A. "Classification of Handicapped Children as It
Affects Indian Children." Position Paper presented at the
National Indian Education Association, undated.

Discusses the effect of the current model for identification and placement of handicapped children on Indian students.
The author states that there may be more handicapped children
among Indian populations than have been identified and less
reliability in the identification of those who need special
education services.

Ramirez, B.A., and B.J. Smith. "Federal Mandates for the
Handicapped: Implications for American Indian Children."
Exceptional Children, 1978, 44:521-528.

Discuss the implications of Public Law 94-142 and Section
504 of the Vocational Rehabilitation Act on the education of
handicapped American Indian children.

Rich, E. "Bilingual Special Education: Meeting the Needs of
the Non-English-Speaking Mentally Retarded Child." In
LaFontaine, H., B. Persky, and L. Golubchick (eds.), *Bilingual
Education*. Wayne, New Jersey: Avery, 1978.

Presents issues related to the development and implementation of effective bilingual programs for non-English-speaking
mentally retarded children.

Rist, R.C. "Student Social Class and Teacher Expectations: The
Self-Fulfilling Prophecy in Ghetto Education." *Harvard
Educational Review*, 1970, 40:344-368.

The author reports the results of an observational study of
a class of ghetto children during their kindergarten, first-,
and second-grade years. He shows how the kindergarten teacher
placed the children in reading groups which reflected the
social class composition of the class and how these groups
persisted throughout the first several years of elementary
school.

Sabatino, D.A., K. Kelling, and D.L. Hayden. "Special Education and the Culturally Different Child: Implications for
Assessment and Intervention." *Exceptional Children*, 1973,
39:563-567.

A summary of biased assessment techniques is followed by
approaches to accurate testing procedures. The approaches
discussed include translations, use of nonverbal tests, and
use of culture-free tests. The authors conclude that all
these approaches present serious problems, and the ideal
solution is to develop and standardize tests for various
cultural groups. These culturally based tests should be
administered in the children's primary language. In addition,
the examiners must be specifically trained to administer the
instruments. Two basic approaches to providing linguistically different children a more relevant education are given.
First, access to bilingual/multicultural education; and
second, foster children's assimilation so they can function
in the dominant culture, not only linguistically, but culturally.

Sauer, R.A. "Issues in the Education of Migrants and Other
Mobile Handicapped Students." *Exceptional Children*, 1982,
48:503-505.

A discussion of the issues affecting handicapped migrant
students in New York State. Includes problems in the identification and referral process, classification of students,
and placement of handicapped migrant students in local
special education programs. Possible solutions to these
problems are proposed.

Strong, L. "Language Disability in the Hispano-American Child."
Paper presented at the 23rd Annual Conference of the Orton
Society, Seattle, 1972.

The paper focuses on the problems faced by the Spanish-
speaking dyslexic in an English-speaking school system. The
author cites the factors which compound children's basic language problems as inadequate or premature instruction, beginning reading in a second language, frequent migrations between Puerto Rico and the mainland, economic deprivation, mal-
nutrition, inadequate pre- and post-natal care, and the inadequate use of the phonics method in reading. She provides
recommendations to reduce the degree of dyslexia: inclusion
of phonics in reading instruction, having high expectations
for the children, and having children learn to read in the
native tongue to avoid the high incidence of school-created
dyslexia.

Thomas, C.H., and J.L. Thomas. *Bilingual Special Education Resource Guide.* Phoenix: Oryx Press, 1982.
Contains background articles on the bilingual special education student. Lists information sources.

Wagner, R.F. "Bilingualism, Multiple Dyslexia and Polyglot Aphasia." *Academic Therapy*, 1976, 12:91-97.
Explores the nature and relationships of cognitive deficiencies and learning problems as they relate to one or more languages. Offers suggestions for remediation of learning problems in bilingual populations,

Chapter 7

BILINGUAL VOCATIONAL EDUCATION

Prior to the Vocational Education Amendment of 1976
(P.L. 94-482), vocational education programs were effectively
closed to most students of limited English proficiency (LEP).
The reason given for this situation was usually summed up in
one word: language. Students of LEP could not participate in
vocational programs until they had acquired sufficient mastery
of English to be able to profit from instruction solely through
the medium of English. A bilingual vocational teacher was
virtually unheard of throughout most of the country. Unfortunately, many students did not stay in school long enough to
achieve the requisite proficiency in English to gain access to
vocational programs.

The 1976 amendment identified vocational education for
persons of LEP as a national priority. Most bilingual vocational training (BVT) programs, whether federally or state
funded, have been established since passage of P.L. 94-482.
The law allocated 380 million dollars for the period 1977
through 1982 for programs to focus on three activities: (a)
the implementation of bilingual vocational training programs
for persons of LEP (65 percent of the total funds were allocated for this activity); (b) training of bilingual vocational
instructors (25 percent); and (c) research, and development of
materials, methods, and techniques (10 percent).

Since the first federal appropriations in 1975, through
1981, 112 vocational training programs, and 17 bilingual instructor training programs have been funded. These programs
have served a total of 658 vocational instructors, and 3,217
LEP individuals from nine language backgrounds.

Participants have been trained in food technology, welding,
dental assistance, building maintenance, clerical, construction, boiler maintenance, micro-computer technology, Chinese
cooking, and other areas.

The BVT programs that are implemented according to sound
principles of both vocational and bilingual education prove to
be very effective, as measured by retention and placement rates.

Nine successful BVT programs studied by Troike, et al. (1981) had retention and placement rates of 95 percent. This is remarkable for any type of program, but when it is considered that they are serving populations who traditionally have the highest dropout and unemployment rates, it is amazing.

BVT programs are surprisingly cost effective. The Miami Dade Community College program cost $112,000 for twelve months of training. They placed 100 percent of the participants. During the first 12 months of employment, they paid an aggregate amount of $66,000 in taxes. At that rate held constant, the program would pay back its cost in a little over a year.

The principles on which BVT programs are based are:

> Vocational training
> - Sound task analysis.
> - Individualized and small group instruction.
> - Demonstration and hands-on experience.
> The bilingual approach is designed to ensure that
> - Every participant understands the instruction and is understood when she or he responds to instruction.
> - Instructional materials are appropriate for students being served.
> - Instruction is based on strengths of two cultures: the student's own culture and that of the workplace.
> - Students use their own language while they are learning English as a second language.
> (*Human Resources*, 1983, p. 2)

BVT PROGRAMS

Bilingual vocational training programs in the United States stress skills development and have a basic two-fold goal: (1) to provide education and training in an employable skill, while (2) developing vocation-specific English language skills in a manner which respects and incorporates into instructional delivery the students' language and cultural identity, so that successful participants may find, get, and keep a job in an English-speaking workplace.

Bilingual vocational instruction is presented both in English and the dominant language of the student to the extent necessary to assure the effective and safe acquisition of vocational skills, while job-specific English skills are being learned and the use of English in all areas of instruction is increased as the student progresses. For purposes of BVT, LEP participants are individuals from a particular language and cultural background whose limited English ability for a specific vocation has been identified, this determination being influenced by two factors: (1) the length of the vocational skills program, and (2) the language demands of a particular occupation. For example, in a short-term training program, the clerical cluster poses greater language learning requirements, and, therefore, a higher level of English proficiency of participants at the outset than would be the case for the machining cluster.

Job-specific English as a second language provides language skills development in comprehending, speaking, reading, and writing English which utilizes the specific vocabulary and the most prevalent communicative situation necessary to successfully function in a particular vocational field and, ultimately, a job.

A typical BVT program will have four interrelated areas: the vocational, the related skills, the job-specific ESL, and the life skills counseling areas. Each area has a bilingual instructional capacity, either through the bilingual abilities of individual instructors, or with the assistance of bilingual resource instructors, preferably with a trade-oriented background, who mediate or interpret instructional delivery.

Each area has a primary function which is clearly defined. but all areas perform important secondary, collaborative, functions if the BVT program is to be successful.

The vocational area develops occupational skills in English and the native language or through an interpreter/mediator. Instructors also reinforce job-specific English learning, coordinate their efforts with related-skills instructors, and work closely with the life-skills instructor. Occupational demands are constantly changing in response to advances in technology, and every member of the program staff needs to be aware of the primary job skills required for the target occupation. The vocational area instructor, therefore, provides a significant measure of leadership in determining the curriculum in coordination with other area instructors. One of the most useful types of information that the vocational instructor can offer the job-specific ESL area will be step-by-step procedures for the completion of basic job tasks; the vocational instructor can also provide considerable insight into the most frequent vocational communication situations which arise at the worksite.

Obviously, the related-skills instructor will look to the vocational area for direction in planning the theoretical and critical ancillary skills development so necessary to work in each specific vocational field. Finally, as experienced practitioners of a particular occupation, vocational-area instructors have a key role in developing positive student attitudes for long-term employment and must work closely with life-skills area instructors to insure that participants are aware of the demands of the "world of work."

The related-skills area provides instruction in such key

ancillary skills as theory, occupational math and science, blueprint reading, or any other skill indispensable for effective functioning in a specific job, while also playing a key role in English language development and life-skills acquisition for the workplace. Upon consultation with the vocational area staff, the related-skills instructor knows, for example, that specific skills in applied mathematics are required to meet work-relevant computational needs. For example, a machine operator must have a thorough knowledge of a particular array of fractions, that is, halves, quarters, eighths, sixteenths, thirty-seconds, sixty-fourths, and thousandths of an inch and their metric equivalents and would rarely, if ever, deal with the variety of math skills required of food service trainees, involving thirds of cups or doubling of recipes. The theoretical conceptual development, which must often accompany applied skills acquisition, makes the effective use of the students' dominant language as an instructional mode particularly important in the related-skills area.

The job-specific ESL area develops work-relevant English skills, while stressing and reinforcing training given in the vocational and related-skills areas, and complementing--especially in the English language demands of the job search, application, and the job interview--the work of the life-skills instructor. ESL instruction in these programs takes a cognitive approach to language learning, primarily owing to time constraint and a job-specific focus. It is assumed that the better a student understands what he or she is practicing, the faster will vocational language competence be acquired. Therefore, the students' preexisting skills in their first language are brought to the level of awareness and used to build skills in the second language, English, around an occupational focus. Whenever necessary, and particularly in presenting grammar concepts, the students' dominant language is utilized directly in order to make helpful comparisons between languages. Of course, vocational English receives a major part of the attention when the primary concern is practice.

Pronunciation is typically de-emphasized if communication is not affected. Vocabulary is developed in coordination with the vocational area, which provides detailed task analyses that allow the ESL instructor to develop lists of verbs and associated vocabulary for language practice. Vocabulary development in a bilingual vocational training program is particularly challenging since, although the occupational lexicon is specific, it is at the same time very broad in its denotational field. Students may need to know every possible inflectional and derivational form of the root "LUBRICAT - (E)": lubricate, lubricates, lubricated, lubricant, lubrication, etc. Grammar is taught but in a very comprehensive manner; it is very likely that a student will have to learn all the question forms from the outset of a program, including "What for?," so critical to occupational language, which is often left to the end of a "general" ESL course, owing to its supposed complexity. In a bilingual training program, the students will require a working model of English, perhaps unsophisticated initially, to deal with the broad yet focused language needs of the occupation. Often ESL instructors participate with trainees in selected vocational skills projects in order to sensitize themselves to occupational English demands.

The life-skills area helps develop individual and group awareness of the students' own culture—with both strengths and weaknesses—in order to build a cross-cultural awareness of the challenges posed by the English-speaking workplace and to develop skills and strategies to effectively deal with those challenges. Life skills will include such concerns as life analysis and planning, career awareness, consumer education, and related multicultural and world of work skills as well as the provision of extensive ancillary supportive services. Cross-cultural issues are often identified by interviewing employers or personnel directors who have had contact with persons from the students' cultural background as well as indivduals of similar background who are familiar with the world of work in a particular occupation.

Beyond the survival skills typically taught in life-skills courses, this area stresses problem-solving, decision making, and assertiveness strategies essential for long-term employment in the target occupation. Yet the emphasis of the life-skills area is not solely on individual "coping" skills; very often, the pooling of the collective support resources available to students from a common culture in order to resolve problems and remove obstacles to skills development and employment all serve to reinforce the bicultural character of life-skills development and to create what is often termed a sense of "family."

Numerous BVT programs have been established which employ this basic program design throughout the United States. The program studied by Troike, et al., successfully integrated ESL and vocational instruction. The programs all exhibited the following characteristics:

1. The ESL instructor was:
   - bilingual;
   - trained and experienced in ESL methodology;
   - flexible;
   - able to modify and create methods and materials; and
   - cooperative and team-oriented.

2. The ESL instructor regularly observed vocational classes in order to learn as much as possible about the skills being taught.
3. The ESL instructor and counselor-job developer visited potential job sites to observe working conditions and functional language use in actual settings.
4. The vocational instructor visited ESL classes periodically to observe and learn about methods and materials.
5. The ESL and vocational instructors met together regularly (daily or several times a week) to plan and coordinate classroom activities.
6. The ESL instructor used the trainees' native language in class, whenever necessary to explain, clarify, check comprehension, and conduct translation activities.
7. ESL instructional content was meaningfully related to the vocational class content and the eventual functional needs of the work place.
8. Minimum attention was given to pronunciation and grammar, particularly at lower English ability levels, and maximum attention to vocabulary and functionally important verbal routines and message forms (especially safety language); pronunciation practice was not effective with adults.
9. Reading in job-related English was introduced as early as possible both as an important skill in itself (e.g., for reading vocational manuals) and as a reinforcement for oral practice; writing and typing were used as appropriate.
10. Instructional activities in ESL reinforced vocabulary and conceptual learning of the vocational class. Audio-lingual "pattern practice" and "memorized conversations" were reduced to a minimum and used only when meaningful. (Human Resources Management, Inc., 1983, p. 36)

It is clear that the successful programs are in concert with the latest thinking in ESL instruction. All the skills, listening, speaking, reading, and writing are stressed. Language is functional and mastery of the functions of language is paramount.

In addition to the integration of ESL and vocational education training, it was found that all nine programs included the following eight features:

1. Team teaching and planning
2. Incorporation and sequencing of instruction in job-

related English language skills with vocational
skills
3. Job-placement and follow-up
4. Awareness and teaching of similarities and differences
of cultural patterns
5. Instructor/trainee interactions
6. Coordination of counseling and job development
7. Staff consensus in the selection of vocational and
language materials, and
8. Instruction in survival skills for the workplace.
(Troike, et al., 1981, p. 1)

Bilingual vocational education programs differ significantly from other bilingual programs in one major respect: No
attempt is made to teach the native language. This is used
only to the extent necessary to teach job skills and for counseling. ESL, in turn, is job- or skills-specific.

A factor which is critical to the success or failure of
a program is the initial phase of outreach, assessment, and
placement. LEP students historically do not have access to
information on available services and programs. New and innovative outreach techniques must be developed if affirmative
recruitment is desired.

The test generally used for placement is the Bilingual
Vocational Oral Proficiency Test. A low score on this test
indicates a need for bilingual instruction. The test also
gives information on which to base job-skills assignment. A
person with a very low score obviously would not do well in a
secretarial or clerical program.

The nine programs studied all included life skills training
and counseling. "It included not merely employment and personal
advising, but such things as intervening with landlords to have
roofs repaired, arranging for babysitters, taking children to
doctors when they were ill, helping trainees secure food stamps
or make consumer complaints, and working out alternative transportation or changing class schedules when bus schedules changed.
Counseling then embraced all of the trainees' needs which might
have affected participation and achievement in the program"
(Troike, et al., 1981).

The best programs are those whose personnel understand their
target population, linguistically and culturally. The ideal program would draw staff from the cultural/linguistic group which
the students represent. If that is not possible, the next best
alternative is to train bilingual craftspersons to teach. Bar-
ring that, members of the students' native language group can be
trained as aides.

A very obvious characteristic of a successful program is
reliable job-market analysis information. The best instructional

and counseling components will not guarantee success for a
program teaching non-marketable skills.

PERSONNEL FOR BVE

BVE is at the point where bilingual education programs
were a decade ago in terms of the availability of trained personnel. The language of the BVE Act of 1976 stated: "that
there is a critical shortage of instructors possessing both
the job knowledge and skills and the dual language capabilities
required for adequate vocational instruction of such language-
handicapped persons and to prepare such persons to perform
adequately in a work environment requiring English language
skills, and a corresponding shortage of instructional materials
and of instructional methods and techniques suitable for such
instruction" (Subpart 3, Sec. 181).

A successful BVT program at a minimum requires a vocational
instructor and an ESL or language instructor. Kirschner Associates, Inc. (1981) defined these as follows:

> Vocational Instructor--the individual with primary
> responsibility for providing instruction in the occu-
> pational skills, such as welding, culinary arts, busi-
> ness education, or construction. This term does not in-
> clude persons who assist the vocational instructor by
> supervising skills practice, developing job opportuni-
> ties, or translating instruction from English into the
> trainees' native language.

> ESL or language instructor--the individual with pri-
> mary responsibility for providing instruction in the use
> of the English required for specific job and job environ-
> ment. Frequently, this instructor is called the English-
> as-a-Second-Language instructor or the ESL instructor.
> This term does not include persons who provide general
> training for improving the English language proficiency
> of trainees, nor does it include persons who assist the
> language instructor by supervising skills practice.

The State of Connecticut has established several successful bilingual vocational training programs which include the
features of BVT programs discussed here.

Bilingual pre-vocational programs have increased awareness
and access of the Hispanic community to further vocational and
training opportunities. The collaboration of a local regional
vocational-technical school and a local education agency in the
bilingual career exploration project for eighth graders of
New London's Centro de la Comunidad demonstrates that in-
school youth benefit from bilingual vocational opportunities.

Similarly, the Bilingual Pre-Vocational Training Program in Allied Health at Hartford Hospital has shown the effectiveness of this model with adults and youth with a high school or GED diploma.

There are also bilingual vocational education services provided in seven of the State's regional educational-technical schools, which are dealing with the unique challenges posed by counseling, occupational exploration for ninth graders, and simultaneous English and vocational and related skills development in grades 9-12.

Two programs illustrate the potential for BVE approaches in private sector training and employment. The National Puerto Rican Forum/Aetna Life Insurance Bilingual Office Skills Program utilizes bilingual vocational techniques to realize a corporation's commitment to the Hispanic community in the training and employment of successful participants. The Metal Machine Program of the Hartford Area Training Center provides machine operator skills instruction to all sectors of the community with 50 percent Hispanic participation. What is unique about this program is its effort to meet the training needs of limited English-proficient Hispanic trainees as well as those of the English-speaking participants from a variety of language and cultural backgrounds, and to this end the program utilizes the services of a bilingual training specialist, bilingual instructors, and bilingual counselors, as well as a job-specific ESL instructor. This program demonstrates the effectiveness of BVT approaches as components of mainstream training programs. Vocational education administrators are learning that a bilingual instructor increases a program's ability to serve all sectors of the community.

The State of Illinois has developed curricula in English, Spanish, and Laotian in automotive mechanics, autobody repair, maintenance mechanics, fiberglass, food service, clerical work, welding, and machine trades.

The China Institute in America trains LEP Chinese-Americans for work as chefs, with a 95 to 100 percent placement rate. The Bronx Community College Housing Maintenance and Repair Program trains participants in carpentry, plumbing, boilers and heating, electricity, and pest control in English, Spanish, and Italian.

Little Wound School on the Oglala Sioux Reservation in Kyle, South Dakota, trains Lakota speakers in building trades and secretarial skills. This is the first program designed for American Indians, a group that was traditionally excluded from vocational training programs.

The University of California at Los Angeles Dental Assistants Training Program has trained 142 students, 80 percent of

whom were employed in their field or a related field. This
program is designed for bilingual students, not students of
LEP. The program does offer job-related ESL, but not instruction in a language other than English.

THE FUTURE OF BVE

        Bilingual vocational materials and staff development will
be future priorities for BVE. Teacher training and pre- and
in-service staff development will generate the human resources,
which, in turn, can produce the instructional materials required to serve more languages and vocations. There is an
urgent need for a central repository of information on BVE in
general and bilingual vocational instructional materials in
particular at one of the major clearinghouses of educational
research, bilingual education or vocational education, which
would issue a regular bulletin serving as a much-needed vehicle
of communication in this relatively new and expanding field.
        Efforts must also continue to increase access of LEP per-
sons to training and educational opportunities offered by local
education agencies at the secondary level, in vocational-
technical schools, adult education programs, and technical and
community colleges. The institutionalization of bilingual
vocational programs in public education and through private
sector training is a critical priority.
        The realities of employment in an information age will
necessitate an increased use of computers in BVE. This should
include computer literacy, computer-assisted instruction, and
automatic data processing analyses of vocational language, with
a view toward more efficient instructional delivery.
        Finally, while BVE is a programmatic response to the em-
ployment and training requirements of one "Special needs" population, the LEP, it is important to remember that BVE must
ultimately deal with all the "special needs" of the LEP themselves. This includes a programmatic response for displaced
homemakers (or bilingual components of existing programs, as
have been utilized in some projects) and for women in non-
traditional employment—recognizing that for many LEP women,
paid employment in itself is "non-traditional"—bilingual
special education, bilingual rehabilitation programs for the
handicapped, and bilingual vocational training programs for the
hearing impaired.

CONCLUSION

Bilingual vocational education programs have been found to be consistently effective in teaching job skills and English to participants in projects in many languages and diverse fields. Models with clear guidelines for implementation have been developed. Programs have been found to be cost effective, with participants often returning more in taxes within one year than the cost of their training.

Bilingual vocational programs are not yet available to all who need them. There are many vocational fields where curriculum and materials are not available in all the languages necessary. There is a serious lack of bilingual personnel in vocational education, and most teacher training programs do not train vocational teachers.

Some good beginnings have been made. The federal government and state and local education agencies need to move quickly to build on them and continue to expand opportunities in vocational education for students of LEP.

REFERENCES

Human Resources Management, Inc. "Job Training for the Limited English Proficient: A Leadership Institute." Washington, D.C., 1983.

Kirschner Associates, Inc. *A Monograph for Bilingual Vocational Instructor Competencies.* California: National Assessment Center, 1981.

Public Law 94-482. Vocational Educational Amendment of 1976.

Troike, R., Lester Golub, and Ismael Lugo. *Assessing Successful Strategies in Bilingual Vocational Training Programs.* Washington, D.C.: U.S. Department of Education, 1981.

ANNOTATED BIBLIOGRAPHY

Adams, S., and S. Taylor. *Bibliography of Currently Available Vocational Education Curriculum Materials for Use with Students of Limited English Proficiency.* Center for Career and Vocational Teacher Education. June 1979. 152 pp.

A supplement to a project to provide teacher training and resources for vocational educators of limited English-speaking students, final report. Includes listings of monolingual and bilingual vocational materials for related areas, career guidance resources, survival and consumer skills, and vocational ESL materials. A list of publishers and suppliers is appended.

Crandall, J. *Adult Vocational ESL. Language in Education: Theory and Practice #22.* Center for Applied Linguistics ERIC Clearinghouse on Language and Linguistics, September 1979. 51 pp.

Discusses language content in ESL, including literacy training. Describes the various program models. The discussion of materials includes adapting, creating, and field-testing and evaluation. Research needs in vocational ESL and characteristics of successful programs conclude the monograph. Includes a good bibliography.

Connecticut State Department of Education. Division of Vocational and Adult Education, Bureau of Vocational Program Planning and Development. *English for Speakers of Other Languages (ESOL) for Connecticut Vocational-Technical Schools: Curriculum Guide.* August 1982.

A curriculum for teaching ESL to vocational and prevocational LEP students. Includes an extensive list of vocational-technical terms, a checklist for each level, and a bibliography.

East Central Network and Illinois Vocational Curriculum Center, Staff. *Bilingual Materials, A Bibliography.* 1982. 16 pp.

A listing of holdings available on-loan from the East Central Curriculum Management Center in Bilingual Vocational
Education.

Galvan, M. *Helpful Hints for Implementing Individualized Instruction and Bilingual Vocational Education.* Bilingual
Vocational Instructor Training Project. 1979. 80 pp.

A useful outline of bilingual vocational program models
which maximize individualized instruction, by an accomplished
applied linguist who is a forerunner and a leading intellect
in the field of bilingual vocational education.

Hepburn, L., M. Shin, and Project staff. *Multi-Cultural
Competency-Based Vocational Curricula Series.* Illinois State
Board of Education, Department of Vocational, Adult, and
Technical Education, 1982.

A multi-media program in 9 parts: 1. Autobody repair specialist; 2. Automotive mechanic; 3. Cook; 4. Fiberglass tech-
nician; 5. Machinist; 6. Maintenance mechanic; 7. Office
worker; 8. Welder; 9. The world of work. All curricula are
in English with Spanish and Laotian introductions and glossaries.

Hurwitz, A. *Bilingual Vocational Instructor Training.* National
Center for Research in Vocational Education. 1980. 42 pp.

Discusses background, needs, and major issues involved in
preparing bilingual vocational instructors and training programs.

King, J.E. *Bilingual Vocational Education in the United States:
A Survey.* Illinois State Board of Education. Department of
Adult, Vocational and Technical Education. 1976. 109 pp.

An early survey detailing data collected from two questionnaires on then-existing bilingual vocational training programs for Spanish-speaking LEP students. Includes a review
of literature.

Kirschner Associates. *A Monograph for Bilingual Vocational
Instructor Competencies.* May 1980. 120 pp.

Delineates the investigation by a panel of expert practitioners in bilingual vocational education into the most critical components of instructor competencies. Presented in
usable format, this monograph also includes findings on vocational ESL instructor competencies. A test was developed to
assess bilingual vocational instructor competencies.

Kotesky, A. "Implementing College Regular Vocational Programs into a Bilingual Mode." Elgin Community College, 1979.

Describes two instructional design models in operation at the bilingual access program.

Lopez-Valadez, L., and Staff. *Bilingual Vocational Education Human Resources Directory.* Bilingual Vocational Education Project. Revised, January 1982.

A detailed listing of professionals available to provide consultation services in bilingual vocational education.

Lopez-Valadez, L., and Staff. *Bibliography of Bilingual Materials for Career/Vocational Education: A List of BESC Library Holdings.* Bilingual Vocational Education Project. Revised, February 1980. 67 pp.

An annotated bibliography of on-loan materials available from the Bilingual Education Service Center Library. Materials listed include career awareness, pre-vocational and vocational, vocational English as a second language (VESL), professional, and bibliographic resources. A list of publishers is appended.

Lopez-Valadez, L., and Staff. *Bilingual Vocational Education Project (Final Report).* Illinois State Board of Education. Department of Adult, Vocational and Technical Education, 1979.

A report by one of the pioneers and leaders of the bilingual vocational education movement outlining the coordinated delivery of support services to bilingual vocational programs in Illinois.

Lopez-Valadez, L., and Staff. *Vocational Education for the Limited English Speaking: A Handbook for Administrators.* Illinois State Board of Education, Department of Adult, Vocational and Technical Education, 1979. 25 pp.

For vocational administrators and practitioners on the design of bilingual vocational education programs which successfully meet the employment and training needs of LEP learners.

McCarthy, Dr. J. *An Exemplary Teacher Education Program for Vocational Teachers of Bilingual Students.* Two Volumes. Illinois State University, 1977, 1978. 302 pp., 278 pp.

A report discussing a workshop for in-service training of bilingual vocational instructors.

MacDonald, R., R. Troike, M. Galvan, A. McCray, L. Shaefer, and P. Stupp. *Improving Techniques in Teaching English for the Job.* Interamerican Research Associates, 1982. 134 pp.

A landmark work. From the preface of the National Clearinghouse for Bilingual Education: "Using a non-technical presentation, the authors show how computer analysis of job-relevant text materials can be used in developing language instruction for LEP students. This practical approach is also designed to help the ESL instructor coordinate activities with the vocational curriculum. In addition, the special applications of data processing to functional language teaching--procedures for obtaining and using various types of text analysis--are appropriate for native speakers of English whose language skills may need to be strengthened."

Maryland Vocational Curriculum Research & Development Center. *Vocational Curriculum Resources for Bilingual Students.* 1979. 100 pp.

Assesses numerous instructional materials for bilingual training and education programs in terms of design and instructional utility.

Mrowicki, L., and P. Dehesus. *Handbook for the VESL Instructor.* Illinois Adult Indochinese Refugee Center, Northwest Educational Cooperative, 1981. 33 pp.

A practical handbook focusing on the content of a vocational English-as-a-second-language class. Includes information on scheduling, native language support, resources, steps for preparing and writing a VESL lesson, a sample machine tool lesson, and criteria for evaluating a VESL lesson.

National Center for Research in Vocational Education. *Alliance for Career and Vocational Education.* Career Education Curriculum Materials, Bilingual Editions, 1979. 5 pp.

Career education materials for trade and finance, personal services, construction, and product services, to be used in conjunction with the "Career Planning System," a career exploration curriculum for twelve occupational clusters. All four clusters and the "Career Planning System" are available in Spanish, with glossaries in Spanish, Greek, Italian, Chinese, and Portuguese.

National Center for Research in Vocational Education. *ERIC Update on Bilingual Curriculum Materials for Vocational and Adult Education.* 1982. 52 pp.

Includes resources identified through an ERIC search, which consists of input from the data base of 16 ERIC Clearinghouses. The search includes resumes from resources in education and current index to journals in education.

National Clearinghouse for Bilingual Education (periodically revised by staff and Harpreet Sandhu). *Information Packet for Bilingual Vocational Programs*. Approximately 60 pp.

Updated information on opportunities in bilingual vocational education, funding agencies, state officials with responsibilities for vocational education for disadvantaged youth and adults, training projects, sources of information, resource materials, and search services.

Pergamon Press, Inc. *Dictionaries of the World*. Revised periodically.

A listing of dictionaries, particularly technical dictionaries, published in many languages, that are available through Pergamon Press.

Peterson, M., and D. Barry. *Strategies for Outreach Services in Bilingual Vocational Training Programs*. Kirschner Associates, 1983.

"Provides information on the types of community resources available for trainees, the procedures for establishing coordinated delivery service programs, and successful practices for enhancing the impact of bilingual vocational training and for improving the employability of trainees" (from the Project Abstract).

Rios, E., and W. Hansen. *Career and Vocational Development of Bilingual Students*. National Educational Laboratory Publishers, Inc., 1978. 50 pp.

A brief overview of issues and implications for the career and vocational development of limited English proficient students.

Sayers, D., Project Director; S. Melendez, University of Hartford, Supervisor. *Bilingual Vocational Instructional Materials: Curriculum Development Resources and Priority Areas*. 1. Summary of Research. 2. Final Report. Connecticut State Department of Education, Division of Vocational Technical Schools, August 1982.

A survey of bilingual vocational instructional materials available in career education, related skills, vocational ESL, and 9 occupational clusters in Cambodian, Greek, Haitian Creole, Italian, Laotian and Hmong, Polish, Portuguese, Spanish and Vietnamese.

Sayers, D. *Bilingual Vocational Training with Trainers and Trainees: Concepts and Applications.* Division of Vocational Technical Schools, Connecticut State Department of Education, 1980. 45 pp.

A report on exemplary instructional and staff development techniques utilized in Connecticut's first public-funded bilingual training program.

Schriber, P. *Training Modules for Vocational Education of Students with Special Needs; Module II.* Illinois State Board of Education, Department of Adult, Vocational and Technical Education, 1979.

One of 13 modules treating successful teaching strategies for students with special needs, module II focuses on disadvantaged students and students with limited-English proficiency.

Sibirsky, S. *Bilingual Vocational Education Library: Bibliographical List.* Division of Vocational Technical Schools, Connecticut State Department of Education. Revised periodically.

A listing of on-loan materials, including instructional materials and professional resources.

Thatcher, G.M. *Bilingual Vocational Education; National Workshop to Increase Spanish Speaking American Participation in Vocational Education at All Levels.* Kean College of New Jersey, ECCME. 27 pp.

A report from one of the earliest conferences on bilingual vocational education.

TPC Training Systems. *Catalog of Industrial Training Programs.* 1982. 58 pp.

A most ambitious publishing effort providing Spanish translations of training courses in industrial fundamentals, electrical maintenance, industrial electronics, mechanical maintenance, machine shop practices, maintenance welding, and rigging and installation. Each course consists of from 5 to 10 units, with 5 to 10 16-page lessons plus a trainee guide and a reveal key in a notebook binding. Units include pre- and post-test, and incorporate programmed learning features. Video units are available.

Troike, R., L. Golub, and I. Lugo. *Assessing Successful Strategies in Bilingual Vocational Training Programs*. U.S. Department of Education, 1981. 240 pp.

A most helpful practical study of successful exemplary practices in nine existing bilingual training programs. Includes extensive sections on strategies, criteria, and planning for successful bilingual vocational training programs. Bibliography and appendices detail resources and programs.

Chapter 8
PROGRAM EVALUATION

Evaluation is a decision-making tool. Legislators want to know whether a program should continue to be funded. Funding agencies must decide whether particular projects should continue to be funded. Local education agencies must "sell" the projects to parents, school boards, teacher groups, etc. Finally, project administrators and staff must decide which components to keep, which to eliminate, change, or modify.

Carol Weiss (1972) defined evaluation research as follows: "The purpose of evaluation research is to measure the effects of a program against the goals it set out to accomplish as a means of contributing to subsequent decision-making about the program and improving future programming" (p. 4).

Evaluations, then, usually have many audiences, each with a particular interest which may lead to different emphases. Legislators are interested in outcomes: does the program solve the problem it was designed to solve? Funding agencies, federal and state, want to know whether a particular project met its stated objectives. Very often, the concern of funding agencies is for outcomes. School boards, parents, and critics are also outcome oriented. Project directors are also concerned with outcomes, as that is how their effectiveness will be evaluated by all the interested parties. Project staff are also interested in evaluation of the process. Which features of the project are working well? Which are having difficulties? How can the project be improved to insure the achievement of its stated objectives?

Louise Comfort (1982) described the changing role of evaluation in Title I of the Elementary and Secondary Education Act (ESEA). Her description, discussion of the problems and issues, and conclusions apply to Title VII as well. She states, about the intended role of evaluation: "Program evaluation was intended as a rational means to determine the effectiveness of the ESEA programs in order to permit Congress to make informed decisions regarding its continuance" (p. 124).

In the early years, evaluation in Title I was essentially

description, according to Comfort. The administration's goal was to get money into the hands of the school districts as quickly as possible. School districts, in turn, hurried to implement activities and the year-end reports were essentially descriptions of what had taken place. Many of the stated objectives of most projects were, in fact, difficult, if not impossible, to measure.

This situation was probably inevitable given that "Districts were given the money for their programs with high hopes and great expectations but little guidance or direction on how to spend it" (p. 130).

The transition years were years spent by state agencies attempting to develop uniform evaluation procedures and forms that would yield information on program effectiveness. This came about, to some extent, as a result of pressure from Congress for evaluation of program effectiveness. According to Comfort, the evaluations did not demonstrate that Title I was making much difference in improving the achievement of disadvantaged children. By that time, however, Title I had become another way of funding education and the evaluations were not to be used for decisions on whether to continue funding. The questions changed from whether funding should continue to "how much and in what form" (p. 135).

A persistent phenomenon throughout the evolutionary process of evaluation in Title I was that "The perception by program staff regarding who was making which decisions based upon what kinds of information influenced the gathering of information and the rigor of the evaluation practices" (p. 129).

There are many parallels between the evaluation history of Title I and Title VII. Title VII funds were also distributed for program implementation without much attention to evaluation. Evaluation, however, was required. Project staff were implementing projects, training staff, developing materials, attempting to improve projects on the basis of data they were attempting to gather. Objectives were often difficult to measure. Evaluations were originally intended for the Congress and the program officers, but it was soon obvious that there were many audiences--school boards, parents, teacher groups, critics, and the media.

Comfort concludes that evaluation has failed to provide the basis for rational decision making on educational policy. Policy makers and others, however, continue to require evaluations at the same time that they continue to criticize them. Sometimes evaluations play a role in the debate and decision about funding. Critics of bilingual education constantly point to evaluations that conclude that bilingual education makes no difference in the achievement of LEP children. They also criticize evaluations as flawed. At the same time, they ignore evaluations that conclude that bilingual education is effective in helping LEP students achieve performance gains.

In part, evaluation has failed to form the basis for rational decision making on educational policy because it has been plagued by apparently insoluble problems which Comfort identified as timing, distortion inherent in the process when project staff know that decisions on funding are to be based on the evaluations, resentment on the part of staff to the extra work, lack of adequate training for staff, and, finally, the different needs for data of the different audiences.

Evaluation has always been required for federally funded bilingual programs. These evaluations have been problematical because they have had two or more intended audiences and several purposes. The evaluations go to the Office of Bilingual Education, where funding decisions are made. They often go to the local school board and are reported in the local press. Each of these constituencies has a different educational philosophy and political agenda.

Very serious questions arise for the evaluator. Are evaluators influenced by the intended audience? Will evaluations deal forthrightly with problems if evaluators know that funding decisions will be influenced by them?

Most of the information that goes into an evaluation has to do with what happens in the classroom between teacher and students. Teachers, however, have very little, if any, input into evaluations, besides administering tests and recording results, which they resent. They are often not aware of project goals, evaluation design, or even what data are being collected and analyzed. Needless to say, they very often do not see evaluation results and when they do, there is no discussion of them or of how to use them to improve instruction.

Bissell (1980) lists some caveats for those concerned with evaluation of bilingual programs which help shed light on some of the problems they face. One caveat is, "How realistic are the guidelines?" She claims that Title VII

> guidelines assume an optimum situation: valid instruments available to measure language growth and proficiency; Technical Assistance Centers with resources and competencies to provide help; multiple objectives that can be assumed using multiple measures without evaluation dominating the programs; and resources and time to carry out the guidelines. Many Title VII projects do not enjoy these conditions. (p. XVII)

Bissell also asks about the feasibility of evaluation procedures in highly mobile populations. Bilingual education has been plagued with a student mobility rate so high that it makes cumulative data or standardized test scores meaningless. Needless to say, longitudinal studies become impossible.

Evaluation of bilingual programs is, of necessity, beset
with numerous problems which are not amenable to easy solutions.
Some of the problems stem from a conflict in educational philosophy between bilingual educators and the federal, state,
and local authorities. For the most part, these authorities
judge bilingual program effectiveness on the basis of the speed
with which students are mainstreamed and on their educational
outcomes as measured by standardized English-language tests.
Bilingual educators are often committed to developing native
language proficiency before making the transition into instruction solely through the medium of English. English language
proficiency sometimes lags behind that of students instructed
monolingually in English. The lag is usually compensated for
in successive years. However, bilingual programs are criticized
for the first two years when students do appear to be performing in English at levels lower than their peers.

Another problem with evaluations of bilingual programs has
been the failure to consider student differences such as language proficiency at the beginning of a program. In a typical
first-grade Portuguese class, there may be children who have
been born in the United States, some who have been in the country for several years, and others who are recent arrivals.
Most evaluations do not deal with this problem and, therefore,
cannot make definitive claims about project effectiveness.

With older students who are recent arrivals, there has
traditionally been no assessment of proficiency in the native
language either. Obviously, students with fully developed
skills in their native language will find the transition into
English easier than students who may be functionally illiterate
or totally illiterate.

While no one would question that the educational level of
parents has a bearing on the students' proficiency in their
native language and, consequently, on their experience in learning a second language, program evaluations, by and large, have
not controlled for this factor. Although language minority
students in bilingual education programs tend to be from lower
socioeconomic levels and, therefore, from homes with low educational attainment, this is not an absolute situation and there
is sufficient diversity in home background to require control-
ling for that factor in evaluation.

Federal regulations require that the performance of program participants be compared with what their performance would
have been without the program. This is problematic in states
where bilingual education is mandated and all comparable children are, therefore, enrolled in some type of bilingual program.

The data required present problems for some projects. For
some, group pre- and post-test score analyses are virtually im-

possible due to high student mobility. Teachers have been known to complain in some inner-city programs about student turnover of 50 percent or more in one year.

EVALUATION DESIGN

Opponents of bilingual education have criticized evaluations of projects claiming that evaluation designs have been seriously flawed. The U.S. Commission on Civil Rights declared in 1975 that "one of the weaknesses of some of the early bilingual programs was inadequate evaluation: relatively few projects collected useful baseline data. The absence of clearly defined objectives, the lack of tests translated into the non-English language and of new instruments appropriate for the target population, and the failure to measure, rather than to merely identify, language dominance were some of the marks of inadequacy" (Andersson and Boyer, 1978, p. 38). These criticisms are still true of many bilingual program evaluations.

The Center for Applied Linguistics found that only seven of 150 evaluation reports surveyed met minimal criteria for sound evaluation designs. Dulay and Burt (1979) surveyed 179 evaluations and 38 research studies and rejected all but three of the evaluations and nine of the studies.

Troike (1978) blames the dearth of quality research and evaluation data on the lack of adequate funds. He claimed that only one-half of 1 percent of the $500 million spent on bilingual education in a decade had been spent on research and evaluation. He concludes:

> Educators, legislators, and others concerned with quality programs and with the future of bilingual education should insist on the adequate funding of research, even at the expense of other activities if necessary, because the achievement of equal educational opportunity for children from non-English speaking backgrounds crucially depends upon it.

Baker and de Kanter (1983) reviewed several hundred studies of Title VII bilingual programs and discarded all but 39 as methodologically unacceptable. Critics of the report (which was later published in book form) charged that the authors' methodology was also seriously flawed. Baker and deKanter concluded that there was no justification, based on the 39 studies, for the federal government to require TBE as the sole instructional method for teaching LEP children. This conclusion coincided with the Reagan administration position of allowing flexibility in selecting program design, and their plan for a Bilingual Education Improvement Act including support "of a broadened range of instructional approaches...."

TESTING AND TESTS

A very important part of program evaluations is the information provided by test scores. All evaluation plans include objectives for student achievement. The degree to which students achieve gains in standardized test scores has become the most important criterion for determining program success or failure. Testing, tests, their validity, reliability, relevance, and cultural bias have been subjects of much debate for the last fifteen years.

Testing is an ever-present, time- and resource-consuming issue in bilingual education. Students are tested for language dominance for placement in bilingual programs. (Language dominance refers to the language in which users have greater facility, i.e., can understand and use better than their "other" language. Language dominance implies some degree of bilinguality.) They are tested for language proficiency to determine their first and second language instructional needs and exit from transitional bilingual programs. (Language proficiency refers to students' competence in a language, the degree to which they understand and use the language in all the skills: listening, speaking, reading, and writing.) Reading tests are administered in English and the students' native languages. Mathematics tests usually round out the testing battery. Some programs administer attitude and self-concept inventories, questionnaires, or surveys.

All of this testing is occurring concurrently with the debate about the adequacy of the available tests. To questions of reliability and validity have been added questions of the differences between measuring language dominance and language proficiency. In the early days of bilingual education, many tests were merely translated into non-English languages. This led to criticisms of the cultural and class bias inherent in testing and the inappropriateness of translations. In the intervening fifteen years, tests have been developed, primarily in Spanish, which attempt to remedy the inadequacies of the translations.

The debate on testing and tests in bilingual education is now closer to the general debate on the issue of testing. Questions as to whether tests really measure what they purport to and whether tests should play an important role in decision-making continue to be debated. While the debate goes on, testing also continues.

LANGUAGE TESTS

Most of the testing in bilingual education involves some form of language testing. Oller (1979) believes that testing, in general, is language testing: "In one way or another, practically every kind of significant testing of human beings depends on a surreptitious test of ability to use a particular language" (p. 2).

Many educators question the validity of achievement and intelligence testing of linguistic minorities, and blacks who speak black English claim that tests do not measure intelligence or achievement but proficiency in the English language.

Tests specifically developed to measure the amount of language acquired are of three types--discrete point, integrative, or pragmatic. Discrete point tests are developed to test one language skill at a time (e.g., reading, speaking, listening, or writing). Each test item focuses on one aspect of language at a time, such as grammar or phonology. Discrete point tests take language skill apart. Minimal pairs test items are discrete point items. Students are asked to listen to pairs of words which sound very similar except for one phoneme (e.g., bat/pat) and tell whether they are the same or different.

Integrative tests are at the opposite end of the testing continuum: they put language skill together. They test many skills and aspects of language at the same time.

Pragmatic tests are integrative tests that require more of the students. The tests require students to use language contextually and to comprehend language. Language learners can do relatively well on some discrete point test items with little proficiency in the language. In pragmatic tests, it is not possible to do well without some comprehension. Dictation and cloze tests are examples of pragmatic tests. Cloze tests delete every fourth, fifth, or other word from a passage and the examinee is asked to fill in the missing word.

Language testing for dominance, proficiency, and achievement continues to be an issue in the bilingual program evaluations. Some educators believe that criterion-referenced tests which measure student achievement specifically in terms of project objectives may be more appropriate than norm-referenced tests. It is difficult to find anyone perfectly satisfied with any one test of language dominance, proficiency, or achievement. It is becoming increasingly clear that tests form only one part of an evaluation and that many types of data need to be compiled and analyzed in order to measure the true effectiveness of bilingual education.

EFFECTIVENESS OF BILINGUAL PROGRAMS

Evaluations of bilingual programs have been found to be effective by some researchers and ineffective by others in teaching students English, native language, mathematics, and other subject matter. They have been found to do no better or worse than monolingual programs in teaching basic skills. They have been found both to improve student self-concepts and to make no difference in student self-concepts. They have been found to improve attitudes toward the two cultures involved and to make no difference.

Noel Epstein (1977) claims that there is no evidence that proves the effectiveness of bilingual programs. However, Epstein reached this conclusion through interviews with politicians and administrators in bilingual education. He did not conduct research or review the existing research.

The AIR (American Institute for Research) study also concluded that "students participating in Title VII projects did not show significant differences in achievement or attitudes when compared with non-Title VII students." The study covered 38 Spanish-English bilingual programs and found that program students did not perform as well as non-bilingual program students in English language arts. They performed as well as non-project students in mathematics.

The AIR study has been analyzed and criticized as seriously flawed by several researchers (Cervantes, 1979; Cardenas, 1977). The study's findings have been found invalid for reasons such as lack of comparability between the groups being compared, inappropriate tests, failure to define "bilingual program" and control for the level of implementation. Despite the weaknesses in the study and, consequently, the inconclusiveness, if not error, of its findings, the study has received a great deal of attention. (See Chapter 11 for an analysis of the AIR study.)

Although many bilingual program evaluation designs are so flawed as to make any conclusions open to question, there have been a substantial number of sound evaluations that have found bilingual education to be effective for students of limited ability or no ability in speaking English. Dulay and Burt (1976) reviewed 175 evaluations and 38 research projects and excluded any that had any of the following weaknesses in the design:

     (1) No control for subjects' socioeconomic status
     (2) No control for initial language proficiency or
         dominance
     (3) No baseline comparison data or control group
     (4) Inadequate sample size

    (5) Excessive attrition rate
    (6) Significant differences in teacher qualification
        for control and experimental groups
    (7) Insufficient data and/or statistics reported (p. 2)

Only nine projects and three studies met the criteria.
The study yielded 59 findings on variables such as reading and
language arts in the first and second languages, math, and
social studies achievement in the second language, cognitive
function in both languages, attitude, and attendance. The
findings were categorized as positive if "(1) The experimental
group performed significantly better than a comparison group;
(2) Pre-post gains during treatment were significantly greater
than gains before treatment; or (3) Results of comparison to
district or national norms were significantly better than before treatment." If no significant differences were found,
it was said that the treatment had "no effect." If subjects
performed significantly worse in one of the three comparisons,
the effect was said to be negative.

Of the 59 findings, 34 or 58 percent were found to be
positive, i.e., students made significant gains compared to
the control group from pre- to post-test or compared to national
norms. Twenty-four findings, 41 percent, were neutral, i.e.,
there was no significant difference in the three comparisons.
In looking at this set of neutral findings, it must be kept in
mind that neutral can be considered positive. Students of
limited or no English speaking ability, participating in a bilingual program were performing in English, math, social studies, attitude, etc., as well as comparable children in monolingual programs with one exception—they were also learning
native language arts.

There was only one finding of a negative effect in the
twelve projects or studies and 59 findings.

Troike (1978) maintains that there is sufficient evidence
on the effectiveness of quality bilingual programs:

> Despite the lack of research and the inadequacy of
> evaluation reports, enough evidence has now accumulated
> to make it possible to say with confidence that quality
> bilingual programs can meet the goal of providing equal
> educational opportunity for students from non-English-
> speaking backgrounds. In fact, the evidence is suffi-
> ciently strong to permit the statement that if a pro-
> gram is not producing such results, something is wrong
> (though not necessarily with the program) and needs to
> be changed. (pp. 13-14)

ENGLISH LANGUAGE ACHIEVEMENT

Achievement in the English language is usually the criterion of most interest to school boards, state education agencies, and critics of bilingual education. There is evidence that bilingual education programs can result in significant gains in the English language.

Troike's analysis of a survey of bilingual program evaluations revealed that:

(1) In San Francisco, Chinese-dominant students in the Title VII bilingual program scored at or above local and national norms in English.

(2) In Artesia, New Mexico, Spanish-dominant and English-dominant students in the bilingual program scored significantly higher than the control group students in English and reading.

(3) French-dominant students in the bilingual program in St. John Valley, Minnesota, were matched with students of comparable I.Q. and socioeconomic status in the monolingual English program. After five years, students in the bilingual program out-performed the students in the control groups in English language skills.

(4) Navajo students in the bilingual program in Rock Point, Arizona, were 1.3 and 1.6 years below national norms when the program began. Three years later, they were only .6 and .5 years below national norms for the 4th and 5th grades respectively and four years later they were one month (.1) below and one month above national norms for the 5th and 6th grades respectively.

(5) Spanish-dominant 5th and 6th grade students in the Santa Fe, New Mexico, bilingual program scored above the comparison groups and close to national norms in English reading.

(6) Spanish-dominant students in grades 2 and 3 in the New Haven, Connecticut, bilingual program experienced greater growth in English reading than the control students. In addition, the bilingual class tested at grade level in English whereas the control group did not.

(7) In the Douglas, Arizona, Spanish-English bilingual program second-grade students scored slightly lower than the control group on the English Metropolitan Achievement Test after two years. By the third grade bilingual program students scored higher than the control group in English reading and higher than the norm.

The results of the St. John Valley French-English program, the Navajo program in Rock Point, Arizona, and the Spanish-English programs in Santa Fe, New Mexico, and Douglas, Arizona, point to the cumulative effects of bilingual education. Although, in some cases, bilingual program students lagged behind control group students in English reading, they caught up with and, in some cases, surpassed them after three to five years in the program.

Cohen and Laosa (1976) found that Spanish-dominant students in the bilingual program in Redwood City, California, scored significantly lower than control-group students instructed solely in English. Bilingual program students, however, were introduced to reading in English and Spanish simultaneously, a practice which is, unfortunately, very common in transition-type bilingual programs.

Fischer and Cabello (1978) found that the most stable predictor for English reading proficiency is Spanish reading proficiency. In a similar vein, Finnish immigrant students in Sweden were found to perform closer to Swedish norms in Swedish if they had had five to six years of education in their native language. Students who immigrated at the ages of ten to twelve years achieved greater proficiency in Swedish language skills than students who immigrated at the pre-school level or in the early grades. Math and science achievement was also higher where Finnish language skills were greater.

CONCLUSION

Evaluation of bilingual programs continues to be a problematic area. Perceptions of evaluation uses, many audiences with different agendas, inadequate or inappropriate assessment instruments, inability of school districts to assign students randomly or provide control groups, resistance on the part of teachers and staff to testing and record-keeping, and the lack of adequate training of staff on evaluation purposes, design, methodology and their role continue to make evaluation an unwelcome but necessary evil.

Perhaps a reassessment of the limits of evaluation and of its realistic uses and less emphasis on using evaluation results for future decisions and greater use for program improvement might begin to move evaluation in the right direction and make it a useful educational tool.

REFERENCES

Andersson, T., and M. Boyer. *Bilingual Schooling in the United States*. 2d ed. Austin: National Educational Laboratory Publishers, 1978.

Baker, K.A., and A.A. deKanter. *Bilingual Education: A Reappraisal of Federal Policy*. Toronto: Lexington Books, 1983.

Bissell, J. *Program Impact Evaluations: An Introduction for Managers of Title VII Projects*. Los Alamitos, Calif.: SWRL Educational Research and Development, 1980.

Cardenas, J. "AIR Evaluation of Bilingual Education." *IDRA Newsletter*, 1977, San Antonio, Texas: Intracultural Research Association.

Cervantes, R.A. *An Exemplary Consafic Chingatropic Assessment: The AIR Report*. Bilingual Education Paper Series, Vol. 2, No. 8. California: National Assessment and Dissemination Center, 1979.

Cohen, A.D., and L.M. Laosa. "Second Language Instruction: Some Research Considerations." *Curriculum Studies*, 1976, 8:149–165.

Cohen, A.D., and M. Swain. "Bilingual Education: The Immersion Model in the North American Context." In Alatis and Twaddell (eds.). *ESL and Bilingual Education*. Washington, D.C.: TESOL, 1976.

Comfort, L.K. *Education Policy and Evaluation: A Context for Change*. New York: Pergamon Press, 1982.

Dulay, H., and M. Burt. "Bilingual Education: A Close Look at Its Effects." *Focus*, 1979, NCBE, #1.

Epstein, N. *Language, Ethnicity, and the Schools: Policy Alternatives for Bilingual-Bicultural Education*. Washington, D.C.: Institute for Educational Leadership, The George Washington University, 1977.

Fischer, K.B., and B. Cabello. "Predicting Student Success Following Transition from Bilingual Programs." Paper presented at AERA Meeting, Toronto. Los Angeles Center for Study of Evaluation, UCLA, 1978.

Oller, J.W., Jr. *Language Tests at School*. London: Longman Group, 1979.

Troike, R.C. "Research Evidence for the Effectiveness of Bilingual Education." *NABE Journal*, 1978, 3:13-24.

Weiss, C. *Evaluation Research: Methods for Assessing Program Effectiveness*. Englewood Cliffs, N.J.: Prentice-Hall, 1972.

ANNOTATED BIBLIOGRAPHY

Cohen, A.D. *Describing Bilingual Education Classrooms. The Role of the Teacher in Evaluation.* Rosslyn, VA: National Clearinghouse for Bilingual Education, 1980.

This paper distinguishes the types of evaluation applied to bilingual education programs. The purpose of the monograph is to highlight for administrators, evaluators, and teachers the relevant kinds of descriptive information contributed by the teacher which accurately reflects classroom characteristics in the evaluation of a bilingual program. Six principles are selected for discussion. Each principle is accompanied by a brief case study which focuses on the evaluation of a language-related, classroom-centered issue. An exercise follows each case study in which the reader assumes the role of classroom teacher and provides an interpretation and/or recommendation. A discussion concludes each exercise. A bibliography is included.

Erickson, F. "The Politics of Speaking: An Approach to Evaluating Bilingual-Bicultural Schools." Los Angeles: National Dissemination and Assessment Center, 1978.

This paper suggests alternative approaches to traditional program evaluation design. A sociolinguistic approach is described for the evaluation of bilingual language-maintenance programs. Such an evaluation would examine social variants influencing the speech communication acts in a program setting. The author would identify (1) what kinds of social costs and benefits accrue to different ways of speaking in different situations, (2) which member of the conversation defines what ways of speaking are situationally appropriate, and (3) the power and authority relationship between the definer of appropriateness and the speaker. Analysis of such data could determine the impact of both the formal curriculum and the social organization in relation to first-language maintenance.

Evaluation Instruments for Bilingual Education: An Annotated

Bibliography. Dissemination and Assessment Center for Bilingual Education, Austin, Texas, 1977.

This bibliography is designed to provide information on evaluation instruments available for use in bilingual education programs. The instruments are organized into three categories: project-developed instruments (79 citations), commercially published instruments (139 citations), and instruments from non-commercial sources (40 citations). Each category groups individual entries according to the skill area measured.

Irizarry, R.A. *Bilingual Education: State and Federal Legislative Mandates. Implications for Program Design and Evaluation.* Los Angeles: National Dissemination and Assessment Center, undated.

Identifies characteristics of bilingual education programs mandated by current and federal legislation which are of importance to the evaluation of the programs. These characteristics may differ in regard to program implementation from state to state and are, therefore, important for consideration in evaluation. Two summaries are presented. The first is an across-state summary of 14 provisions which may vary in the implementation of bilingual education programs. These provisions include: type of program, population to be served, participation of English-speaking students, census, census mandate, description of the program, student/teacher ratio, teacher/staff requirements and qualifications, staff training, material requirements, community participation and evaluation reporting requirements. The second part is a summary of the content of federal legislation and that of 20 states that have adopted legislation in bilingual education pursuant to federal provisions.

Irizarry, R.A., et al. *Final Evaluation Report. Newton High School, Queens, N.Y. Chinese/Korean Bilingual Language Arts Resource Center.* ESEA, Title VII, 1979-80. ERIC Document.

A final evaluation report on a New York City high school Chinese/Korean, Title VII, bilingual education program. A demographic context of the target population is provided. The diversity of student characteristics is discussed in relation to entry criteria, ethnic composition, and language proficiency. Program description includes information on the project background, organization, and structure. Instructional components are presented in terms of program philosophy and goals, program funding, and instructional courses offered. Non-instructional components considered in the report include curriculum and materials development, supportive services, staff development, parent/community involvement, and affective domain. Reported and interpreted are the results of both criterion-referenced tests and norm-referenced tests. Conclusions and recommendations are provided.

Irizarry, R.A., et al. *South Shore High School Project BLAST. Bilingual Assistance for Students. Final Evaluation Report, 1979-1980.* New York City Board of Education, Brooklyn, N.Y. ERIC Document, Arlington, Virginia, 1980.

A final evaluation report of a transitional bilingual education high school program serving Spanish, Russian, and French/Creole speaking students in Brooklyn, N.Y. Students in both public and private schools are served. The report provides demographic information, a description of student characteristics, and a program description. Instructional components are presented on programming and transition, funding, bilingual classes, and mainstream classes. Non-instructional components include curriculum and materials development, supportive services, staff characteristics, staff development, parent/community involvement and affective domain. The private school component is described. Provided are types of assessment procedures used and interpretation of their findings in the areas of English language development, native language growth, mathematics, social studies and science. Results are presented in separate tables for each language group. Conclusions note that Project BLAST is designed and implemented to meet the needs of students in several language groups of disproportionate numbers. The report recommends that other Title VII programs replicate this project's inclusion of American-born students in native language arts classes as well as the practice of inviting program students to speak in mainstream social studies classes.

Norris, C.A., and L. Wheeler. *Title IV-A/Johnson O'Malley Indian Education Program. Final Evaluation Report, 1980-1981.* ERIC Document, Arlington, Virginia, 1981.

A final report of a Title IV Johnson O'Malley Indian Education Program in the Phoenix Union High School District. Seven goals are identified and evaluated for the planning, development, and implementation of the program. Goals are established in the areas of home/school liaison services, supplemental education programs, Indian studies curriculum, cross-cultural experiences and communication, awareness of career and post-secondary alternative, overall management, and increased parental involvement. It is recommended that program objectives and activities be revised to be more concrete and realistic in relation to student needs, funding, and available staff. Appendices include opinion surveys and needs assessments designed for parents, students, principals, assistant principals, head counseolors, and book store managers.

Oller, J.W., and K. Perkins (eds.). *Research in Language Testing*. Rowley, MA: Newbury House, 1980.

A compilation of 24 research studies which investigate the nature of language proficiency in adult second-language learners. These investigations consider: factors which are supposed to contribute to success for second-language learning, differences between native and non-native performance of language tasks, and investigations of listening, speaking, reading, and writing tasks. The editors suggest that a single factor of global language proficiency may account for most variance in a wide variety of educational testing instruments and that language skill pervades every area of the school curriculum.

Roby, W.R. *The 1979-80 Evaluation of the Title VII Bilingual Program, Project Cumbre, at the Ann Street Bilingual School of Hartford, Connecticut*. ERIC Document, Arlington.

An evaluation report of a Title VII Spanish-English bilingual program at the Ann Street School in Hartford, Connecticut. The opening section provides background information, summarizes findings, and reports conclusions and recommendations. Educational objectives established for kindergarten students were to increase Spanish and English language skills and proficiency and to demonstrate high self-concept. Educational objectives for students in grades 1-6 were in the areas of Spanish and English language skills, English reading, social sciences, mathematics, and social studies. Results of criterion-referenced testing and norm-referenced testing for each grade level are reported and integrated. The impact of the program is compared to the impact of other Hartford bilingual programs on mean number of years students receive continuous bilingual education, mean age-per-grade level, and academic achievement. The progress of students who have graduated from the program and continue in middle school is discussed in the areas of reading and mathematics. Program objectives were established for instructional personnel and parents of bilingual students. Provided is a description of how these objectives were met. The report describes some of the expanded school opportunities available to students during the 1979-80 school year.

Silverman, R.J., J.K. Noa, and R.H. Russel. *Oral Language Tests for Bilingual Students: An Evaluation of Language Dominance and Proficiency Instruments.* Center for Bilingual Education, Northwest Regional Educational Laboratory, Portland, Oregon, second printing, 1977.

This report evaluates individually 24 currently available oral language assessment instruments for use with bilingual students. Thirty-eight criterion measures are employed. Per each test, these measures are grouped into 4 major criterion areas: measurement validity, examinee appropriateness, technical excellence, and administrative usability. A point value is assigned to each criterion according to a format defined in the text and an overall rating is provided in each criterion area. Results of this rating format are matrixed into an evaluation rating chart. Test descriptions are grouped into three categories: commercially available tests, tests undergoing development and/or field testing, and experimental tests. The majority of the instruments evaluated are for use in determining Spanish/English oral language proficiency. Two tests are intended for use with Portuguese/English-speaking populations and one test is designed for use with English/Spanish, Mandarin, Cantonese, Tagalog, and Ilokano-speaking populations. An appendix identifies test development efforts in ten other major languages and provides developers contact information.

Singado, I.C. *District 30 Queens, Chapter 720, Greek-English, Korean-English. Final Report.* ERIC Document, Arlington, 1981.

A final evaluation report of a New York City Greek-English, Korean-English bilingual program for students in grades K-6. The program was formulated to aid the educational and cultural development of limited-English proficiency students in the program. Educational objectives include: the ability to understand and to speak English, native language proficiency, academic gains in social studies, science and mathematics due to instruction in the dominant language, and increased student participation in classroom activities and extracurricular activities. Sources of curriculum materials are discussed. Other topics included in this report refer to class-

room observations, teacher training, parent activities and
activities of the Parent Advisory Committee.

Tucker, R.G. "Implications for U.S. Bilingual Education:
Evidence from Canadian Research." *Focus*, 1980, National
Clearinghouse for Bilingual Education #2.

Discusses conclusions of empirical research on the effectiveness of Canadian bilingual education (immersion) programs. Salient characteristics of the Canadian programs are
interfaced with the treatment of similar factors as they
exist in U.S. bilingual education programs. These factors
include: types of bilingual education programs which are
federally legislated and funded, availability of teachers
trained to work in bilingual programs, degree of parental
understanding of and development of program objectives, social
and economic status of the native language, degree of homogeneous entry-level language skills of children participating
in bilingual programs and the assumption that children will
succeed. While the author maintains that there are no
empirical data to indicate transitional programs to be more
effective than maintenance programs, he concludes that the
Canadian studies suggest that when certain linguistic criteria are met and combined with community understanding and
parental support, second-language instruction can be implemented without detriment to the child.

Ulbarri, D.M., M.L. Spencer, and G.A. Rivas. "Language Proficiency and Academic Achievement: A Study of Language Proficiency Tests and Their Relationship to School Ratings as
Predictors of Academic Achievement." *NABE Journal*, 5:47–80,
1981.

Investigates the comparability of results obtained from
use of the Language Assessment Scale (LAS), the Bilingual
Syntax Measure (BSM), and the Basic Inventory of Natural
Languages (BINL) and their relationship to achievement tests.
There are two purposes to the study: (1) to compare these
tests in terms of their language classification levels and
(2) to determine the relationship of the language categories
of each test to standard achievement test data.

Chapter 9

PARENTAL INVOLVEMENT AND PARTICIPATION

Since the beginning of public education in the United
States, the issue of its control has been hotly contested.
Ravitch (1974) traces the history of public education in New
York City and characterizes the issue of control as essentially
one of political struggle between new and previous immigrant
groups. She calls each major struggle for control "school
wars."

The first "war" was between the Catholic clergy and the
Protestant philanthropic organizations that controlled the
publicly funded free schools. That struggle resulted in public control. The next struggle was for centralization, an
attempt to wrest control from local school boards. This was
followed, in the early twentieth century, with professionaliza-
tion or control by educators. The last major struggle for
control was decentralization, followed closely by community
control.

The decentralization movement was an attempt to bring
control of the schools to the local level where it could be
more responsive to community needs. This movement was supported by the professionals in many cities, but some communities
felt that nothing changed as a result of decentralization.

> In forcing the passage of the decentralization law of
> 1969, the United Federation of Teachers and other oppo-
> nents of community control wrote into the law the re-
> structuring of the same old failing system behind a new,
> decentralized facade. (Fuentes, 1976, p. 692)

Fuentes describes the efforts of the minority communities
of District I in New York City at gaining control of the school
system. He claims that community control did not fail, as many
opponents charge, but that it was never allowed to occur. Some
researchers have found that neither the decentralization nor
community control movements resulted in any significant increases in the power of parents to influence educational decisions.

Edwards (1979) maintains that parents have little power
in public schools and that, except for children, they have the
least authority regarding their children's education. Although
parents can vote for board members, exert pressure on issues,
and be part of advisory groups, they have no access to important education decisions.

In fact, the teachers and administrators who want parents
to go to school board meetings and speak out against school
closings and budget cuts often do not want parents involved in
decisions on hiring, curriculum, or budgets. They claim that
parents are not qualified to make certain educational decisions.
It often appears as if the decision and policymaking system is
unnecessarily complicated and inaccessible to parents.

> The last few years of urban crises have generated a new
> concern about the citizen's role in the planning process.
> Given the complexity of the issues and the growing so-
> phistication of techniques in urban and social planning,
> many writers have argued that community groups, espe-
> cially in low income neighborhoods, need the expertise
> of professionals to defend their interests in the policy
> process. (Guskin and Ross, 1974, p. 340)

There are several terms used in connection with the educational decisionmaking process which might be worth defining.
Davies, et al. (1979) define citizen participation as "taking
part in activities in order to exercise power or influence--
to have impact on decisionmaking" by "parents and other adult
residents in a city or town." Educators and students are
excluded in this term. The term "involvement" is used where
there is "no clear intent to exercise power or to have an
effect on decisionmaking."

Involvement, which was originally "citizen-initiated,"
has increasingly become "mandated" by state and federal stat-
ute, in their requirements for advisory councils. There is
some question as to whether the mandating of community involvement or participation has been beneficial or whether it
has eroded parents' power. Most federally mandated participation requires "evidence of consultation with client representa-
tives in the process of proposal preparation" (Davies, et al,,
1979). That consultation often becomes the extent of the
participation.

Many states also mandate advisory groups for specific
programs. Clasby (1979) found that "State-level advisory
councils or committees represent a well-established tradition
of appointing selected professionals and/or elite citizens to
offer advice on a selected program or activity" (p. 32). In
a study of 22 documents on state initiatives for citizen participation, she concluded that participation usually meant
advising and consultation.

While most teachers and administrators will espouse the importance of parental involvement, many balk at parental participation in educational decisionmaking. They believe the role of parents should be limited to advocacy under the leadership and tutelage of the professionals. Educators often adhere strictly to the letter in terms like "advisory board" or "advisory council." Parents may advise, but educators are under no obligation to heed the advice.

Gittell, et al. (1979) studied sixteen community organizations in three cities to determine "how poor and working-class groups can exercise power in educational policies in urban school districts" (p. 4).

The study found three types of community organizations: service, advisory, and advocacy. Service organizations engage in direct delivery of services such as referral, education, counseling, etc. Advisory groups consult with agencies and local officials and advise--they have no decision-making power. Advocacy groups deal with specific issues and attempt to influence decisionmaking.

It was found that advocacy groups were the most effective in influencing decisionmaking. Not surprising was the finding that of the sixteen groups studied, not one poor or working-class group was an advocacy group. The lower-class groups were of either the service or advisory types. Of the four middle-class groups, three were advocacy groups.

These findings have particular relevance to the communities involved in bilingual education since, by and large, they are poor and working-class communities.

PARENTAL INVOLVEMENT IN BILINGUAL EDUCATION

Although parental involvement has been a part of bilingual education since the earliest programs, bilingual educators often suffer from the same narrow view of the parental role in education--they see it as one of involvement and not participation. "Real involvement can be promoted by listening carefully to the parents' comments and by giving volunteers a chance to make classroom supplies according to specifications provided by teachers. These can include charts, simple educational toys, blocks, bean-bags, pencil or crayon holders, etc." (Andersson and Boyer, 1978, pp. 79-80)

The quantity and quality of parental involvement and community participation in bilingual education varies greatly from state to state, district to district, and program to program. The Cuban community in Dade County was very active in lobbying, raising funds, and planning for the Dade County bilingual programs. The initiative came from parents who did not want their children to lose their native language and culture (Mackey and Beebe, 1977).

In Boston, the Puerto Rican community took the initiative, working with a Catholic nun in lobbying, planning, and implementing the bilingual program. They were successful not only in securing a bilingual program for the City of Boston, but in pushing the state legislature to enact the first state bilingual education law.

Many bilingual programs encourage parental involvement that enlists the aid of parents in improving student achievement. Parent training programs are conducted to help them understand how children learn and what they can do at home to help them. Parents are often invited to share their culture and folklore with the students and to serve as volunteer teacher aides. These programs often include native language, English literacy instruction for parents.

The parental involvement component of the Mississippi Choctaw Bilingual Education Program for Native Americans offered parent training that included orientation to bilingual education, literacy training in the native language, and training for parent aides who assisted in mainly cultural activities and events (York, 1979).

The Chicago Parent Leadership Training Program attempted to train parents to serve on bilingual program advisory councils (Cerda and Schensul, 1978). The training was designed to give parents skills needed for participation in the planning, implementation, and evaluation of bilingual programs in a consultative, advisory capacity.

Rodriguez (1981) studied fifteen Title VII Advisory Committees in Texas public schools "to determine the extent and significance of community participation in programmatic decision-making." The participation was analyzed in terms of a five-level typology developed by the Recruitment and Leadership Training Institute of Temple University. The five levels posited by the typology are roles that the groups play or are expected to play by those exercising power. These are:

(1) The placation role. This is meant for minimal compliance with requirements of participation and to avoid possible complaints and investigations.
(2) Sanctions. This is essentially a rubber-stamping role. Participants are selected by the authorities for their visibility. The goals, programs, and policies are developed by the school boards.
(3) Information. Participants in this role are selected by school boards because of the information they possess, e.g., knowledge of the community and its native culture.

(4) Checks and balances. This is the first level at
which some power is exercised. Participants can
approve or veto decisions.

(5) Change-agent. This is the highest level of participation. Participants can veto but can also
initiate action leading to change. (pp. 1-21)

Rodriguez found that community involvement in the bilingual programs he studied was, by and large, limited to lists
of attendees at meetings called by school officials to disseminate information about the program.

The school districts' plans were in conformity with
federal expectations at the placation/sanctions level. It was
only in court-ordered desegregation cases that participation
escalated to a checks and balances level. This was achieved
only through intensive pressure from the courts and the
federal guidelines for bilingual education and desegregation
projects.

Desegregation has perhaps been the single issue most responsible for parental involvement in bilingual education.
When a desegregation plan has not made provisions for bilingual
education, parents have intervened in many cities, Denver and
Boston being two of the most notable.

Melendez (1981) found that Puerto Rican parents in Boston
were not actively involved in the desegregation case until the
first order was issued without any provision for the bilingual
program. The parents organized and intervened as plaintiffs-
intervenors in the case. In fact, they developed strategies
that were characteristic of the successful advocacy groups
found by Gittell (1979) to be used by middle-class groups.
They were aware that attorneys usually made the decisions in
litigated cases, and they jealously guarded their leadership
and decisionmaking role.

Rodriguez (1981) found that proposal writers talked about
parents' need for training in "lettering, coloring, operating
the duplicating and laminating machines ...," and to "improve
their skills, techniques and self-confidence."

Some members of advisory committees responded to the
question, "What, in your opinion, is the most important con-
tribution your committee has made to the bilingual program?"
with: judging of a Holiday Spirit Contest, making Christmas
decorations, and trying to help children get home assistance.

Matute-Bianchi (1979) studied parental involvement in the
San Jose Title VII program. She declared that, despite language on parental involvement in the 1977-78 reauthorization
of Title VII, the federal mandate for parental involvement is
weak. She maintains that there is no consensus in what the
purpose, goals, or function of advisory groups should be; that

the federal government has no policy on citizen or parental
participation in educational decisionmaking, that no theory of
parental involvement has emerged on which to base policies,
and that there are no reliable data on which to base policy.

In her study of the community participation in the San
Jose Consortium for bilingual education, Matute-Bianchi describes in detail the events leading to the submission of the
Title VII proposal for funding. The officials involved ad-
hered to the letter of the law in holding meetings for consultation. There were three meetings held to discuss the
proposal that was to be prepared. Two of those meetings were
for educators and those who would participate in the consortium. Only one meeting was announced as open to the public.

The announcement of the public hearing to discuss the
proposal appeared five days before the scheduled meeting
(federal guidelines require seven days' notice). 80 persons
attended the public hearing, most of them teachers, administrators, and teacher aides--very few parents attended. There
was no written proposal or draft provided for comment. The
audience was informed of the intention to submit a proposal
and were asked to write one objective each "in a variety of
content areas, ranging from reading, math and language arts to
culture, arts and music." Such a request was obviously not
intended for parents. That meeting produced more than 600
pages of suggestions and comments from the participants.

Federal regulations require that such comments and suggestions be given "meaningful consideration" in the preparation
of the proposal. According to Matute-Bianchi the 600 pages of
comments and suggestions sat in the office until one week after
the consultant had delivered a draft of the proposal. He had
not seen the results of that meeting.

Federal guidelines do not require evidence of efforts to
seek out and encourage parental participation. The only requirements are copies of the notice of hearing and a list of
advisory board members, half of whom must be parents of children who will be served by the project. It is easy for local
school districts to adhere to the letter of the regulations
and for meaningful parental participation not to exist.

*The courts and parental involvement in bilingual
education*

The issue of parental and community involvement in educational decisionmaking often ends up in the courts. Federal
courts, much more than state courts, have been the battleground
for the issue of parental participation in education decisions.
Federal court decisions, by and large, have tended to limit
citizen participation. "The keystone to these decisions is the

principle that the management, administration, establishment, and maintenance of public schools are primarily the affairs of the State, subject to constitutional limitations, which the State may delegate to appropriate administrative bodies" (Baxter, 1979). Baxter found that desegregation cases have generally been favorable to parental and community participation. Indeed, some desegregation decisions have mandated biracial citizens' advisory groups.

Since the *Lau* decision, bilingual communities have increasingly looked to the courts to force school districts to implement bilingual education programs. They have also intervened in desegregation cases to protect bilingual programs. Courts have generally been responsive to the demands of linguistic minorities for bilingual education within the context of desegregation. In *Keyes v. School District No. 1* (1973) the court ordered one of the most far-reaching bilingual programs. It would have, in effect, left some schools almost totally Hispanic. That case was reversed by a higher court which declared that bilingual education must be subordinated to desegregation and not substituted for it.

In Boston, Puerto Rican parents intervened when the first desegregation order issued made no provision for the bilingual program (*Morgan v. Hennigan*, 1974). As a result of their intervention, the court ordered a census to determine the extent of the need for bilingual education and the assignment of students with such need before assignments for racial balance.

Melendez (1981) reached two major conclusions in her study of the Boston desegregation case and parental involvement. In the first place, she claimed that the success of the parents in securing the bilingual program was directly attributable to the federal court presence. Boston public schools had been successfully opposing desegregation under the state's Racial Imbalance Act since its enactment in 1965. In fact, the first lawsuit for the desegregation of Boston's schools had been brought well over a hundred years before the Morgan case.

Secondly, Melendez found that the parents in Boston exhibited most of the characteristics of the middle-class advocacy groups found by Gittell to be the most effective in influencing school policy. This, although the members of the Boston parents' group were mostly poor and working class.

Instituting lawsuits is parental involvement in a very limited sense. It is lawyers who lead, and parents and community groups usually just sign papers as plaintiffs and testify in court. Most often, once the lawsuit has been settled or tried, and the court order issued, parents have no further role to play--the educators then resume the leadership. It is only when courts mandate parent monitoring and advisory groups that parental involvement continues. However, such involvement is usually of the "checks and balances" type, not participation in decisionmaking.

The future of parental involvement in bilingual education

Schooling has the longest and most powerful influence on our lives, except for that of our homes and families. For many poor and economically disadvantaged linguistic minority children, it offers the only opportunity for empowerment and integration into the economic mainstream of society. Without meaningful parental participation in the decisionmaking process, schooling will continue to be a tool for perpetuating the status quo and dooming a significant proportion of linguistic minority students to a permanent underclass.

Matute-Bianchi (1979) concluded her study of the San Jose Consortium with a list of questions that must be answered if participation is to be substantive and not merely symbolic. The questions she asked could have been answered already if federal, state, and local authorities had been sincere about the desirability of parental involvement. Parent groups and the educational establishment need to discuss the issues and hammer out a policy on parental participation. There is certain to be disagreement on questions such as the "proper" areas for parental and community involvement. Are budgeting, personnel, and curriculum legitimate areas for parental involvement or participation? Who will represent parents and the community? How will they be selected and by whom? What skills do they need and how will they acquire them? What resources do they need? How will differences and grievances between parent groups and the school or district be resolved?

The literature on parental and community participation in bilingual education to date does not answer most of the questions raised by Matute-Bianchi. Parent groups and bilingual educators need to work together to find answers to those questions and develop models for such participation. Failure to do so will give the lie to the rhetoric on the importance of parental participation in bilingual education and justifiably subject bilingual educators to charges of the same insensitivity and lack of responsiveness that they have attributed to the educational establishment.

The literature to date does not deal very much with language groups other than Spanish. This, too, will change with the increasing number of other language groups, particularly Southeast Asians, enrolling in bilingual programs.

CONCLUSION

Educators continue to pay lip service to the merits of parental participation in educational decisionmaking. Often, all they want from parents is rubber stamping of their decisions and political pressure for funding for programs. Title VII continues to require participation of parents in an advisory capacity but requires little accountability to ensure such participation.

There is a need for models of parental participation in bilingual education. Participation needs definition. What areas or issues are appropriate for parental involvement? Do parents need training? What kind of training? Should involvement be strictly advisory or should they have substantive power?

If the federal government continues to diminish its role in education, it may be necessary for parents to begin to become more involved at the state and local levels if these are to be held accountable for the needs of LEP children.

REFERENCES

Andersson, T., and M. Boyer. *Bilingual Schooling in the United States*. Austin: National Educational Laboratory Publishers, Inc., 1978.

Baxter, F.V. "Judicial Activism and Citizen Participation: A Survey and Analysis from 1970 to Presnt." In Davies, D., et al. *Federal and State Impact on Citizen Participation in the Schools*. Boston: Institute for Responsive Education, 1979.

Brisk, M.E. "The Role of the Bilingual Community in Mandated Bilingual Education." In *Working with the Bilingual Community*. Rosslyn, Virginia: National Clearinghouse for Bilingual Education, 1978.

Cerda, M.B., and J.J. Schensul. "The Chicago Parent Leadership Training Program." In *Working with the Bilingual Community*. Rosslyn, Virginia: National Clearinghouse for Bilingual Education, 1978.

Clasby, Miriam. "State Legislation for Citizen Participation." In Davies, D., et al. *Federal and State Impact on Citizen Participation in the Schools*. Boston: Institute for Responsive Education, 1979.

Davies, Don, James Upton, Miriam Clasby, Felix Baxter, Brian Powers, and Ross Zerchykov. *Federal and State Impact on Citizen Participation in the Schools*. Boston: Institute for Responsive Education, 1979.

Edwards, J. "Rights of Parents in Public Schools: What They Are, What They Are Not, and What They Should Be." In Hunt, T.C. (ed.). *Society, Culture and Schools: The American Approach*. Garrett Park, Maryland: Garrett Park Press, 1979.

Fuentes, Luis. "Community Control Did Not Fail in New York: It Wasn't Tried." *Phi Delta Kappan*, June 1976.

Gittell, M., et al. *Citizen Organizations: Citizen Participation in Educational Decisionmaking*. Boston: Institute for Responsive Education, 1979.

Guskin, A.E., and R. Ross. "Advocacy and Democracy: The Long View." In Fred M. Cox, et al. (eds.). *Strategies of Community Organization*. Itasca, IL: F.E. Peacock, 1974.

Keyes v. School District No. 1, Denver 413 U.S. 189 (1973).

Mackey, W.F., and V.N. Beebe. *Bilingual Schools for a Bicultural Community: Miami's Adaptation to Cuban Refugees.* Rowley, MA: Newbury House Publishers, Inc., 1977.

Matute-Bianchi, M.B. *Parent and Community Participation in Federally-Funded Bilingual Education: A View from the Bottom Up*. Unpublished doctoral dissertation. Stanford: Stanford University, 1979.

Melendez, S.E. *Hispanos, Desegregation and Bilingual Education: A Case of the Role of "El Comite de Padres" in the Court Ordered Desegregation of the Boston Public Schools (1974-1975)*. Unpublished doctoral dissertation. Cambridge, MA: Harvard University, 1981.

Morgan v. Hennigan, C.A. 72-911-G (1974).

Ravitch, D. *The Great School Wars*. New York: Basic Books, 1974.

Rodriguez, R. "Citizen Participation in Selected Bilingual Education Advisory Committees." *NABE Journal*, 1981, 5:1-21.

York, K.H. "Parent/Community Involvement in the Mississippi Choctaw Bilingual Education Program." In *Working with the Bilingual Community*. Rosslyn, Virginia: National Clearinghouse for Bilingual Education, 1979.

ANNOTATED BIBLIOGRAPHY

Chavez, E. *Parental Involvement and Participation in Bilingual Education: A Guide*. *(El envolvimiento y la Partici-
pacion de los Padres en la Educacion Bilingue. Una Guia)*.
Albuquerque, New Mexico: National Institute for Multicultural Education, 1980.

This is a two-part document on parental involvement in bilingual education. The first section outlines the development of legislative changes in the Title VII Education Amendment as of April 1980, as these changes relate to the role
of parental and community involvement in education. The
second section outlines traditional and non-traditional activities through which parents participate in the educational
process.

Coca, B. *Actividades Para Padres: A Parent Handbook (Activities
for Parents: A Parent Handbook)*. Montezuma, N.M.: Montezuma
Publications, 1980.

This handbook is a compilation of information and materials
disseminated during a thirteen-session workshop conducted
for parents in Mora, New Mexico. Program components emphasized knowledge of Mexican-American culture, lessons in the
history of New Mexico, the development of communication
techniques and the presentation of non-school activities
designed to enhance children's reading skills. The handbook
provides parents with a glossary of educational terms, a list
of government-related abbreviations and acronyms, and a reference list of educational literature and materials designed
for parents.

Cohen, B., et al. *Project PIE: Parent Involvement in Evaluation*. New York: Impact Institute, Inc., 1981.

This handbook describes a training program designed for
parents, administrators, and evaluators to assist them in implementing a parental involvement component in the evaluation
of local bilingual education programs. Four levels of parent

participation are considered: the parents as advisors to the evaluation team, parents evaluating the parental involvement component, parents observing bilingual classroom activities, and parents as writers. Appendices provide a Project P.I.E. training outline, a parent interview questionnaire, a parents' survey, a parent classroom visitation checklist and a glossary of bilingual education evaluation terms.

Collins, L.F., and M. Obregon-Pagan. *Parent Involvement in Education: A Planning Manual.* Mesa, Arizona: Mesa Community College Bilingual Program, 1980.

A manual for parents, written in English and Spanish. It deals with skills in developing the child's cognitive and linguistic skills in the home; the parent as classroom observer and participant, and organizing meetings and workshops. It includes Title VII regulations requiring the establishment of a Parent Advisory Council. Also includes a fact sheet of bilingual education terminology.

Community and Working with Parents in the Multicultural Classroom. San Francisco: Far West Lab for Educational Research and Development, 1977.

This learning unit is designed to train teachers in developing effective communication with parents. The unit activities address teacher goals and verbal and non-verbal communication and facilitating techniques of communication. The unit includes a teacher attitude survey toward parental roles in the classroom and a parent survey designed to explore parental attitudes toward parental roles in the classroom.

Gold, N.C. "Evaluation of Community Involvement in Curriculum Development in Bilingual Schools." Paper presented at the Annual New York State English for Speakers of Other Languages/Bilingual Education Conference, Albany, New York, October 22-24, 1976.

This paper reports results of a project conducted in the Spring of 1975 which included field interviews and observations in ten bilingual programs in Connecticut and Massachusetts. The author presents a rationale for community involvement, describes barriers which must be overcome in order for such participation to take place, and suggests a framework for evaluation of that involvement. Included as Appendix B is an Interview Guide which is seen as a possible facilitator for community organization as well as an instrument for data collection. A bibliographic essay completes the work.

*Guidelines for Parental Involvement in Transitional Bilingual
Education.* Boston: Massachusetts State Department of Education, 1976.

This handbook of guidelines was developed by the Bureau of
Transitional Bilingual Education, members of the local Parent
Advisory Councils (PAC), and school officials. A rationale
for parental involvement in education is presented. Guidelines include PAC regulations for the organization of parent
councils and PAC guidelines defining parents' rights and
responsibilities as PAC members.

Hayes Mizell, M. "Maintaining Parent Interest in Title I
Parent Advisory Councils." *The Urban Review*, 1979, 2:81-88.

This article describes motivating factors in maintaining
parent interest in serving on a Parent Advisory Council
(PAC). General observations are presented regarding the
nature of parental involvement in Title I PACs. Practices
are identified which promote parents' perceptions that their
opinions do not matter and they have nothing to contribute.
Recommended are alternative approaches to these practices
which are more likely to stimulate parent interest and participation in PACs.

Lisjon, G. *Parent Interviews, ESES Title VII Bilingual Project.*
Formative Evaluation Report #8. Fall 1974. Austin Indepen-
dent School District, Texas. ERIC document. Arlington,
Virginia.

This is the initial report of a two-part evaluation of the
Parental Involvement Program component of a Title VII bilingual education project in the Austin Independent School
District, Texas. A random sample of parents with children
in grades K, 3, and 6 are interviewed in an attempt to measure the degree of home support for students' school activities and to measure the degree of change in this support as a
result of project activities. It is concluded that parents
are expressing a general support of and knowledge of their
children's school activities. Areas targeted as high priority
for improvement are knowledge of child's teacher, principal
and aide, communication among parents regarding school activities, and parent's knowledge of the project and of bilingual education.

Matute-Bianchi, M.E. "Parent and Community Participation in
Federally Funded Bilingual Education: A View from the Bottom
Up." Unpublished doctoral dissertation. Stanford: Stanford
University, 1979.

The focus of this paper is on two parent-community participation groups within a California school district. One
group is described as dependent on and internally organized
by the school system in response to Title VII regulations.
The other is described as an independently organized group
external to the school system. Each group is examined in
terms of its developmental history, political orientation,
educational objectives, and organization of resources. Discussed is how each group perceives its effectiveness as an
informed decision maker in educational policy. The author
argues that the federal mandate for parent-community involvement in bilingual education is weak. She concludes that the
impact of federal aid to education has been to create, at the
local level, an educational bureaucracy which removes the
family and community to a peripheral role in educational
decisionmaking.

Melendez, S.E. "Hispanos, Desegregation and Bilingual Education: A Case Analysis of the Role of 'El Comite de Padres'
in the Court-Ordered Desegregation of the Boston Public
Schools (1974-1975)." Unpublished doctoral dissertation.
Cambridge, Massachusetts: Harvard University, 1981.

Analyzes the role of "El Comite de Padres" as plaintiff-
intervenor in the Boston desegregation lawsuit *Morgan v.
Hennigan, et al.* The potential for conflict between bilingual education and desegregation is discussed. "El Comite"
is described as a low-income, single-issue group with a few
middle-class members. The group, without access to power or
decisionmakers, was successful in influencing educational
policy. The group's emergence, membership, leadership,
dynamics, and intervention strategies are discussed and compared to Gittell's study on community participation in educational decisionmaking. The author concludes that while "El
Comite's" intervention in the outcome of educational policy
was effective, its goals could not have been achieved without the presence of the court.

National Clearinghouse for Bilingual Education. *Working with
the Bilingual Community.* Rosslyn, Virginia: National
Clearinghouse for Bilingual Education, 1979.

A collection of five papers dealing with parental/community
involvement in bilingual education. Maria Estela Brisk discusses the subject in light of legislative and judicial
issues. Maria B. Cerda and Jean J. Schensul describe a
Chicago program designed to train parental leaders in the
Hispanic community. Kenneth York discusses the Mississippi
Choctaw Bilingual Education Program and how parents and com-

munity members have contributed to its initiation, growth,
and success. Norberto Cruz summarizes his recent research
identifying roles and functions of parent advisory councils
serving Title VII Spanish-English programs. In the final
paper, Alberto Ochoa examines the need for parental participation, presents three approaches for involving the community
in educational programs and suggests activities for generat-
ing parental interest and support.

Nieto, S., and R. Sinclair. *Curriculum Decision Making: The
Puerto Rican Family and the Bilingual Child.* April 1980.
Paper presented at the Annual Meeting of the American Educa-
tional Research Association, Boston, MA.

This study was designed to develop procedures for involving
Puerto Rican parents in curriculum decision making. A review
of the literature in related areas establishes a rationale
for parental involvement and forms the basis for developing
the procedures. Two procedures, a questionnaire, and a
parent interview were developed for the purpose of obtaining
input from Puerto Rican parents as to their perceptions of
the responsiveness of school curriculum to the needs of the
children. Results of the field testing of the questionnaire
are reported and recommendations for future research are
discussed.

Phelps. S. *Filipino Bilingual/Bicultural Program--Parents
Handbook.* Arlington, Virginia. ERIC Document, 1979.

This is a handbook written for parents whose children are
participants in a Filipino bilingual-bicultural program. The
handbook provides a description of the program, guidelines
for the establishment of the program, outcomes expected from
the program, and a student checklist.

*Project Parents: Awareness, Education, Involvement Program.
ESEA Title VII. Final Evaluation Report 1980-1981.* New York
City Board of Education, Brooklyn, NY. ERIC Document.
Washington, D.C.

This report describes an educational program for parents
with children enrolled in bilingual education programs. The
program addresses parental needs for instruction in English
as a second language. Instruction for a general equivalency
diploma and instruction in the language of the educational
system. Target language groups served are Spanish, French/
Creole, Italian, Greek, and Chinese. An overview of the program is presented, and characteristics of program participants
are described. Topics discussed include staffing, program
implementation, instruction, materials acquisition and de-

velopment, and staff development. It is concluded that the program is conceptually well-grounded. Recommendations are made for more effective program implementation.

Rodriquez, R. "Citizen Participation in Selected Bilingual Education Advisory Committees." *NABE Journal*, 1980, 5:1-21.

This study investigates the degree of citizen participation planned for by school districts of 15 Texas Title VII Advisory Committees. A five-level typology developed at Temple University was the primary research tool used to analyze the extent of influence exerted by Citizen Advisory Committees in formulating educational decisions. Research results indicate that no committee achieved the level of program decisionmaking participation established in P.L. 93-380. It was further observed that local school authorities tended to resist high levels of citizen participation and made provisions for increased participation only when pressured to do so by external forces.

Rothing, I.C. "Federal Policy in Bilingual Education." *American Education*, 1982, 30:30-40.

The author suggests that federal policy regarding the education of minority-language children has tended to favor bilingual-bicultural programs over alternative educational approaches which emphasize English-language instruction despite a lack of conclusive research evidence to support the effectiveness of one instructional approach over another. Mandates established by The Lau Remedies and Title VII legislation are cited as examples of federal measures which have exceeded the position adopted by the Supreme Court in *Lau v. Nichols*.

Valbuena, F.M., et al. *The Parent's Guide to Bilingual/Bicultural Education. Home, Child, School.* Detroit Public Schools, Michigan Department of Bilingual Education. ERIC Document. Washington, D.C., 1978.

This guide is the result of a parent-community workshop sponsored by the Detroit Public School System. The guide provides parents with the following information: a rationale for bilingual education, specifics of the 1974 Michigan Bilingual Education Law; information and techniques for effective parental involvement, the composition and function of the Detroit Public School network of Bilingual Education Advisory Committees, and a directory of Detroit Public School administrative and bilingual education staff.

Walker, M.P., and E.J. Ogletree. *Puerto Rican Parents' Knowledge of Attitudes Toward Bilingual Education.* ERIC Document.
Washington, D.C., 1978.

This study examines Puerto Rican parents' understanding of
and attitudes toward bilingual education. Responses were
obtained from an attitude survey administered to Puerto Rican
parents with children enrolled in bilingual programs and
Puerto Rican parents with children enrolled in English-only
programs. Responses indicated that parents whose children
were in bilingual programs had higher identity with and
higher expectations of the programs than parents with children
in English-only programs.

Your Children--Sus Niños: Your Schools--Sus Escuelas. Centennial School District, San Luis, Colorado. ERIC Document.
Arlington, Virginia, 1976.

This handbook, written in English and in Spanish, is developed for parents whose children are in a Title I bilingual
education program in the Centennial School District, San
Luis, Colorado. The functions of various education committees are described which serve to give parents a voice in
all phases of the decisionmaking process. These committees
include the Accountability Committee, the Title I Advisory
Council, the Bilingual/Bicultural Community Committee, and
the School Community Council. Parents are invited to attend
meetings on how to become active committee members.

Chapter 10

TEACHERS AND TEACHER TRAINING

One of the first problems encountered by those implementing the early bilingual programs was that of recruiting qualified personnel. Indeed, the problem was more basic than that.
There were many questions that needed to be answered before
establishing qualifications criteria. What is a qualified
bilingual teacher? What skills, competencies, and characteristics must teachers in bilingual programs have that teachers
in a monolingual program do not need? Is there more to teaching in a bilingual program than being able to transmit information in two languages? Is there a difference, besides language,
between teaching science in English and Chinese? Must teachers
be bilingual? Must they be bicultural?

These questions are still being debated and probably will
continue to be for a long time. Teacher preparation and certification is not an issue for which there will ever be a definitive solution or answer in bilingual or in any other approach
to education.

When the Cuban community in Miami began planning a bilingual program in the early 1960's, there were no Cuban teachers in the Dade County Public Schools. Six refugee teachers,
participating in the Cuban Teacher Retraining Program, were
selected to take twelve graduate credits and teach under temporary certificates (Mackey and Beebe, 1977).

The same problem faced Puerto Ricans in the northeast and
Chicanos in the southwest. Foreign-language programs in the
United States have been notoriously unsuccessful in producing
bilingual individuals. There were, therefore, very few certified teachers who could speak Spanish, much less teach it as a
language or use it as a medium of instruction. Teachers from
minority language groups were often bilingual but not biliterate. The latter presented two kinds of situations. On the
one hand, there were bilingual teachers, e.g., Chicanos, Puerto
Ricans, who could speak Spanish but could not read or write it,
never having studied it formally. Furthermore, they did not
know the terminology in Spanish for subjects like math and sci-

ence. On the other hand, this was not a problem for Cubans in
Miami, since that community included many teachers who had
been trained and worked as teachers in Cuba. The problem for
the Cuban teachers was that they were often weak in English.

School districts found several short-term solutions to
the problem of lack of bilingual personnel. Some districts
hired para-professionals, or aides, from the students' linguistic group. The aides would work with small groups of children in the native language. Sometimes the aides served as
interpreters mediating between the teacher and students.

Another solution mostly for Puerto Ricans in the northeast
was to recruit teachers from Puerto Rico. This solution, however, resulted in the same problem that was faced by the Cubans,
that often the teachers were weak in their English skills.
The answer to that problem was team-teaching, with each teacher
teaching only in his/her dominant language. This approach had
the salutary benefit of helping to allay fears of some monolingual English-speaking teachers that there was no place for
them in bilingual education with the implied threat to their jobs.

The issue of two teachers versus one has always been a
critical question. Many factors enter into this decision.
Philosophy is one important aspect of this issue. Many have
argued that teachers in bilingual education should be models of
bilingualism and should, therefore, be proficient at a college-
educated level of each language.

Although most bilingual education advocates would agree
that this is a worthy ideal, it was and remains a very difficult one to attain. Most teachers educated in Puerto Rico and
Cuba would be dominant in Spanish and significantly weaker in
English. On the other hand, teacher preparation programs in
the United States were not producing teachers proficient and
capable of teaching in two languages. For Miami, the answer
was two teachers and a team-teaching model. This was facilitated by the fact that the program would be a two-way model,
i.e., English-speaking children would participate in the program and learn Spanish as a second language. The model adopted
used a method that was sometimes called the "preview-review"
method. Subject matter was taught in the native language, by
native-language speaking teachers, in the morning. In the
afternoon, the teachers would exchange classes and review, or
reinforce, the subject matter in the second language.

This model has several advantages in terms of staffing.
First, teachers teach only in their dominant language, so students are hearing native-like language. In addition, teachers
are teaching in a language in which they have had experience
teaching: the educational terminology presents no problems.
Third, the fact that equal time is allocated to each language
serves to enhance the status of the target language.

In the first federally-funded bilingual programs in New York City, all teachers were bilingual and classes were self-contained. Instruction was begun in the students' native language (English or Spanish, since the programs were of the two-way maintenance model). ESL was taught by a specialist, and subject matter was gradually introduced in the second language by the bilingual classroom teacher, as students were deemed able to benefit from it.

HISTORY OF TEACHER PREPARATION FOR BILINGUAL EDUCATION

When the Bilingual Education Act was passed in 1968, there was no bilingual teacher training program anywhere in the United States. There was no bilingual teacher certification in fact. Many states still do not have bilingual certification. The large-scale experiment with bilingual education began with teachers who were bilingual and teachers who were monolingual, or clearly dominant in one of the two languages, and committed to the concept, but none had any training in teaching content matter in two languages.

The 1968 Bilingual Education Act included funds for:

> (b) providing preservice training designed to prepare persons to participate in bilingual education programs as teachers, teacher-aides, or other ancillary education personnel such as counselors, and in-service training development programs designed to enable such persons to continue to improve their qualifications while participating in such programs; P.L. 90-247, Jan. 2, 1968, Sec. 704 (b).

Two years later, Gaarder evaluated the first 76 federally funded bilingual programs and found: "To a large extent the projects expect to depend on the teaching services of aides, sometimes called para-professional, 'bilingual' individuals usually drawn from the community, rarely required to be literate in the non-English tongue and paid disproportionately low wages" (Andersson and Boyer, 1978).

The 1974 Amendment to the Bilingual Education Act attempted to remedy the shortage of qualified bilingual personnel by providing continued funding for training. It added a section on "Training" (Sec. 723) which contained very specific language and provisions. The law would provide funds for training teachers, administrators, para-professionals, teacher aides, and parents, as well as persons to teach and counsel such persons. It also provided for special training programs designed to meet individual needs and encourage reform and innovation.

272   Teachers and Teacher Training

In addition to undergraduate training programs, funds were provided for graduate programs, fellowships, and short-term training institutes.

The situation has improved somewhat since Gaarder's 1970 evaluation, largely as a result of the 1974 amendment, but there remains a large, unmet need for bilingual teachers. It is difficult to estimate both the demand and the supply of bilingual teachers (Kaskowitz, et al., 1981). The estimates of supply change depending on the qualifications requirements used. The Kaskowitz study found that if the most stringent qualifications requirements were applied ("language proficiency and training to teach language arts and other subjects to students whose language is other than English; post-secondary course work both in teaching English as a second language and in history, culture, or ethnic studies associated with students whose language is other than English"), the supply of available teachers nationally was 7,900. When minimal criteria were applied ("language proficiency and training to teach either language arts or other subjects to students whose language is other than English"), the supply jumped to 27,500 (p. 3).

The estimates of the need also vary according to the criteria used. If all students of LEP in public schools, grades K-12, were to be served, the need for bilingual teachers would be 112,000. However, if the criteria were the greatest need, elementary grades, and reasonable concentration of students, the need dropped to 24,300.

The study also found that, at most, 1,900 graduates of teacher-training programs enter the bilingual education field yearly. Furthermore, using the lowest estimate of need, holding the need constant, and allowing for attrition, at the rate at which bilingual teachers are being produced, it would take 19 years to fulfill the need found in 1980. If the number of LEP students increases as expected, they concluded that the need for qualified bilingual teachers would be greater in the year 2000 than it is at present.

The report of the Office of Bilingual Education and Minority Languages Affairs, of October 21, 1983, listed a total of 126 teacher-training programs at 128 institutions of higher education, funded under Title VII for 1983-84. Of these, 16 were continuation projects and 42 were new. The total amount awarded for all teacher-training programs was $10,259,012.

Most of the teacher-training programs funded by Title VII provide fellowships that pay tuition and, in some cases, stipends, fees, and books. State-funded institutions of higher education, which have relatively low tuition rates, can often maintain a viable bilingual teacher-training program once funds are no longer available. Private institutions, particularly those that are tuition-driven, often find it difficult to attract students when they must pay full tuition. If this trend continues, it is conceivable that there will be very few bilingual teacher-training programs in private institutions. Indeed, there are virtually no bilingual education degree programs in prestigious institutions. Those prestigious institutions that are producing professors and researchers active in bilingual education grant degrees in Teaching English as a Second Language, sociolinguistics, administration, etc., with an emphasis on bilingual education.

A review of the program descriptions of those institutions listed in the *Directory of Teacher Preparation Programs in TESOL and Bilingual Education* (1982) as granting degrees in bilingual education, reveals that most programs grant a degree in elementary or secondary education, with a concentration in bilingual education. Of the sixteen institutions listed as granting bachelor's degrees in bilingual education, only five have bilingual education majors. The remainder offer majors in elementary and secondary education with "special emphasis," "endorsement," or "concentrations" in bilingual education.

STATE CERTIFICATION REQUIREMENTS

Undergraduate or pre-service teacher-training programs are, to a great extent, designed to prepare students for certification. Most states have certification in early childhood, elementary, secondary, and special education. For the most part, states that have bilingual teacher certification have a "standard" or "regular" certificate with a "bilingual endorsement." The bilingual endorsement requirements from state to state run the gamut from Illinois, which in addition to a current valid certificate requires only evidence of capacity in ˙English and the target language, to states like Michigan, New Jersey, New Mexico, New York, and Wisconsin, all of which require 24 semester hours of work in bilingual education.

By 1982, 29 states had adopted certification requirements for teachers in bilingual programs. In general, they require teachers to have "regular" certification and some additional requirements. Most states require proficiency in English and in the students' native language although for the most part proficiency is not defined.

In the absence of stricter certification requirements, it is unlikely that institutions of higher education will offer undergraduate majors in bilingual education. It is easier for colleges and universities to design master's-level programs which are usually of 30 to 36 semester hours, approximately half of which are specifically in bilingual education. Indeed, even some of those courses are sometimes standard university courses

in linguistics, cultural anthropology, TESL, etc. Very often,
an institution needs to design only two or three new courses
and hire adjunct instructors.

This situation has resulted in extreme variation, not only
in the academic preparation of teachers in bilingual programs
but also in their skills and competencies.

Waggoner (1980) analyzed the findings of a 1976-77 survey
of teachers in bilingual programs conducted by the National
Center for Education Statistics "to determine whether their
backgrounds, experience, education, and skills qualified them
for teaching in bilingual education programs."

The survey revealed that fewer than half of the 42,000
teachers reporting that they were teaching through a language
other than English had had at least one course in bilingual
education. Furthermore, only 14 percent were prepared for
(a) teaching language arts in a non-English language, (b) teaching other subject areas through the minority language, and
(c) teaching ESL.

*What are the characteristics of a qualified
bilingual teacher?*

In 1974, the Center for Applied Linguistics (CAL) sponsored a conference for the purpose of developing guidelines
for the preparation and certification of teachers for bilingual
education programs. It provides the base for most of the certification documents and teacher training programs which have
been developed since. The CAL guidelines (appendix in Blatchford [1982]) stated "one cardinal principle which must be
rigidly observed throughout, namely that the teacher of bilingual-bicultural education should have the same quality academic
preparation as teachers of other subjects at comparable levels"
(p. 151). In addition, they listed the following as necessary
personal qualities:

1. A thorough knowledge of the philosophy and theory
   concerning bilingual-bicultural education and its
   application.
2. A genuine and sincere interest in the education of
   children regardless of their linguistic and cultural
   background, and personal qualities which contribute
   to success as a classroom teacher.
3. A thorough knowledge of and proficiency in the child's
   home language and the ability to teach content
   through it; and understanding of the nature of the
   language the child brings with him and the ability
   to utilize it as a positive tool in his teaching.
4. Cultural awareness and sensitivity and a thorough

knowledge of the cultures reflected in the two languages involved.

5. The proper professional and academic preparation obtained from a well-designed teacher training program
in bilingual bicultural education. (p. 151)

The competencies that would fulfill these personal characteristics are identified and listed under seven categories:

I. Language Proficiency--This is necessary in English and
the target language of the program. It is necessary to have
communicative skills for effective communication with parents
and children, as well as the ability to teach content matter
through both languages and the language arts of each language.

II. Linguistics--A knowledge of language in general, how
it works, who speaks what language, when, and to whom, regis-
ters, and styles, as well as specific knowledge about the English language and the target language are necessary for effective teaching in a bilingual program.

III. Culture--Study of cultural anthropology is desirable
if not necessary. Knowledge of what culture is, how it evolves,
how cultures conflict, and the interrelatedness of language and
culture are important for any teacher teaching students from
cultural backgrounds different from his/her own but particularly
so in bilingual-bicultural programs where the culture associated
with the students' native language is to be taught and reflected in the curriculum.

IV. Instructional methods--The teacher in a bilingual program must have a repertoire of methods in order to individualize
instruction to meet the needs of children at different levels
of first and second language development, and acculturation.
Methods have to be adapted and modified to fit the learning
styles of the students.

V. Curriculum utilization and adaptation--All teachers
need skills in this competency, but it is of particular importance to teachers of bilingual education. Curriculum is not
always available in the target language, and mere translation
has been found to be inadequate for the task. Teachers must be
able to insure that bilingual education students receive the
same quality of education as mainstream students.

VI. Assessment--Students' placement in a bilingual program, exit from the program and mainstreaming as well as progress throughout their participation in the program must be
assessed continually. Teachers must know how to administer,
interpret, and use the results of different types of test instruments. They must know how to develop tests to evaluate
classroom instruction.

VII. School-Community Relations--There is probably no program in the history of education in the United States that has

required more parental involvement than bilingual education. Parents throughout the country were instrumental in the struggle for securing legislation and funds to implement programs. Bilingual education teachers, more than teachers in any other type of program, need to have skills in developing positive school-community relations.

The literature on teacher preparation for bilingual education has increased significantly since CAL issued its guidelines. As new theories, methods, and techniques of teaching and of teacher training evolve, it is natural and necessary that bilingual educators discuss and study the implications for bilingual education.

Pascual (1979) believes that the competencies for bilingual education written into the existing "bilingual endorsements" that several state education agencies have adopted were problematical. "As one reviews these documents, it is impressive to see that most states emphasize competence in the non-English language, culture, and history of the students. However, very few states require verification of that competence through objective measurements" (p. 202).

In a survey of 136 bilingual teachers and aides in New Mexico, he found that 90 percent could not perform at a third-grade level of reading on the New Mexico State Department of Education Placement Test in Spanish. However, the responsibility for such a state of affairs, according to Pascual, lies with the teacher training institutions.

> Teachers go to universities to get credentials. It is there that the quality of preparation should provide for competence and performance. But in the universities we find that many professors also lack skills and content knowledge. They, like teachers, are victims, of the very system they are trying to correct. At this level one does not have to worry about certification, endorsement, or direct supervision. The result has been a terrible disregard for academic standards when dealing with the Spanish language and most aspects of the culture. (p. 222)

Of course, if bilingual education is viewed solely as a means to teach students English in order to mainstream them quickly, the situation found by Pascual will not be viewed as seriously as when the aim of the program is to develop bilingualism and biliteracy. In either case, however, Spanish-language instruction will suffer, as will the students' native language development which is important for second-language learning.

The issue of teacher competence in communication skills and content is probably the same for bilingual education as for

mainstream education. Much has been written in the popular
media recently about teacher difficulties in basic communication skills and in content area preparation. Most new teachers,
however, have a great deal of preparation in the theory and
practice of teaching. Pascual said of the teachers surveyed in
New Mexico, "In the area of pedagogy, a different picture
emerges. All possible aspects of methodology are dealt with,
and teachers' credentials seem to be replete with courses dealing with bilingual children and how to teach them."

A great deal of discussion has taken place about the need
to use, include, and reflect the students' culture in the bilingual program curriculum. However, this often translates
into celebrating holidays, food tastings, and musical programs.
The more difficult task of infusing the curriculum with the
values of the minority culture was largely left untouched.
Cazden and Leggett (1978) wrote: "The most important factor in
achieving culturally responsive education is the school staff.
It creates the learning environment in which children succeed
or fail." They continued:

> Because culture is largely a matter of implicit knowl-
> edge, it is not sufficient for Anglo teachers to take
> formal courses on non-Anglo language and culture. The
> Proposed Approach to Implement Bilingual Programs pre-
> pared by the National Puerto Rican Development and
> Training Institute is very clear on this point. Accept-
> ing the importance of ethnic foods, festivals, and
> courses on cultural history, the institute states:
>
>> But this is a limited interpretation of the concept
>> of culture. What seems to be forgotten is that cul-
>> ture is acquired by direct, frequent, varied parti-
>> cipation and experience in all aspects of the life
>> of a group of people. A very large part of this ac-
>> quisition occurs outside of the learner's awareness.
>> It follows that culture in this deep sense cannot be
>> taught in culture classes.
>
>> Culture can only be "taught" or transmitted if special
>> efforts are made to incorporate into the school, its
>> curriculum, its staff and activities as many aspects as
>> possible of the life of the cultural group to which
>> the learner belongs.... (pp. 32-33)

Banks (1981) discusses the necessary characteristics for
a teacher for multiethnic education in terms of what he describes as a multiethnic environment.

> A multiethnic environment does not necessarily have stu-
> dents within it from diverse ethnic and racial groups.
> It promotes norms, values, and behaviors that reflect

the ethnic and racial diversity in American society.
Such an environment can exist within an all-white sub-
urban school as well as within an inner-city school
that has a multiethnic student population. However,
many schools which have multiethnic student populations
cannot be characterized as multiethnic because of their
Anglo-centric norms, behaviors, and values.

He continues, elaborating on the characteristics teachers
need to acquire in order to be successful in a multiethnic
environment:

To function effectively within multiethnic educational
environments, teachers need to acquire: (1) more democratic attitudes and values; (2) a multiethnic philosophy; (3) the ability to view events and situations from
diverse ethnic perspectives and points of view; (4) an
understanding of the complex and multi-dimensional nature
of ethnicity in American society; (5) knowledge of the
stages of ethnicity and their curricular and teaching
implications; and (6) the ability to function at increasingly higher stages of ethnicity.

Although Banks talks about multiethnic educational environments, his remarks have relevance for bilingual settings as
well.

Rodriguez (1980) studied the apparent differences between
outstanding and mediocre bilingual education instructors at the
elementary level, in an attempt to lay the foundation for defining "generic and causal competencies for effective bilingual
teachers." She found several areas of competency in successful
elementary level bilingual teachers:

(1) High level of communication skills, "that is the
    ability to relate effectively with children and
    parents."
(2) Positive regard for students--"effective bilingual
    teachers put themselves in the child's situation.
    They recognize and at times even anticipate what
    the child's emotional reaction to a situation might
    be."
(3) Flexibility in both curricular content and methodol-
    ogy. This included a non-authoritarian and egali-
    tarian style.
(4) "Socio-cultural knowledge"--Sufficient fluency in
    the target language to communicate effectively
    through it, is required. Knowledge of and apprecia-
    tion of the children's cultural lifestyle and valu-
    ing the importance of the children's first language
    are important, as is commitment to the philosophy
    and theory of bilingual education.

Migdail (1979) found little difference among university programs in bilingual-bicultural education, except for regional differences in emphasizing "local ethnic folklore or history." She identified 18 courses as representative of the courses being offered in bilingual teacher education programs around the country. Respondents from institutions of higher education around the country rank-ordered the 18 courses from very important to never important. The list of courses by order of importance for all respondents was:

1. The Teaching of Reading--Spanish
2. The Teaching of Reading--English
3. Study of the Language Least Known
4. Study of Sociocultural Differences
5. Content Courses Made Available in Spanish and in English
6. Home-Family Relations of the Spanish-Speaking Population (local)
7. Bilingual Diagnostic--Prescriptive Techniques
8. Oral Language Assessment Techniques
9. History of the Local Ethnic Community
10. The Teaching of Mathematics--English
11. Bilingual Implications--Educational Psychology
12. Bilingual Implications--Classroom Management
13. The Teaching of Mathematics--Spanish
14. Literature of the Local Ethnic Community
15. Contrastive Linguistics
16. Research Methods--Bilingual
17. Philosophy of Education Related to Latin America
18. Practicum of Intern Training Given in Puerto Rico or Mexico. (p. 119)

It is interesting that there were no course offerings in TESL or in language development. One of the recurring criticisms of bilingual education is that students are not learning English quickly enough and are, consequently, being held in bilingual programs too long. The criticism may or may not be valid, depending on the program and the evaluation. Where there may be validity to the criticism, there may be a conflict between the philosophy of the educators and the letter of the law mandating the transitional programs. Nevertheless, whether a program aims for quick transition or for bilingual-bicultural maintenance, teaching English as a second language is crucial, and an understanding of language acquisition, development, and learning is critical to successful teaching of ESL.

There was an understandable amount of agreement among geographic regions on the rank ordering of three courses--Teaching Reading in English and Spanish and Content Courses Made Available in Spanish and in English. These were ranked among the

top five by respondents in the Southwest, Northeast, and the
Southeast. The Midwest ranked Content Courses Made Available
in Spanish and in English as No. 6.

It is not surprising that there were no courses among the
18 dealing with any language other than English and Spanish.
This situation will probably need to be addressed in the near
future as increasing numbers of Southeast Asians continue to
enter the country.

The MERIT Center at Temple University developed a teacher
training model for multicultural settings (Sutman, et al.,
1979). Six premises serve as the foundation of the model:

1. It is unrealistic to think that the conventional
   undergraduate four-year curriculum will include all
   of the experience essential to the many competencies
   expected of the beginning teacher in any classroom,
   much less the bilingual classroom.

This implies both the need for reform of the conventional
four-year curriculum, as well as the need for in-service training. Out of 178 programs in TESOL and/or Bilingual-Bicultural
Education listed in the 1981-1984 Directory of Teacher Preparation Programs in TESOL and Bilingual Education, only 16 offered
a baccalaureate program in Bilingual Education and 18 in TESL.
This means that very few new teachers will be prepared, at
graduation, for the specific requirements for teaching in bilingual education. These must be addressed in inservice programs.

2. A mature and effective approach to teaching evolves
   only over a period of several years.

This, too, implies the need for continued inservice education. Teachers need time to implement what they learned in the
preservice (baccalaureate) programs. They need to try out varied
styles and decide on what their own style is. It is only in the
classroom what they can begin to see the practical issues and
problems of current trends and techniques.

3. To develop effective teacher education programs it is
   essential to distinguish among different levels of
   competencies.

While elementary school teachers in a bilingual program
need to have some knowledge of tests, their administration, and
uses, they do not need to go into a great deal of depth into
issues such as reliability, and validity, item contruction, etc.
A low level of competency is sufficient. On the other hand,
an elementary school teacher should have a much higher level
of competency in teaching reading.

4. Competencies generally considered essential for outstanding teaching in most academic areas are also essential for the bilingual teacher. Additional competencies, however, are needed for effective performance in bilingual situations.

The additional competencies are all target-language related. Bilingual teachers need to know the native language and culture of their students. Ideally, they ought to be able to teach through the medium of their students' L_1, as well as the language arts, history, and culture associated with it.

5. In any bilingual program the teaching of English is an important and integral part of helping students to be able to use English as well as their mother tongue.

It is important that every teacher in a bilingual program, not just the ESL teacher, have minimal competency in teaching ESL. The high school subject teacher can use ESL techniques in social science courses to help students develop their English language skills as they learn content. The elementary-school classroom teacher can incorporate ESL techniques in the content area so that the ESL component is an integrative one. Helping students learn English will help them improve their native language because the formal study of a foreign language always reinforces one's native language.

6. Quality teaching is sustained and burnout is minimized by teachers who maintain a reasonable balance between the art of teaching and the science of education. (p. 45)

According to Sutman, et al., most beginning teachers "reveal a larger emphasis on the artistic aspect of their work." Experience and quality inservice training are required for teachers to develop this balance.

These premises form the foundation of the teacher training model developed at the MERIT Center. The model incorporates the managerial teaching strategy as appropriate for bilingual education. Teachers using this strategy become "managers of educational activity" or "organizers of learning experiences." Students assume much of the responsibility for their learning, mainly by asking questions and seeking answers.

Managerial teaching with emphasis on personalization of instruction assumes optimum significance in classrooms where there are children speaking in two, three, or more different languages—a situation not at all uncommon in urban schools and becoming more common in rural schools.

Two issues emerge as possible problems in terms of manage-

rial teaching in bilingual education. In the first place,
most teaching in institutions of higher education uses the
lecture and discussion format. Therefore, teachers will not
have any experience in either learning or teaching via the
strategy. "Teacher education programs for bilingual teachers
must not only exemplify managerial teaching strategy, but must
also provide future bilingual teachers with opportunity, under
supervision, to test out their competence to handle it themselves" (Sutman, 1979, p. 51).

Secondly, managerial teaching leaves a great deal of the
responsibility for learning to the students. This can create
problems since students already conditioned to learning in
more traditional ways may find the managerial strategy difficult.

INSERVICE TRAINING

Although the literature on teacher training for bilingual
education does not deal in great depth with inservice training,
most of the training which takes place is, in fact, inservice.
As we discussed earlier in this chapter, most of the training
is conducted at the master's degree level. Most of those participating are full-time teachers in bilingual programs. Many
master's degree students pursue the degree to fulfill requirements necessary for tenure and salary increases.

Very few school districts have clearly defined inservice
training requirements and programs in place. By and large,
the requirements deal only with semester hours beyond the
bachelor's degree in the teacher's major subject or area.

Arawak (1982), in a study of inservice training needs in
Title VII programs, stated that inservice education has been
controlled by colleges and universities. This study concluded
that inservice training should be planned on the basis of a
local needs assessment which should involve the school board,
administration, teachers, staff, parents, and professional
associations.

In a study of the inservice training components of 72
funding proposals for Title VII grants, the researchers found
that most needs assessments were conducted without any systematic criteria. They were unable to assess the extent or participation in the needs assessments of a broader community, i.e.,
teachers, other staff, and parents. They argue that teacher-
training programs should be collaborative ventures among all
these parties. They should also make greater use of district
staff, rather than rely solely on the colleges and universities,
and consultants.

It is clear that if inservice training is to have real

value, it must prepare teachers to apply new methods and techniques, use new materials and technology, adapt and utilize
new concepts in the classroom. This can only be achieved
through inservice training that is designed to respond to
clearly identified and articulated needs in a process that involves all the parties with a stake in the outcome.

SUPERVISION OF BILINGUAL TEACHERS

There is a dearth of literature and research on supervision and evaluation of teacher performance in bilingual education. There is a need for research to study the supervision
needs with a view toward answering questions such as whether
there is a difference between supervising, observing, and evaluating teachers in bilingual education and teachers in monolingual programs. What professional and personal characteristics
and qualifications must a supervisor in bilingual education
have? Is the supervisory relationship in bilingual education
programs essentially similar to or different from that in monolingual programs?

In addition, evaluation instruments must be developed that
reflect the competencies and skills in culture, language, linguistics, and bilingual teaching methods and techniques that
distinguish teaching in bilingual education programs from
teaching in monolingual programs. The MERIT Center at Temple
University developed an "Evaluation Profile for Areas of Performance for Teachers in Bilingual Settings" which contains ten
items, each of which has from five to nine operational definitions. The profile analyzes teacher performance in a good deal
of detail. As with every instrument for evaluating behavior
or performance, not every criterion is objectively measurable.
For example, one operational definition states: "Conducts self
with enthusiasm and animation." Such a statement is clearly
vulnerable to supervisor subjectivity. However, the instrument
does deal with the areas specific to bilingual education, such
as use of the native language, understanding the role of ESL,
and use of appropriate bilingual materials.

Another instrument adopted by the Temple University program is the "Self-Evaluation Profile for Teachers in Multicultural and Bilingual Situations" (Sutman, 1979). This profile deals with the issues of knowledge and understanding of
the culture. It can be used by Anglo teachers to evaluate
their knowledge about their students' culture, as well as by
language-minority teachers to evaluate their knowledge and
understanding of the Anglo culture. Each question is posed in
terms of "How much do I know about...?" There is a need for a
strategy, protocol, instrument or method for evaluating to what

extent the "knowledge" in the self-evaluation profile is reflected in the teaching performance.

TEACHER AIDES

     Teacher aides have been part of bilingual education pro-
grams in the United States since the beginning. Many programs
hired teacher aides from the students' linguistic group to work
with monolingual English-speaking teachers. The use of aides
has varied widely from program to program, depending on the
aides' educational level and experience, and on the teachers'
attitudes and skills in working with aides.
     Gaarder (1970) found that projects in the first two years
of federally funded programs depended on aides who were sometimes not literate in either language. On the other hand, some
aides had been experienced teachers in Cuba and Puerto Rico.
They often worked as aides while they took courses preparatory
for certification and some went on to become teachers.
     Many aides are relegated to doing the type of task that
will free the teacher to spend more time on teaching and planning. Aides are used to take attendance, collect milk and lunch
money, take children to the bathroom, duplicate materials, correct papers, and supervise lunchrooms and playgrounds.
     When teachers feel comfortable, and know how to utilize
them, aides can be used for working with small groups in arithmetic, reading, reading readiness skills, storytelling, and
much more. Teachers need to learn how to work with aides.
Aides usually need guidance, instruction, and time to plan with
the teacher if they are to be used to assist in instruction.
     Unfortunately, aides who assume, or are given, a great
deal of responsibility for teaching are not compensated adequately. "Ironically, while the role of the aide is being
modified out of necessity, attitudes, pay, and educational
advantages are not. The marked change in responsibility has
not been accompanied by increased salary, professional respect,
or educational opportunity" (Seymann, 1979, p. 4).
     Although many training programs for bilingual teachers
have been implemented since the passage of Title VII, the same
is not the case for bilingual aides. Much has been written on
teacher preparation and certification and models of teacher
training have been developed, but very little has been written
about and for teacher aides. LaFontaine (1971), advocating the
use of aides, stated that requirements were minimal since they
were used for non-instructional purposes.
     Perez (1971) talked of a larger role for aides and men-
tioned the need for planning, training, and certification.
     The most in-depth treatment of the topic of teacher aides

in bilingual education was undertaken by Seymann (1979). She developed a grid of competencies for aides in four categories. A questionnaire was then developed containing 341 questions stated as tasks in the four categories of language skills, cultural attitudes, knowledge of bilingual processes, and educational skills. It was found that the skills, or competencies, needed by bilingual teacher aides were:

A. Speaking Spanish
B. Reading Spanish
C. Writing Spanish
D. Analyzing the sound system of English and Spanish
E. Teaching history, culture, and music of the Mexican-American people
F. Identifying how culture manifests itself in behavior
G. Articulating the basic theory of bilingual education
H. Explaining current methodology and testing in bilingual education
I. Planning lessons
J. Developing bilingual materials
K. Teaching subject matter in Spanish
L. Teaching reading in Spanish. (pp. 51-52)

Obviously the responsibilities of aides have changed if the above list is a true reflection of the skills aides need to have to function in bilingual classrooms.

It is also obvious that aides will not develop the necessary skills without programs of preservice and inservice training. However, if we are going to require aides to pursue more education and develop higher level skills, it will be necessary to compensate them, certify them, and give their profession some respect and status.

CONCLUSION

An educational program is only as good as its teachers-- bilingual education is no exception. Although the federal government has put some funds into teacher training, it has been found that at the present rate of producing bilingual teachers, the need will be greater by the year 2000 than it is now. It is clear that a greater commitment to preparing the necessary teachers is needed at the federal and state levels. Although the need continues to be great for Spanish-speaking teachers, there is also an increasing need for qualified certified teachers in many other languages. States need to develop more stringent certification criteria which will lead to the institutionalization of the necessary programs at the undergraduate level. Inservice teacher and aide training needs to

be planned based on an assessment of needs at the local level
which includes broad-based participation to ensure that the
community's goals and needs are addressed.

REFERENCES

Andersson, T., and M. Boyer. *Bilingual Schooling in the United States.* Texas: National Educational Laboratory Publishers, 1978.

Arawak Consulting Corporation. "A Study of the Inservice Training Needs Assessment Activities and Procedures in Title VII Basic Bilingual Education Programs." Washington, D.C., National Institute of Education, 1982.

Banks, J.A. *Multiethnic Education: Theory and Practice.* Boston: Allyn and Bacon, 1981.

Blatchford, C.H. *Directory of Teacher Preparation Programs in TESOL and Bilingual Education: 1981-1984.* Washington, D.C.: TESOL, 1982.

Cazden, C.B., and E.L. Leggett. "Culturally Responsive Education: A Discussion of Lau Remedies." In *Bilingual Education Paper Series,* 1978, Vol. 2, No. 2, September. National Assessment and Dissemination Center, California.

Center for Applied Linguistics. *Guidelines for the Preparation and Certification of Teachers of Bilingual-Bicultural Education.* Arlington, Virginia: Center for Applied Linguistics, 1974.

Gaarder, B.A. "The First Seventy-Six Bilingual Education Projects." In Alatis, J.E. (ed.), *Report of the Twenty-First Annual Round Table Meeting on Languages and Linguistics: Georgetown University.* Monograph Series on Languages and Linguistics. No. 23. Georgetown University Press, Washington, D.C., 1970.

Irizarry, R.A. *Bilingual Education: State and Federal Legislative Mandates: Implications for Program Design and Evaluation.* Los Angeles: National Dissemination and Assessment Center, undated.

Kaskowitz, D., J.L. Binkley, and D.M. Johnson. *Study of Teacher Training Programs in Bilingual Education.* California: RMC Research Corp., 1981.

288   *Teachers and Teacher Training*

LaFontaine, H. "Paraprofessionals: Their Role in ESOL and Bilingual Education." *TESOL Quarterly*, 1971, 5:309-314.

Mackey, W.F., and Beebe, V.N. *Bilingual Schools for a Bicultural Community: Miami's Adaptation to Cuban Refugees*. Rowley, MA: Newbury House, 1977.

Migdail, S.R. *An Analysis of Current Select Teacher Training
Programs in Bilingual/Bicultural Education and the Develop-
ment of New Teacher Training Designs*. California: R & E
Research Associates, 1979.

Pascual, H.W. "Clients and Teachers in Bilingual Education
Programs." In *Bilingual Education Paper Series*. Vol. 3,
1979, No. 5, December. National Dissemination and Assessment
Center, Los Angeles.

Perez, C. "Auxiliary Personnel in Bilingual Education." Paper
presented at the Fifth Annual TESOL Convention in New Orleans,
March (ERIC Doc. ED 052648) 1971.

Rodriguez, A.M. "Empirically Defining Competencies for Effec-
tive Bilingual Teachers: A Preliminary Study." In *Bilingual
Education Paper Series*, Vol. 3, No. 12, July 1980. National
Dissemination and Assessment Center, Los Angeles.

Seymann, M.R. *The Bilingual Teacher Aide: Competencies and
Training*. Texas: Dissemination and Assessment Center for
Bilingual Education, 1979.

Sutman, F.X., E.L. Sandstrom, and F. Shoemaker. *Educating
Personnel for Bilingual Settings: Present and Future*. The
American Association of Colleges for Teacher Education,
1979.

Waggoner, D. *State Certification Requirements for Teachers
for Bilingual Education Programs*. National Center for
Education Statistics. U.S. Department of H.E.W. NCES 77-239,
1976.

ANNOTATED BIBLIOGRAPHY

Acosta, R.K., and G. Blanco. *Competencies for University Programs in Bilingual Education*. U.S. Office of Education (DHEW), 1978.

Guidelines for bilingual programs in institutions of higher education. Includes competencies for undergraduate, Master's, and doctoral levels. Covers the planning of bilingual teacher training programs including fiscal, personnel, facilities, collaboration with community, and selection of students. Useful for institutions contemplating instituting bilingual teacher training programs.

Brisk, M.E. "Bilingual Higher Education Programs. Their Impact on Institutions and Community." *Bilingual Education Paper Series*, Vol. 2, No. 3. October, 1978. National Dissemination and Assessment Center.

Describes the status of bilingual teacher-training programs. Discusses the type of personnel needed to serve the needs of bilingual children and the kinds of training programs needed to train the personnel. States that evaluation of programs should consider their effects on the school, the community, and the institution.

Carrillo, F.M. *The Development of a Rationale and Model Program to Prepare Teachers for the Bilingual-Bicultural Secondary School Programs*. California: R & E Research Associates, 1977.

This monograph attempts to fill the void in terms of teacher training for bilingual secondary education. Most teacher training programs have concentrated on elementary education. Discusses rationale and provides general objectives and minimum levels of performance for participants. Lists and describes suggested courses. The model is targeted to bilingual education for Mexican-Americans.

Fonselon, J.F., and R.L. Light, eds. *Bilingual, TESOL and*

*Foreign Language Teacher Preparation: Models, Practices,
Issues.* TESOL, Washington, D.C. Georgetown University,
1977.

Twenty-six papers divided into two groups reflecting two
positions--the first that teacher training programs are
adequate and the second, that there is a need for strict
guidelines and reform of programs. Section 2 describes the
practices in teacher preparation programs. Section 3 presents arguments for and against the issues in the previous
sections.

Fantini, M.D., and R. Gardenas, eds. *Parenting in a Multicultural Society.* New York: Longman, 1980.

A book of readings that looks at parenting across cultures.
Teachers in bilingual education should find the papers on
Puerto Rican, Mexican-American, Asian, and Native American
parenting of particular interest. Part 4: "Improving Parenting at Home and in the School" should be of interest to bilingual educators.

Gonzalez, E.S. *A Bibliography of Bilingual Teachers: Competencies, Certification, and Training.* Virginia. National
Clearinghouse for Bilingual Education, 1981.

Approximately 40 entries list requirements for certification, training models, teacher supply and demand, and much
more. Each entry has an abstract and information on availability of material.

Hidalgo, F. "Bilingual Teacher Education: An Assortment of
Emerging Issues." *California Journal of Teacher Education,*
8:56-68.

Examines bilingual teacher education in California. The
issues discussed include the status of bilingual teachers;
competencies for bilingual teachers; and bilingual secondary
and vocational teacher education. Recommendations are given
for teacher training institutions. Individuals and departments concerned with the education of bilingual teachers may
wish to learn from the experiences in California which are
described here.

Jones, P.A. "Teaching the Bilingual Reader." *Bilingual Journal*, 1980, 5:6-8.

A survey of 98 teachers to determine their needs in terms
of reading instruction. Fewer than half were prepared to
teach reading and ESOL. Concludes that there is need for

inservice training in 5 specific areas. Of interest to program administrators in planning training activities.

Lee, M. *Multicultural Teacher Education: An Annotated Bibliography of Selected Resources.* Vol. III. Washington, D.C. American Association of Colleges for Teacher Education, 1980.

Compiles resources and references for use in teacher education programs, appropriate for inservice, preservice, and graduate classes. Materials cited were drawn from various sources, including journals and newsletters, and special articles dealing with multicultural education. A list of organization resources is included in the volume. (ERIC, June 1982, p. 22446)

National Clearinghouse for Bilingual Education. *Bibliography of Resources in Bilingual Education.* Curricular Materials. National Clearinghouse for Bilingual Education, 1980.

Lists and describes over 400 products for bilingual education. Five indexes facilitate locating the material desired. The indexes are Author, Languages, Subjects, Series Titles, and Titles. Each entry includes the language(s), target grades, and annotation.

National Clearinghouse for Bilingual Education. *Guide to State Education Agencies.* Washington, D.C. Resources in Bilingual Education Series, 1979.

Lists persons, telephone numbers, addresses in 50 states and territories in bilingual education at SEA. Includes Title VII programs, types, and funding. Summarizes state bilingual education laws and teacher certification requirements. Includes lists of required textbooks in bilingual education programs.

Politzer, R.L. *Some Reflections on the Role of Linguistics, in the Preparation of Bilingual/Cross-Cultural Teachers.* Bilingual Education Paper Series, Vol. 1, No. 12, July 1978. 16 pp. California. National Dissemination and Assessment Center.

Highlights the important changes in linguistics theory and research which have surfaced since 1958. The author warns that no one component of bilingual education preparations (i.e., linguistics, cultural understanding, teaching methodology, nor knowledge of the target language) is "sufficient" or "overwhelmingly important" by itself. The bilingual/cross-cultural specialist must have comprehension training, and all the components are interrelated.

Reilly, M.T., M. Libb, and D. Suave, compilers. *Guide to Resource Organizations for Minority Language Groups*. Virginia. National Clearinghouse for Bilingual Education, 1981.

A very useful guide to 242 organizations. For each organization, a contact person, purpose, funding sources, geographical area, and publications, if any, are given. Four indexes, Language, Location, Target Cultural Groups, and Subjects, are provided.

Trueba, H.T., and C.B. Mizrahi. *Bilingual Multicultural Education and the Professional*. Massachusetts: Newbury House Publishers, Inc., 1979.

Readings on the major topics in bilingual education. Teachers will find section 6 on "The Teaching of Content Areas" of particular interest. It deals with topics such as "Science Teaching in the Bilingual Classroom," "Cultural Diversity and Science Teaching," and mathematics and learning a second language.

Waggoner, D. "Teacher Resources in Bilingual Education: A National Survey." *NABE Journal*, 3:53-60, 1979.

An analysis of the 1976-77 survey of teachers in bilingual education. The findings, based on response from 42,000 teachers involved in bilingual education programs, present the gap between stated desired qualifications and the reality.

Whitmore, D.R. "Partners for Bilingual Education." *Bulletin of the Association of Departments of Foreign Languages*. Vol. 7, No. 2, pp. 17-19. November 1975.

Discusses the role of professional educators outside of the field of bilingual education--such as foreign language professors and linguists--who have the expertise to play an important part in the education of bilingual-bicultural teachers. Administrators of all university departments may be enlightened by this article, as educational departments and their bilingual components may need the cooperation and instruction of all university departments to improve the quality of education for all the students, bilingual and monolingual as well. (June 1982, ERIC p. 2240)

Wisconsin University School of Education. *An Urban-Oriented Fieldwork and In-Circuit Television Based Teacher Training Program for Bilingual/Bicultural Education Focusing on Teachers of Limited English Speaking Ability School Age Students: A Model Program for the Urban Midwest Schools*, 1977.

Details a program for the preparation of certified teachers of limited-English-speaking-ability students for bilingual/ bicultural education programs. The four-year degree program leads to Wisconsin certification. This comprehensive report describes the process utilized for the selection of trainees, coordination between university and local educational agencies, and collaboration with the center for Latin America. The text appendices provide sample correspondence and forms to implement similar programs.

Young, J., and J. Lum. *Asian Bilingual Education Teacher Handbook*. Cambridge, Massachusetts: Evaluation, Dissemination and Assessment Center for Bilingual Education, 1982.

This handbook contains useful information for teachers of Asian students. The chapter on "The Asian and the Asian-American Learner" provides an extensive list of sources of information as well as references on Chinese, Japanese, and Korean. The appendices provide a wealth of information.

Chapter 11

ANTIBILINGUALISM

For many decades the United States was regarded as the great melting pot of the world. Although the Constitution of the United States does not designate an official language, immigrants were expected to shed their native languages and cultures and assume a new identity: that of the English-speaking North American. With time the melting pot theory has yielded to a wider acceptance of cultural diversity in American society, and the usage of languages other than English is tolerated though not always accepted. To a great extent, the changes in attitudes and expectations about linguistic minorities occurred through the efforts of community activists and legislators who brought to the fore the inequities suffered by limited-English-speaking persons (see Chapter 2).

Although today limitations in the ability to function in the English language are tolerated slightly more than in the past in this country, bilingual education continues to be a controversial educational alternative which raises numerous pedagogical, political, and social issues. Opponents of bilingual education level serious criticisms against an educational approach which utilizes a language minority child's mother tongue as an instructional medium. It has been said that bilingual programs hinder children's development of English language skills; constitute a barrier to assimilation into North American society; offer preferential treatment to language-different children; segregate ethnic minorities; lead to political fragmentation and promote anti-American attitudes. Let us look at these criticisms in detail.

BILINGUAL PROGRAMS HINDER CHILDREN'S DEVELOPMENT
OF ENGLISH LANGUAGE SKILLS

A claim which has not been supported by research is the misconception that teaching limited English proficient children in the native language while they acquire English will retard

or impede their acquisition of the second language. What the
research on bilingualism has shown is that language minority
children who have a strong foundation in the native language
will acquire a second language effectively and with minimal
effort. Schooling should be started in the child's dominant
language and the second language introduced later. Research
has consistently confirmed this pedagogical theory in the
United States (Arnold, 1968; Dube and Hebert, 1975; Ehrlich,
1971; Golub, 1978; Pryor, 1968; Rosier and Farella, 1976), in
Mexico (Castro de la Fuente, 1966; Modiano, 1968; Vasquez-
Barrera, 1953), and Sweden (Skutnabb-Kangas, 1979). Children
who have succeeded in learning a second language in school
before receiving instruction in the native language are children enrolled in immersion programs in Canada and the United
States. In these cases, the children spoke the language of
the majority (they were not ethnic or linguistic minorities).
They were respected members of society who spoke the dominant
language. It has been found that in immersion programs, the
status of the language and the students' attitudes toward the
first and second languages influence the success of these programs (Barik, Swain and McTavish, 1974; Lambert and Tucker,
1972; Cohen, 1974).

Children who have difficulty mastering the second language
are usually those whose native language skills have not developed well before the second language is introduced. This may
occur in situations where children are placed in submersion
or sink-or-swim programs when they start school, children who
are shifted back and forth between bilingual and monolingual
English programs, and children who attend schools in which educational policies require the introduction of English as a
second language regardless of whether the child is ready. If
a LEP child enters school and is allowed to develop strong
linguistic skills in the dominant language, including reading
and writing skills, the acquisition of English as a second language will occur effortlessly.

BILINGUAL PROGRAMS CONSTITUTE A BARRIER TO
ASSIMILATION INTO AMERICAN SOCIETY

The use of the native language in bilingual education programs is seen as an attempt to obstruct the assimilation of
linguistic minorities into the mainstream. Yet an important
component of any bilingual program in the United States is the
English-as-a-second-language (ESL) program. The most common
bilingual education model is transitional in nature, that is,
the use of the mother tongue is used only to the extent that
it is necessary for the child's acquisition of content area

knowledge. Instruction in English is gradually augmented until
the child has made a transition into the monolingual English
class. The goal of bilingual education is precisely to ease
the transition from one language to another, from one culture
to another. In this context, bilingual education programs may
constitute direct and powerful tools to further assimilation.

The fact that a number of linguistic minorities continue
to seemingly defy assimilation is a result of several factors.
First, although it is expected that language minorities assimilate, this assimiliation is often made very difficult. Linguistic minorities are often segregated from the mainstream,
regarded as marginal beings and usually not respected members
of society. Because of this lack of acceptance by the mainstream, assimilation is difficult if not impossible for many.
Second, many linguistic minorities have consciously opted not
to assimilate, understanding that it is possible to live within
the context of two languages and two cultures without the
compulsion to sacrifice the native language and culture. Third,
the United States is increasingly becoming a pluralistic society
as waves of immigrants continue to arrive at its shores and
existing ethnic populations multiply. The 1980 U.S. Census
reveals that during the last decade there was a 71.8 percent
increase in the American Indian, Eskimo, and Aleut populations;
a 127.6 percent increase in Asians and Pacific Islanders; and
a 61 percent increase in Hispanics. In comparison there was a
5.8 percent increase in the White population and a 17.3 percent
increase in Blacks. As more limited-English-speaking persons
populate the country and cultural diversity becomes more prevalent, the pressures to assimilate are reduced.

BILINGUAL PROGRAMS OFFER PREFERENTIAL TREATMENT
TO LANGUAGE-DIFFERENT CHILDREN

When masses of immigrants arrived in the United States at
the beginning of the century no special treatment was accorded
by the educational system to their children. Today, linguistic
minorities are offered an education in the native language.
This "preferential treatment" to the linguistic minority groups
of today is viewed with resentment. What is frequently over-
looked is that the school populations have changed drastically
over the past decades because of compulsory attendance laws.
The progeny of early immigrants worked in the fields, in the
shops, in the factories, and very few had opportunities to attend school. Today linguistic minority children are attending
schools in massive proportions. Educational problems which did
not arise at the turn of the century acquired relevance as
school demographics changed drastically.

BILINGUAL EDUCATION PROGRAMS SEGREGATE
ETHNIC MINORITIES

It is true that bilingual education programs tend to segregate linguistic minority children from the mainstream. For
the most part, this is a temporary measure which must be weighed
against the cost of placing LEP children in monolingual classrooms where they will be unable to learn effectively. Eventually, children in bilingual programs are mainstreamed into
the English language classroom. Now, even when placed in
monolingual English classrooms, linguistic minority children
continue to experience segregation for reasons that have nothing
to do with bilingual education. The segregation of ethnic
minorities in our schools is a reflection of the segregation
they experience in housing and in jobs. Poverty and prejudice
play the crucial roles in segregating minorities in this
society.

BILINGUAL PROGRAMS LEAD TO POLITICAL FRAGMENTATION
AND PROMOTE ANTI-AMERICAN ATTITUDES

If language differences are allowed to prevail in the
United States, this will lead to extreme political differences
and secession movements. The strife between English-speaking
and French-speaking Québecois is heralded as an example of
what can occur in this country if bilingual education continues
to promote linguistic differences. Bilingual education is
often associated with activist, anti-American groups.

Bilingual education programs, notwithstanding their
secessionist, activist reputation, continue to foster an understanding of the American history and culture in linguistic
minority children. Bilingual education's philosophy of bilingualism and biculturalism is not a separatist notion of linguistic supremacy, but an attempt to provide linguistic minority
children with a dual language and dual cultural background.

The criticisms leveled against bilingual education are
frequently not the result of carefully researched studies or
systematic observations of bilingual classrooms. It appears
that where bilingual education is concerned, persons with no
qualifications are eager to utter outlandish opinions which are
published and disseminated throughout the country. Noel Epstein and Ricardo Rodriguez are two bilingual education critics
whose books have been used by bilingual education foes to jus-
tify antibilingual positions.

EPSTEIN

In 1977, Noel Epstein, a Washington journalist, published a scathing indictment against bilingual education (Epstein, 1977). In his book Epstein articulates many of the prevalent misconceptions of bilingual education.

Epstein contends that federal funds should not be used to support an educational approach that has generated no evidence of its effectiveness. According to Epstein, there is virtually no research supporting the effectiveness of bilingual education over other educational techniques for language minority children. Bilingual education, he states, is an experimental technique. Nevertheless, parents are not given alternatives to choose from. On the contrary, specific bilingual approaches are imposed upon their children although there has been no research done to prove that these approaches are the most beneficial. Although the goal of ESEA's Title VII is to identify children of limited-English proficiency and provide educational programs to meet their needs, Epstein argues that there exists a lack of language proficiency tests to determine eligibility for the program. A major consequence of this is that English-proficient children are occupying the places which should go to limited-English proficiency children in bilingual programs. Epstein further contends that bilingual education promotes ethnic segregation, an educationally and socially detrimental policy.

Epstein cites the AIR study results which indicate that bilingual programs had little positive impact on children's achievement. This report will be described in detail.

A shortage of qualified teachers and adequate curricula, according to Epstein, contribute to the low achievement levels of children in bilingual programs. Bilingual education is seen by the author as a means to create jobs for language minorities.

Epstein's major criticism revolves around the language maintenance issue in bilingual education. He feels that language maintenance programs are a problem because funds are allocated to educating English-dominant children instead of limited-English-proficiency children.

> Any federal funds spent to maintain the native languages of students who are proficient or dominant in English takes these limited resources from children who cannot learn in English and who therefore are most in need. (p. 27)

Epstein argues that language maintenance programs increase the segregation of ethnic minority students and teachers and can create political and social difficulties. He believes that if language minority children do not perform well in schools,

it may be due to their socioeconomic backgrounds rather than
their inability to function in English.

He summarizes his critique by stating that

> The USOE has made little progress in achieving the
> program's goals of identifying effective educational
> approaches, training bilingual education teachers and
> developing suitable materials. (p. 11)

He suggests that since immersion models have been so successful in Canada, this educational technique should be attempted in U.S. schools.

Finally, Epstein recommends five alternative policies for
Title VII:

1. A tighter definition of eligible children to ensure
   that students most in need are being reached.
2. Planned variation research to determine which techniques work best for different students.
3. A broadening of techniques tested to include special
   language immersion....
4. Increased funding for teacher training.
5. A federal curriculum role that concentrates on dis-
   seminating ideas and providing funds to local projects
   for adaptation to special needs and desires. (p. 63)

Although numerous research projects have evidenced the
effectiveness of bilingual programs (Troike, 1978), criticisms
such as Epstein's are frequently leveled against this educational option in newspaper editorials, professional journals
and books. Only one study has presented substantial data on
the ineffectiveness of bilingual programs. The study, performed
by the American Institutes for Research (AIR), finds serious
deficits in bilingual education programs nationwide. We will
review the study in detail, since the results have been used
by Epstein and other critics as evidence of the ineffectiveness
of bilingual education programs.

AIR STUDY

In 1974 the United States Office of Education contracted
with the American Institutes for Research (AIR) to conduct a
large-scale evaluation on the impact of the Title VII Spanish/
English bilingual education program at the national level
(Danoff, 1978). The AIR study reported the results of an evaluation performed during the 1975-76 academic year. The goals
of the study were to:

> (1) determine both the cognitive and the affective im-
> pact of bilingual education on students in Spanish/Eng-

lish bilingual education projects funded through ESEA
Title VII, (2) describe the educational practices which
result in greater gains in student achievement, and
(3) determine per-student costs associated with each
project. (pp. 1 and 2)

The bilingual education projects selected for evaluation were
in their fourth or fifth year of funding.

AIR researchers developed a study design in which the performance of two groups of students were contrasted: those enrolled in the bilingual projects and comparable students not
enrolled in the projects. Students from grades two through
six were pretested and post-tested in English oral comprehension
and reading, mathematics, and Spanish oral comprehension and
reading. In addition, information was gathered with student
questionnaires on students' ethnicity, socioeconomic status,
sex, age, as well as student attitudes toward school-related
activities. The training, experience, and bilingual proficiency of teachers and teacher aides were also evaluated
through a questionnaire. Data on classroom educational practices were gathered through staff interviews and on-site observations.

Over 11,500 students in 384 classrooms in 150 schools
across the United States were included in the impact study
sample. Three different methods were used to analyze the
data collected: standardized residual gain score analysis,
analysis of covariance, and comparison of pretest and post-
test percentile ranks.

Four areas of student achievement were evaluated: English
language arts, mathematics, student attitudes, and Spanish
language arts. English language arts and mathematics achievement were assessed by the Comprehensive Tests of Basic Skills
(CTBS), an achievement test. English and Spanish versions of
the mathematics tests were used. Students took the test in the
more appropriate language judged by the classroom teacher. The
Prueba de Comprension Auditiva Ingles (an ESL test) was also
used to measure auditory comprehension of English. Three student attitudes were measured by a student questionnaire administered in either English or Spanish: attitude toward English usage, attitude toward Spanish usage, and attitude toward
school and school-related activities. Two Spanish language
arts measures were analyzed: an orally administered Spanish and
a second language (SSL) test and Prueba de Lectura, a test of
Spanish reading.

Each project director was asked what occurs to a Spanish-
dominant child after he is able to function in school in English. Eighty-six percent reported that the child remains in
the bilingual program; 8 percent responded that the student is
transferred to an English-only classroom with some Spanish lan-

guage follow-up; 5 percent of the project directors responded
that the student is transferred to an English-only classroom
with no Spanish language maintenance. The AIR study concludes
that these findings reflect bilingual project activities which
run counter to the transition approach which is implied by the
ESEA Title VII legislation. Transition is defined in the AIR
study as an approach in which

> the native language of the student with limited English-
> speaking ability is used temporarily as a bridge to
> help the student gain competence in English ... when a
> student is able to function in a regular English instruc-
> tion classroom, he or she is transferred out of the bi-
> lingual project classroom. (p. 12)

Project goals, the AIR study maintains, were more consistent with a maintenance approach to bilingual education. Project goals often included the objective that the English-dominant student become fluent in Spanish as well as in English.
Maintenance is defined as an approach in which

> when a student is able to function in a regular English
> instruction classroom, he or she remains in the bilin-
> gual project to sustain or build competence in the
> native language and in English. (p. 12)

The teacher interviews and on-site observations revealed
that the goals stated by the project directors were being implemented in the program.

Personnel qualifications were also evaluated. It was
found that 85 percent of the Title VII teachers and 71 percent
of the aides said they had been teaching for two or more years;
78 percent of the teachers and 8 percent of the aides said that
they had a regular or bilingual teaching certificate; and 31
percent of the teachers and 1 percent of the aides said they
had a master's degree.

Sixty-five percent of the teachers and 65 percent of the
aides had two or more years of bilingual teaching experience.
Seventy-four percent of the teachers and 55 percent of the
aides had some college course work in bilingual education.
Ninety-four percent of the teachers and 80 percent of the
aides had attended inservice workshops in bilingual/bicultural
education in the last five years. Sixty-three percent of the
teachers and 51 percent of the aides reported having attended
a bilingual/bicultural conference during the last five years.

As far as degree of bilinguality in the staff, 67 percent
of the teachers and 90 percent of the aides said that they used
both Spanish and English in the home. Sixty-nine percent of
the teachers who had children and 88 percent of the aides said
that they used both Spanish and English with their children.

Sixty-nine percent of the teachers and 28 percent of the aides said they used both Spanish and English in speaking with their bilingual friends and 50 percent of the teachers and 66 percent of their aides said that they were proficient in both Spanish and English.

Results of the impact study:

According to the AIR study, the overall cross-grade Title VII student analyses showed that the Title VII Program did not appear to be having a consistent significant impact on student achievement in English language arts or mathematics. In general, across grades, when total Title VII and non-Title VII comparisons were made, the Title VII students in the study were performing in English worse than the non-Title VII students. In mathematics, across grades, they were performing at about the same level as non-Title VII students.

Regarding student attitudes, the AIR study concludes that participation in the Title VII program did not bring about a more positive student attitude toward school and school-related activities. In general, the students appeared to have a fairly neutral attitude (neither strongly positive nor strongly negative) toward school in both Title VII projects and non-Title VII schools.

In Spanish reading, the AIR study concludes that while no appropriate test norms or comparison groups were available to assess the relative impact of Title VII on the acquisition of Spanish reading, there was an increase in the scores on the Spanish Reading Test (Prueba de Lectura) between the pretest and post-test in the 1975-76 school year for Title VII students.

In analyzing classroom procedures, the AIR study found that the extent of grouping was significantly and positively related to gains in one or more of the tests used to assess English proficiency. That is, the greater the grouping and regrouping of students, the greater the gains in student achievement in English. In mathematics it was found that the more whole-class instruction there is, the less mathematics gains, the more grouping or individualized instruction, the greater the gains.

The extent of Spanish used in mathematics class was found generally to be unrelated to student gains in mathematics. That is, the teacher use of Spanish or the student use of Spanish during mathematics instruction does not appear to produce gains in mathematics.

There was also a consistent positive relationship between the extent of grouping and gains in the Spanish-as-a-second-language test scores. That is, the greater the grouping and regrouping of students, the greater the gains in student achievement.

The degree to which English is used in the home and neigh-

borhood, as measured by a parent questionnaire, was also found
to have no consistent relationship with gains in any of the
student test scores in English, Spanish, mathematics, or attitudes across grades.

According to the AIR study, teacher and teacher aide overall teaching qualifications have very little relationship to
student gains in English, mathematics, and Spanish or to a
more positive attitude on the part of students toward school
and school-related activities, attitude toward English usage,
or attitude toward Spanish usage.

An analysis of the AIR study reveals that methodological
flaws mar the evaluation. Serious problems can be identified
in the identification of the target population, the selection
of control groups, the test instruments, adequacy of staff,
to name a few. Specific examples follow:

1. Students were classified by teachers as either
   Spanish-dominant or English-dominant. This was a
   subjective determination, not a reliable measure of
   language proficiency. Furthermore, approximately
   50 percent of the teachers making language classification were monolingual English-speakers, rendering
   the classification invalid.
2. Comparison groups were chosen with no control for
   factors such as teacher training, teacher classification, and financial resource allocation.
3. Almost 50 percent of the projects were pre- and post-
   tested within five months or less.
4. Although programs varied as to instructional time,
   content, and methodologies, these differences were
   not controlled.
5. Only 26 percent of the teachers participating in the
   study had bilingual teaching credentials.
6. An analysis of the study indicates that 49.6 percent
   of the teachers in the study admit to not being proficient in the other language.
7. Only Spanish/English bilingual programs were selected.
8. The bilingual education programs selected for evaluation were in their fourth or fifth year of funding.
   Most studies on the effectiveness of bilingual education indicate that the full benefits of the program
   may not occur until the fifth or sixth year of
   instruction. (Cummins, 1981)

Epstein's treatise represents a lengthy essay propounding
the author's subjective view on bilingual education. He selectively mentions the AIR study as the only systematic and sound
research done on the effectiveness of bilingual programs. Yet
he fails to mention at least 24 methodologically sound studies

in this area. But, as an expression of the author's personal views, the criticisms are not damaging, since they are not based on sound educational research.

The AIR study, on the other hand, is a purportedly scientific study and the only nationwide evaluation of bilingual programs. The results of this study can be damaging. It is unfortunate that a study of this scope and importance does not evaluate what it purports to evaluate. One of its most serious faults is that the effects of bilingual instruction on limited-English-proficiency students were not assessed. Instead, the study's sample consists of predominantly English-proficient or English-dominant students. Therefore, the AIR findings do not provide any evidence, as sustained by Epstein, that bilingual education is ineffective.

Troike (1978), Dulay and Burt (1977), and Engle (1975) have written lengthy analyses of research projects which evidence the effectiveness of bilingual education. The chapter on evaluation in this book discusses the research evidence in depth.

RODRIGUEZ

In the first chapter of his autobiography, *Hunger of Memory*, Richard Rodriguez (1981) launches an attack on bilingual education, claiming that "it is not possible for a child--any child--ever to use his family's language in school" (p. 12). It is sad to read this searing autobiography of an intelligent man who is overwhelmed by a terrible loss. This is really a book about someone who confesses his inability to do two things well. For Rodriguez this is a tragedy because in order to do one thing well, that is acquire English, he had to choose between his parents (who spoke little English) and his second language and culture. Judging from his book, Rodriguez is still struggling with the guilt of abandoning his parents, his language, and his culture which are all the same thing.

Rodriguez's book is not a scholarly study. It is a memoir and a touching one at that. Although it rends the heart, it does not convince the mind. The emotive side in one reaches out to the author in sympathy, but the dedicated scholar finds the book a failure. Not in its intention, for it is an attempt to tell a story, but in its effect which has been to call into question bilingual education. The book has almost nothing to do with bilingual education and represents only one case out of hundreds of thousands. There are many other stories of equal merit and pathos in which the child succeeds in both cultures, in both languages. There are many memoirs that could be written by people who were equally torn apart and who succeeded in mas-

tering two languages and cultures (the authors of this book
are examples). This was not Rodriguez's life, so he did not
happen to write that book.

This is an extraordinary book, and it is sad that a few
disconnected paragraphs dropped irresolutely into the book
reveal Rodriguez's own anger at bilingual programs. Having
looked at many bilingual programs, we can understand his dis-
appointment. This is of course true of English language programs and no one would suggest doing away with English because
Russell Baker or William Safire writes about shabbily run English courses. The problem with Rodriguez's position is that
without conducting any research, he attempts to generalize
from his own sad case to indict bilingual education programs.

Instead of taking Rodriguez seriously as a scholar of
bilingual education, which he clearly is not and does not
claim to be, let us take him seriously as a writer of autobiography and a man who is willing to display both his pride
and his shame.

While we cannot deny that some bilingual education programs
are not working, the failures of these individual programs are
due to improper program implementation and not to bilingual
education's philosophy, pedagogical theories, or programmatic
models. In visiting bilingual education programs throughout
the country we have observed programs functioning under such
heavy constraints that they cannot fail to fail. Some examples:
Hispanic children placed in bilingual programs for the Chinese;
teachers who speak a smattering of the language and either teach
in a broken version of the children's language or teach in English; children who are concurrently taught in two languages with
the teacher switching back and forth between languages throughout the day; teachers hired to teach because they speak the
children's native language not because they have teaching qualifications; lack of materials and supplies; children taught reading and writing skills in English before they are orally proficient in the language; Cantonese children taught by Mandarin-
speaking teachers; English-as-a-second-language teachers with
no certification or training in second language teaching; lack
of supervisory and supportive staff; philosophical and ideologi-
cal opposition to bilingual education by school superintendents,
principals, and other school administrators.

These are just a few examples of improper implementation
of bilingual programs. When bilingual education programs function according to sound pedagogical practices, they are successful in achieving the educational goals and objectives expressed
in the letter and spirit of the law.

CONCLUSION

Americans' unwillingness to learn foreign languages is legendary. A recent article in *Newsweek* reports that less than 3 percent of secondary school students achieve "meaningful" competency in foreign languages, at least 20 percent of high schools do not teach foreign languages and only 8 percent of U.S. colleges have language requirements for admission (*Newsweek*, 1982). It appears that antibilingual sentiment will continue to plague our educational policies and programs as long as bilingualism is considered unimportant. While the political, social, economic, and enrichment benefits of bilingualism remain unrecognized in this country, the rest of the world continues to accept the values of bilingualism and promote its development. In the meantime, bilingual education programs must constantly contend with critics who use weak rationalizations and distorted justifications to selectively see only the weaknesses of the programs while refusing to acknowledge the gains accomplished by bilingual education.

REFERENCES

American Institutes for Research. *The Identification and Description of Exemplary Bilingual Education Programs.* Palo Alto, California, August 1975.

Arnold, R.D. "San Antonio Language Research Project 1956-66 (Year 2) Findings." ERIC Document Reproduction Service No. ED 022528, 1968.

Barik, H., M. Swain, and K. McTavish. "Immersion Classes in an English Setting: One Way for Les Anglais to Learn French." *Working Papers on Bilingualism.* Toronto: Ontario Institute for Studies in Education, 1974.

Castro de la Fuente, A. "La alfabetizacion en lenguas indigenas y los promotores culturales." Instituto Linguistico de Verano, Mexico, 1966.

Cohen, B. "The Culver City Immersion Program: The First Two Years." *Modern Language Journal,* 1974, 3:95-102.

Cummins, J. "Empirical and Theoretical Underpinnings of Bilingual Education." *Boston University Journal of Education,* 1981, 163:16-29.

Danoff, M.N. "Evaluation of the Impact of ESEA Title VII Spanish/English Bilingual Education Program, Volume II: Year Two Impact, Educational Process, and In-Depth Analyses." Palo Alto, CA: American Institutes for Research. ERIC Document Reproduction Service No. ED 154-634, 1978.

Dube, N., and G. Herbert. "Evaluation of St. John Valley Title VII Bilingual Education Project." Madawaska, ME, 1975.

Dulay, H., and M. Burt. *Learning and Teaching Research in Bilingual Education.* Washington, D.C.: National Institute of Education, 1977.

Ehrlich, A. "Bilingual Teaching and Beginning School Success." ERIC Document Reproduction Service No. ED 077279, 1971.

Engle, P.L. "The Use of Vernacular Languages in Education: Lan-

guage Medium in Early School Years for Minority Groups."
Papers in Applied Linguistics, 1975, Bilingual Education
Series No. 3, Arlington, VA: Center for Applied Linguistics.

Epstein, N. *Language, Ethnicity, and the Schools: Policy
Alternatives for Bilingual-Bicultural Education.* Washington,
D.C.: The George Washington University Institute for Educa-
tional Leadership, 1977.

Golub, L. "Evaluation, Design and Implementation in a Bilingual Education Program." *Education and Urban Society*,
1978, 10:363-382.

Lambert, W., and R. Tucker. *Bilingual Education of Children.*
Rowley, Mass.: Newbury House, 1972.

Modiano, N. "National or Mother Language in Beginning Reading:
A Comparative Study." *Research in the Teaching of English*,
1968, 1:32-43.

Newsweek. "The Slow Learners." November 15, 1982.

Pryor, G.C. "Evaluation of the Bilingual Project of Marlandale
Independent School District, San Antonio, Texas." ERIC
Document Reproduction Service No. ED 026158, 1968.

Rodriguez, R. *Hunger of Memory: The Education of Richard
Rodriguez.* Boston: David R. Godine, Publisher, 1981.

Rosier, P., and J. Farella. "Bilingual Education at Rock
Point: Some Early Results." *TESOL Quarterly*, 1976, 10:
379-388.

Skutnabb-Kangas, T. *Language in the Process of Cultural Assimilation and Structural Incorporation of Linguistic Minorities.* Arlington, VA: National Clearinghouse for Bilingual
Education, 1979.

Troike, R. "Research Evidence for the Effectiveness of Bilingual Education." *NABE Journal*, 1978, 3:13-24.

Vazquez-Barrera, A. "The Tarascan Project in Mexico. The Use
of the Vernacular Languages in Education." *UNESCO Monographs
on Fundamental Education VIII*, 1953, 77-86.

ANNOTATED BIBLIOGRAPHY

Cordasco, F. "Bilingual Education in American Schools: A
Bibliographical Essay." *The Immigration History Newsletter*,
1982, 14:16.

   Discusses the controversy surrounding bilingual education
within the context of its historical evolution.

Dulay, H., and M. Burt. "Bilingual Education: A Close Look at
Its Effects." *Focus*, 1979, 1:1-4.

   The authors analyze Epstein's criticism of bilingual education and the shortcomings of the AIR study. They describe
the research which strongly suggests the effectiveness of
bilingual education programs.

Llanes, J. "The Sociology of Bilingual Education in the United
States." *Boston University Journal of Education*, 1981, 103:
70-82.

   The author discusses topics in bilingual education and concludes that: (1) bilingual education is more equitable for
language minority children; (2) bilingual education is more
effective in teaching English; (3) bilingual education is
helpful in attaining functional bilingualism for all children.

Otheguy, R. "Thinking about Bilingual Education: A Critical
Appraisal." *Harvard Educational Review*, 1982, 52:301-314.

   The author examines arguments which have been offered
against using the native language of bilingual children in
the schools.

Padilla, R.V. "A Theoretical Framework for the Analysis of
Bilingual Education Policy Formation." ERIC Document Reproduction Service. No. ED 217 719, undated.

   Analysis of negative journalistic opinion on bilingual
education which has been widespread enough to have formed
the context of public opinion within which national policy

on bilingual education has been set. The author proposes
that in view of this journalistic assault, proponents of bilingual education must develop a well-articulated positive
orientation toward bilingual education to be counterposed to
the negative orientation in the mass media.

Tikunoff, M.J. *Significant Bilingual Instructional Features
Descriptive Study.* San Francisco: Far West Laboratory for
Educational Research and Development, 1982.

A report on research conducted in bilingual classrooms on
the characteristics of effective programs. These characteristics are: (1) effective bilingual teachers display active
teaching behavior; (2) a high level of academic learning
time is maintained; (3) a strong emphasis on the basic skills;
(4) bilingual teachers use language successfully to mediate
instruction.

Troike, R.C. *Research Evidence for the Effectiveness of Bilingual Education.* Rosslyn, Virginia: Interamerica Research
Associates, 1982.

The author analyzes 12 studies which attest to the effectiveness of bilingual education. He concludes that a quality
bilingual education program can be effective in meeting the
goals of equal educational opportunity for minority language
children.

Appendix A

CURRICULUM MATERIALS RESOURCES
ANNOTATED BIBLIOGRAPHY

*A Bibliography of English as a Second Language Materials:
Grades K-3.* National Clearinghouse for Bilingual Education,
Rosslyn, VA, 1978.

The purpose of this bibliography is to provide the ESL
teacher with educational materials for use with the child
who represents a low-incidence linguistic group and who does
not have the advantage of a full bilingual program available.
Bibliographic materials are grouped according to the following format: (1) ESL reading textbooks, (2) ESL readers, (3)
reference materials, (4) supplementary materials: games,
cassettes, visual aids, songs, rhymes, and riddles, and
(5) tests.

*A Bibliography of English as a Second Language Materials:
Grades 4-12.* National Clearinghouse for Bilingual Education,
Rosslyn, VA, 1978.

Provides the ESL teacher with educational materials for
use with the child who represents a low-incidence linguistic
group and who is not in a full bilingual program. The introduction stresses that while teaching English to the non-
native speaker is different from the task of providing the
same skill to native speakers, ESL students should not be
isolated from the educational mainstream. It is also recommended that language learning activities and materials be
adapted so as to reflect the curriculum of the mainstream
group of students. Bibliographic materials are grouped into
the following categories: (1) ESL texts, (2) ESL readers,
(3) writing texts, (4) supplementary materials emphasizing
grammar practice, pronunciation and fluency, vocabulary and
idioms, practical matters and diversions, (5) tests, (6) student references, and (7) aids for the ESL teacher.

Bibliography of Resources in Bilingual Education: Curriculum

Materials. National Clearinghouse for Bilingual Education, Rosslyn, VA, 1980.

A compilation of more than 400 entries describing available curricular materials for use in bilingual education programs. Individual entries provide information on title, author, year of publication, data concerning availability of materials, abstract, target language, and copyright information. Five indices separate citations and group them according to author, language, subject, series title, and title. Materials for 39 language groups are cited.

Bilingual Education for Gifted and Talented Children. National Clearinghouse for Bilingual Education. Rosslyn, VA, 1981.

An information packet designed for use in bilingual education programs for gifted and talented children. The document is organized into six sections. Section I lists federally funded gifted and talented programs. Data provide the name and location of the program, contact information, and a brief description of the program objectives. Some programs have been highlighted as examples of good program design. Section II provides fact sheets and articles on the characteristics and identification of the gifted and talented child; program funding, planning and evaluation; and curriculum concerns. This section also contains useful information for parents of the gifted and talented; problems these children may have and what to do about them; activities parents can provide to foster creativity; and a bibliography for parents. Section III lists, by state, contact information and a brief description of funding sources. Also provided is contact information on state departments of education consultants for gifted and talented students. Section IV contains bibliographies of materials on minority language gifted and talented children. Section V provides more than 170 ERIC one-line bibliographic searches with abstracts on gifted and talented language minority students. Section VI is a reprint of federal legislation.

Bilingual Special Education Packet. National Clearinghouse for Bilingual Education, Rosslyn, VA, 1980.

This document is intended for use by educators in bilingual special education programs. It is organized into seven sections. Section I contains three articles on bilingual special education. Section II contains a text which accompanies a multimedia package designed to explain federal legislation (Public Law 94-142) to educators and parents. This section provides an overview of the Education for All Handicapped

Children Act, a description of the major components of the
Act, excerpts from the law and suggested resources for supplementary reading. Section III includes information sources
and funding agencies for bilingual special education programs.
This section lists agencies, contact information, and a
brief description of the agency goals. Section IV provides
information on teacher training throughout the United States.
It includes the name of the educational institution offering
the program and contact information, type of program, target
language group, and degree conferred by the program. Also
listed is contact information for Title VII Fellowship programs which offer specializations in bilingual special education. This section includes a directory of 19 projects
funded by the Bureau of Education for the Handicapped, Division of Personnel Preparation. These projects are designed
to serve Hispanic, Asian, and Native American communities.
Section V is a directory of sources of materials for use in
bilingual special education programs. Section VI is a collection of bibliographies on bilingual special education
materials (annotated). A collection of bibliographies on
research and programs for limited-English proficiency (LEP)
handicapped children is compiled from ERIC sources (annotated),
dissertation abstracts, general references, and readings.
Section VII contains ERIC abstracts on current literature in
bilingual special education projects and speech and hearing
problems.

Bilingual Vocational Education Library Bibliographic List.
State of Connecticut Department of Education, Division of
Vocational-Technical Schools, Hartford, Connecticut, 1981.

Provides a bibliographic list of all library holdings on
bilingual vocational education at the Connecticut Department of Education. More than 1,300 entries are arranged
alphabetically and cross-referenced according to field(s)
covered by the publication listed. A code number to the
right of the title entry corresponds to the field covered.
Code numbers and their corresponding topic area are as
follows: 1. Adult Education; 2. Assessment; 3. Bibliographies; 4. Bilingual Education (general); 5. Bilingual
Vocational Education (general); 6. Career Education; 7. Connecticut Institutions and Programs; 8. Counseling and Guidance; 9. Cultural and Multicultural; 10. Curriculum and Instructional Materials; 11. ESL; 12. Institutions (nationwide);
13. Legislation; 14. Educational Technology (audiovisuals
and media); 15. Psychosocial; 16. Special Education; 17.
Teacher Training; 18. Vocational Education; 19. Life Coping
Skills; 20. Education; 21. Sex Equity. No indices are pro-

vided. The list user interested in a specific target language population must examine the list entry by entry. Not
annotated.

Cole, L.T., and T. Snope. "Resource Guide to Multicultural
Tests and Materials." *ASHA*, 1981, 639-644.

The American Speech and Hearing Association has established
a Bilingual/Bicultural Resource Exchange. This exchange contributes information on available assessment materials,
clinical materials, pamphlets, bibliographies, and word
lists developed for use with speakers whose dominant language is not standard English. Entries include the name of
the item, publisher, contact information, type of material,
and cost. Although the items listed are largely designed
for use with Hispanic communities, some items are listed for
use with Native American, Asian and black children. ASHA
invites contributors to the exchange. Contributors will receive an updated listing. Inclusion of an item in the listing does not signify an endorsement or qualitative judgment
of the material by ASHA.

Gage, J., compiler. *Directory of Computerized Resources in
Bilingual Education*. National Clearinghouse for Bilingual
Education, Rosslyn, VA, 1981.

A guide to data bases and computerized search services of
use to bilingual educators. Thirty-five computerized data
bases represent a variety of separate information services
such as bibliographies, legislation, statistics, funding
data, and language and behavior. Each data-base description
includes the following information: producer and contact information, scope and content, corresponding printed index,
user aids, vendor, availability of service, type of services
and cost, notes providing additional information, and a sample citation. A separate section describes Title VII network search services followed by a list of Bilingual Education Service Centers (BESCs) and Evaluation, Dissemination
and Assessment Centers (EDACs), as well as contact information and linguistic target groups served by the service
areas.

Greenberg, J., A. Mazzocco, and D. Sauve, compilers. *Guide to
Current Research*. National Clearinghouse for Bilingual Education. Rosslyn, VA, 1980.

Provides 74 abstracts on current research, either in progress or completed, which are of relevance to bilingual education. A wide range of topics is represented, some of

which relate to academic achievement, bilingual programs, bilingual students, cognition, educational policy, first and second language acquisition, linguistics and parent involvement. An alphabetical list of program titles is provided. Four indices group individual citations according to grantee institution, principal investigator, subject and sponsoring agency. Each entry provides information on: classification number, title, grantee, principal investigator, funding agency, contract or grant number, starting date, completion date and abstract. An appendix lists the names and addresses of sponsoring agencies.

Handout Series Bibliographies. Georgetown University Bilingual Education Service Center (BESC), Washington, D.C.

The Georgetown University BESC has published a handout series of bibliographies to disseminate to bilingual education programs. These handouts provide the following information: author and title, type of material, publisher and address, cost and target language group. A selection of topic offerings from the handout series follows:

(1) Blanck, C., compiler. *Materials for Teaching ESL to Children in Grades K-4.* This annotated listing includes 10 textbook citations and six (6) audiovisual material citations.
(2) Ebel, C.W. (ed.). *An Annotated Bibliography of Books on School, Community, and Parents.* A collection of 24 annotated citations. Publication dates range from 1970 to 1978.
(3) *A Bibliography of Materials about Puerto Rico.* 1977. This bibliography cites 161 readers, 21 textbooks, and 12 listings of audiovisual materials. Not annotated.
(4) *A Collection Bibliography of Books on Reading.* 1980. Cites 94 books available for loan from the BESC library. Not annotated.
(5) Rouss, L.L., compiler. *A Selected Annotated Bibliography of Books on Reading Available for Loan from the BESC Library.* 1980. Provides 21 citations.
(6) *An Annotated Bibliography of Books on Chinese Language and Culture.* Lists available texts and stories. Comments are provided for 21 citations.
(7) *An Annotated Bibliography of Books on Guidance and Counseling.* 1979. Provides 29 citations primarily geared to Spanish-speaking populations but also includes entries on rural and urban poor, black youth, and French speakers. One citation discusses all ethnic backgrounds.

   (8) *Bibliography of Books Relating to Vietnam and Vietnamese
       Language and Culture*. Provides 137 citations with
       comments.
   (9) *Selected Bibliography: Educating Linguistic Minority Stu-
       dents*. Contains 31 citations through 1977. Not anno-
       tated.

Hernandez, A., and M. Ortiz de Medina, compilers. *List of
Materials for Teaching Non-English Dominant Special Education Students*. Hartford Board of Education, Hartford, Connecticut, 1982.

   Provides a large selection of books, readers, teaching and
assessment materials. All materials are either designed for
or may be adapted for use with bilingual Spanish-speaking
children with special educational needs. As applicable,
each entry provides information on the name of the material
and its publisher, the area of assessment, and the intended
grade level. Data do not include publisher addresses, location of material, contact information, or material cost. Not
annotated.

Information Packet for Bilingual Vocational Programs. National
Clearinghouse for Bilingual Education. Rosslyn, VA, 1981.

   A collection of current sources of use to bilingual vocational education programs. This document is organized into
seven sections. Section I is a collection of articles on
opportunities in bilingual vocational education. Section II
lists funding agencies for bilingual vocational education
programs. Data provide information on the name of the funding agency and contact information, administering agency,
authorizing legislation, eligible applicants, eligible population, intent of funds, regulations, form of assistance,
and current appropriations. Section III is a directory of
state officials with responsibilities for vocational education for disadvantaged youth and adults. Section IV is a
collection of abstracts compiled by the Office of Bilingual
Education and Minority Language Affairs (OBEMLA). The abstracts describe bilingual vocational training grants, bilingual vocational instructor grants, and contracts for the
development of instructional materials, methods, and techniques. Section V provides sources of information, materials,
publishers, and book distributors. This section also lists
and describes several agencies concerned with career/voca-
tional education. Section VI is a collection of bibliographies
on bilingual vocational education. Section VII describes a
bibliographic search service available through the National
Clearinghouse for Bilingual Education.

"List of Vietnamese Publishers." Center for Applied Linguistics, Washington, D.C., 1981.

Lists six publishers of Vietnamese educational materials. The information is provided bilingually and the bibliography refers to Asian linguistic groups which include the Vietnamese, Laotian, Hmong, Cambodians, and Tai Dam. The Refugee Educational Guides cite 29 entries. Citations are grouped according to intended educational level (preschool to adult) or they are listed according to a general information category. Each entry lists the educational series search number and title, the number of pages of the text, and the cost of the material.

Sandhu, H.K., and L.A. Bukkila, compilers. *Guide to Publishers and Distributors Serving Minority Languages*. National Clearinghouse for Bilingual Education, Rosslyn, VA, 1980.

A list of all publications and distributors cited. The guide contains 310 entries. Each entry format includes the name of the company providing the materials, contact information, intended grade level of material, type of material, content area and target language of the publication. Four indices separately group citations according to content area, grade level, language and type of material available.

Series Holdings. National Clearinghouse for Bilingual Education. Rosslyn, VA, 1982.

All periodicals held by the National Clearinghouse for Bilingual Education (NCBE) library. The listing includes journals, newsletters, indices, and monographic materials.

Sources of Materials for Minority Languages. A Preliminary List. National Clearinghouse for Bilingual Education, Rosslyn, VA, 1978.

A source guide for educational materials for use with students of minority languages other than Spanish. For convenience, entries are classified into four groups: (1) East Asian, (2) Native American, (3) Territories of the Pacific (including Guam and American Samoa), and (4) Other languages. Languages within groups are listed alphabetically. Individual entries provide the name of the organization offering the material and contact information. Also provided is a brief description of the services and the types of materials offered by the organization. The index lists embassy contact information for 33 countries.

Torres-Reilly, M., M. Libby, and D. Sauve. *Guide to Resource*

Appendix B

ORGANIZATIONS

ALEUT LEAGUE
Star Route A, Box 289
Spenard, AK

AMERICAN COUNCIL FOR NATIONALITIES SERVICE
20 W. 40th Street
New York, NY

AMERICAN LITHUANIAN COMMUNITY
6804 South Maplewood Avenue
Chicago, IL 60629

AMERICAN-SCANDINAVIAN FOUNDATION
126 East 73rd Street
New York, NY 10021

ASIA SOCIETY
112 East 64th Street
New York, NY 10021

ASPIRA, INC.
296 Fifth Avenue
New York, NY 10001

ASSOCIATION FOR CHILDHOOD EDUCATION INTERNATIONAL
3615 Washington Avenue, N.W.
Washington, D.C. 20016

ASSOCIATION OF MEXICAN-AMERICAN EDUCATORS, INC. (AMAE)
California State College at San Bernardino
5500 State College Parkway
San Bernardino, CA 92407

ASSOCIATION ON AMERICAN INDIAN AFFAIRS, INC.
432 Park Avenue South
New York, NY 10016

INFORMATION CENTER ON CHILDREN'S CULTURES
U.S. Committee for UNICEF
331 East 38th Street
New York, NY 10016

INTER-AMERICAN INSTITUTE
The University of Texas
El Paso, TX 79999

MAESTROS PARA MAÑANA (Teachers for Tomorrow)
1705 Murchison Drive
Burlingame, CA 94010

MODERN LANGUAGE ASSOCIATION
62 Fifth Avenue
New York, NY 10011

NATIONAL ASSOCIATION FOR BILINGUAL EDUCATION (NABE)
1201 16th Street, N.W.
Washington, DC 20036

NATIONAL CONGRESS OF AMERICAN INDIANS
1346 Connecticut Avenue, N.W.
Washington, DC 20036

POLISH-AMERICAN CONGRESS
1520 West Division
Chicago, IL 60622

PUERTO RICAN FORUM
156 Fifth Avenue
New York, NY 10010

SOCIETY FOR FRENCH AMERICAN CULTURAL SERVICES AND EDUCATIONAL
  AIDS (FACSEA)
972 Fifth Avenue
New York, NY 10010

TEACHERS OF ENGLISH TO SPEAKERS OF OTHER LANGUAGES (TESOL)
School of Languages and Linguistics
Georgetown University
Washington, DC 20007

Appendix C

JOURNALS

BILINGUAL JOURNAL
49 Washington Avenue
Cambridge, MA 02140

HISPANIC JOURNAL OF BEHAVIORAL SCIENCES
Spanish-Speaking Mental Health Research Center
University of California
Los Angeles, CA 90024

JOURNAL OF MULTILINGUAL AND MULTICULTURAL DEVELOPMENT
Tieto Ltd., 4 Bellevue Mansions
Bellevue Road
Clevedon, Avon BS21 7NU
England

LANGUAGE IN EDUCATION: THEORY AND PRACTICE
Directory of Foreign Language Service Organizations
Center for Applied Linguistics
1611 North Kent Street
Arlington, VA 22209

LANGUAGE LEARNING
N5714 University Hospital
University of Michigan
Ann Arbor, MI 48109

NABE JOURNAL
1201 16th Street, N.W.
Washington, DC 20036

TESOL QUARTERLY
Georgetown University
Washington, DC 20057